worship

exploring
the sacred

James **empereur** SJ

The Pastoral Press

Washington, DC

Acknowledgments

I acknowledge with gratitude permissions granted by the following to use again materials for which they hold copyright: *The Catechist* 7:5, 7:7 (1974) for chapters 10 and 11; *Chicago Studies* (Spring 1977) for chapter 6; Resource Publications and Paulist Press (*Modern Liturgy Handbook* © 1976) for chapter 9.

ISBN: 0-912405-33-3

The Pastoral Press
225 Sheridan Street, NW
Washington, D.C. 20011
(202) 723-1254

The Pastoral Press is the publications division of the National Association of Pastoral Musicians, a membership organization of musicians and clergy dedicated to fostering the art of musical liturgy.

Printed in the United States of America

To Massey H. Shepherd, Jr.
Explorer of the Sacred Liturgy

Contents

Introduction

It is now a truism among those concerned with the worship of the church, whether they be academic professionals or practitioners, that the culmination of the modern liturgical movement in our own time has not brought about the hoped for renewal of the Christian worshiper. We have new rites, but do we have new worshipers? This is not to blame those who have labored so arduously over the past quarter of the century to bring the liturgy back to the center of Christian living. The best of scholarship from liturgical historians and theologians as well as sensitive reflection on pastoral practice have been brought to bear on this task. And there have been some spectacular successes as well as the numerous moderate ones. That the movement to restore the primacy of place to the liturgy, which began in the last century, is still an unfulfilled prophecy is not the fault of those who have dedicated their lives to research, reform, revision, and renewal. The problem is that the world has changed. There is much about our present liturgical rites that is too little, too late. At least, this seems to be the case for Western societies.

Recently, cultural analysts have been stressing the triumph of a narcissism which is pervading the United States. I suspect that this judgment could be verified in most other Western countries. Books such as *The Culture of Narcissism* by Christopher Lasch and *Habits of the Heart* by Robert Bellah and his colleagues have overwhelmingly demonstrated that the area of sacrality has moved from the public arena to the area of the private domain. This has tremendous repercussions for the liturgy. Liturgy is a public action or it is nothing. Liturgy is not what we do in the depths of our hearts, or in consultation with a spiritual director, or by means of mudras, breathing, and zen meditation. But, in fact, people find God more outside the liturgical context than within it. The sacred is still identified with public worship but in a more extrinsic and less personally involving way. The liturgy is sacred, to be sure, but the real contact with God takes place with those people and in those places which existentially define our spirituality.

We are still trying to find ways of bringing spirituality and liturgy together. Liturgy may be defined as the symbolic articulation of the Christian community's relationship with God, but the connection between the two is still not clearly made on the theoretical level and is often missing on the level of experience. The liturgies of the middle ages, of the Reformation, and of more recent centuries often carried with them their own kind of spirituality. One assumed a specific spirituality before one worshiped, often as one entered the church building, leaving the world behind. The highly rationalistic process of modern liturgical renewal has made that approach to liturgy and spirituality incredible. This divorce between our relationship with God and our ritualizing about God has only exacerbated the question: how is the liturgy the place of sacrality?

The essays in this volume are directed to this question. The first five investigate the contemporary experience of the holy. They look at the symbols of the sacred, especially the liturgical assembly. They focus this investigation on the meaning of the holy as it is found in the origin of the liturgical symbols.

This articulation of the experience of the sacred is then placed in the context of theological plurality as a way of opening up more sources of finding the holiness in life which can be celebrated in the public forum. Then some attention is given to the practical implications of these liturgical theologies when planning worship. In describing this process there is no attempt to be complete or even adequate. It is merely suggestive in character.

Finally, the last essays deal with directions for the future. Not every possible direction is indicated. After a general discussion of these challenges, there is an expansion on three of them in particular: the liturgical year as the church's program of spirituality, the issue of social justice which is intrinsically linked to the holy in a Christian perspective, and creativity which is what ultimately will make liturgy as the exploration and celebration of the sacred a possibility.

It is with esteem and appreciation that I dedicate these essays to my doctoral director, Dr. Massey Hamilton Shepherd, Jr. He, more than any liturgical scholar I know, let the sacredness of the liturgy be his source and guide in his life and work.

James L. Empereur, S.J.

worship

exploring the sacred

1

Symbols of the Sacred Today

SECULARIZATION IS OFTEN DEFINED AS "THE PROCESS WHEREBY religious thinking, practice and institutions lose social significance." And there is adequate evidence that such is the case both in the areas of human knowledge and structures. For instance our learning has become more and more independent from any religious perspective, and religious knowledge has become privatized. Both conservative and progressive Christians have promoted this secularization of knowledge either by making a too sharp distinction between the sacred and the secular or by the suspicion of any symbols or theological language that is not part of ordinary experience. While conservatives strive to keep the sacred and the profane sharply distinct, thus isolating the sacred dimension of language and experience from the other areas of human existence and endeavors, progressives with their preoccupation for relevance have been working for religious forms that speak primarily to the merely human. In both cases religion is reduced to the purely interior and has nothing to do with this world. Although this might seem to be stated in a way that is not sufficiently nuanced, it is true that at a time when both the church and society are influenced by various forms of fundamentalism and narcissism this distinction between conservatives and progressives is more easily verified.

The secularization of structures is most obvious in the call for the church to stay out of politics. This does not usually mean that Christians should cease to vote or pay taxes, but that the

1

clergy should not criticize the status quo. Often Christians are the ones who most promote this kind of marginalization of the church. The religious institution becomes a private society for only the spiritual welfare of its members. It is tolerated to the degree that it is not an effective public force in society.

Such secularization is to be regretted. But when talking about the need for secularized liturgy today, it is not this meaning of the word that is intended. Another definition of secularization that applies to secularized liturgy would be: "the process whereby, in the course of our cultural history, languages and roles have become increasingly differentiated." This differentiation is what must characterize liturgy in a secular age. Thus, there is a greater need than ever for the inculturation of the liturgy whereby the faith finds a home and is incarnated in any culture. This is as true for countries of the West as it is for what once were considered "mission lands."

The question is how can we engage in this kind of secularization of our liturgical worship without at the same time turning it into an example of the privatization of religion or without pushing liturgy to the margin of the ordinary Christian's existence? In order to deal with what might be called a desacralized liturgy which remains at the heart of the public and personal lives of people today, it is necessary to reexamine our symbol system. There is a problem with the poverty of our symbols. Since Christian faith finds expression in the public language of liturgy, its vitality depends on these symbolic resources. Inculturation is about symbols, their identification in any culture, and their connection with gospel values. To inculturate is to resymbolize. Both sides of the Christian spectrum acknowledge that in recent years there has been an erosion of meaning in our liturgical celebrations. For the conservatives this is due to the changes in liturgical forms and the changes in accompanying attitudes. The progressives attribute it to the halfway measures of these reforms. In actuality, the reason is not found in liturgical texts and reformed rites, but in the impoverishment of the symbolic resources available to the Christian community at the present time. In many ways, the reactualization of liturgy depends on the cultural reform of society at large. Nevertheless, some assistance can be found reexamining the meaning of the sacred in the liturgy and finding areas where either symbolic resources can be retrieved or discovered for the first time.

An abiding criticism of contemporary liturgical reform is that worship has been depleted of any sense of mystery, that it is a celebration not only of the common and ordinary but even of the banal and trivial. For example, at times one hears of church musicians who are vocal in their concerns that we no longer sing Gregorian Chant and Renaissance polyphony but have resorted to country-style ballads, the guitar, and English of less than happy quality. That much of the church's worship today is pedestrian, even squalid, is incontrovertible. Beautiful is not the adjective that most readily describes the Sunday morning experience. The fact that most of our liturgical reforms have been textual rather than dealing with the non-verbal (the new library, rather than a new liturgy) is a partial explanation for the non-symbolic, nonaesthetic quality of so much worship today.

On the other hand it is necessary to remind these critics of the normative liturgy that before the Second Vatican Council there was more Gounod heard than Bach and that most of us cradle Catholics did not grow up with Palestrina but with incompetent organists making their way through what was supposed to be a Requiem Mass. A concerned and balanced view of the scene today does not have to be aligned with the now dated secularistic theology of Harvey Cox's *Secular City* in which liturgy had no place nor with such professional nostalgics as James Hitchcock for whom the past is supposed to be the solution rather than the guide. We should have sufficient perspective in our liturgical renewal some twenty years later to extricate the justifiable components of the criticism of the more conservative contingent in the worshiping community as well as evaluate the claims of those who belong to the left. There is much that is true in the charges that reaction to a triumphalist worship has meant the loss of the sublime, that active particpation has become equated with the lowest common denominator, and that the vernacular is often lacking poetry and inspiration. On the other hand, those who seek to inculturate the liturgy make the legitimate points that mystery is not found on the level of language and musical forms, but rather that these very symbols should be clear in order to lead the worshiper to the true mystery, the paschal mystery, that the same aesthetic requirements do not obtain for worship as for a good concert, and that great strides have been made in improving the translations and original vernacular compositions.

But behind these concerns is the feeling of uncomfortableness with our symbols. Here is where the crisis of liturgical reform is rooted. Just as good people are led astray by the good rather than by evil, so the basically healthy thrust of the renewal, at least as articulated by the Constitution on the Sacred Liturgy, is also its Achilles' heel, namely, the emphasis on intelligibility. The call for brevity, clarity, removal of repetitiousness, ease in understanding and rationality of structure has opened up the liturgy to the possibility that it can be comprehended and engaged in by all worshipers. This intelligibility means not only moving from Latin into English, but moving from English to English. The restructuring of rites which many of the churches share in common was directed by the criterion of intelligibility, although it was often articulated as pastoral availability or relevance. But this emphasis on intelligibility can reinforce an already present fear of feeling and emotion. It is more comfortable dealing with texts than with gestures as any liturgical planner knows. The tendency in liturgical reform has been a form of rationalism. The proof is in the actual Sunday experience which is still more similar to a catechetical course than to a really good meal. This excessively rationalistic approach is seen in the exaggerated solicitude for conceptual accuracy in the texts with little concern for the feeling content of translations and new compositions. Present liturgical renewal is still based on the idea that cultures are unified, even uniformly built up rationally. There has been great fear of the nonrational in the reformed liturgy in its very attempts to open up this liturgy and make it available to all. In attempting to render the symbols clear, the so-called new liturgies have rendered ineffectual precisely those overtones of feeling which are the substance of symbolic reality. Fear of the role of feeling minimizes the importance of religious experience in the liturgy and once worship is no longer rooted in contemporary religious feeling, it becomes uninvolving, removed from ordinary experience; it becomes over sacralized, isolated, and ultimately nonsymbolic. Louis Bouyer in his book, *Rite and Man*, says: "A loss of contact with the living sources of a religious experience seems to go along with the advance of intellectualization."[1] Even the cautious remark of Roman Guar-

1. Louis Bouyer, *Rite and Man* (Notre Dame: University of Notre Dame Press, 1963) 137.

dini that "Liturgy is emotion, but it is emotion under the strictest control" recognizes the problems of the overconceptualization of our worship.

Maslow as well as other psychologists have pointed out the importance of religious experience to people, and thus any approach to liturgy which considers feelings irrelevant is unsatisfactory. It is true that personal mysticism and mass hysteria should not be what characterizes our regular worship, but overconceptualization denegrates the worshipers' personalities. The Charismatic renewal has helped us to realize that religious experience, while very personal, also has communal dimensions. Liturgy is not an attempt to reenact past personal religious feelings but is to create a feeling of community which meets God in and through its communal religious experiences. We have been much too cavalier about the role of the unconscious in the liturgy. For this reason our symbols (which bridge conscious and unconscious feeling) have been ineffective and sterile. The fear of turning the liturgy into a sensitivity session is real and has foundations in some past attempts to do so, but that should not prevent us from so orchestrating the signs and symbols of our worship that they give room for our feelings to emerge and provide opportunities for an intensification of our religious experiences. Because the liturgy is a human action, it is not possible to divest it of its emotional content.

Often the criticism leveled against those who would plan liturgies which trigger feelings and emotions is that they are manipulative. Using different and unapproved eucharistic prayers, changing certain components of the rite such as the gesture of peace to a different part of the liturgy, the use of gestures and certain dramatic arts, all this is seen as playing around with the feelings of the members of the assembly. No doubt such manipulation can and does take place. But then it is also important to realize that anything we do in ritual carries with it feeling-stages and emotional reactions. Manipulation is found not only in the so-called creative attempts at modern liturgy, but also in the use of approved but less poetic vernacular texts and new compositions. And what is more manipulative of people's feelings than attempts to go back to a former liturgy, whether that of the Council of Trent or Cranmer?

There are three bearers of the sacred which have been important in our past liturgical experience which still today can assist us in discovering the mystery of God in worship. This is especially true if these symbols are used in conjunction with the newer emerging symbols of transcendence. The first of these appears to be the weakest. It is our relationship with nature. However, there does appear to be a turnaround because of nuclear, ecological concerns. We had reached the point where the spiritual significance and understanding of the created world had almost been banished from our minds, and we had come to look upon things and creatures as though they had no sacred or numinous quality about them. Light and darkness were not cogent signs of God as they formerly were. They were simply light and darkness, easily controlled by the achievement of modern science. But concerns about pollution, the waste of natural resources, the energy crisis are all making these natural symbols live again. This does not automatically mean that these nature symbols can be used in the same way as before. Turning off the electrical lighting in a church building so that one can light the new fire at the beginning of the Easter Vigil is less than cogent because we are pretending that we are living in a former time when without electricity, fires had to be kindled anew. Such pretense is not to treat light and darkness in a natural way. However, the lit paschal candle can be very effective if one clearly recognizes the importance of the kind of darkness which is created by turning off the lights, namely, it is the darkness which is dispelled by the light of Christ. In other words, we must integrate these nature symbols in the liturgy so that they speak naturally and not because we have previously assigned a meaning to them.

Another bearer of the sacred from the past is the way the unfathomable is expressed in language, gesture, and objects. What cannot be fully expressed, the ineffable, is still part of our experience. There is no question that liturgies have lost much of this quality. In becoming verbose, they have lost the connotative value of words. Gestures are at a minimum and when used are not experienced evocatively. While there is a concern that liturgy must come from the culture and must speak to ordinary human experience, still there are special moments in life, special ways of acting and dressing. Thus, for instance, there is still concern about vesture because ordinary dress will not do anything to enhance worship. To preside at the eucharist in jeans or the three piece suit does not immediately indicate that one has discovered the sacred in contemporary fashion. Perhaps it is our very preoccupation with texts and words that makes us sense a need for what cannot be expressed in words. We feel an imperative for gesture and music. In a recent article, Robert Hovda has expressed something about the ineffability of liturgical garments and gesture that is important at a time when we see that social justice issues are a contemporary entrance into the transcendent, a hint of the sacred in worship.

> I think it is fair to say that the rich and comfortable feel the kinds of liturgical needs I am discussing at this point the least. People who know they are oppressed, who have to struggle for survival, are much more likely to appreciate the need of an outrageous feast in the midst of obvious famine. It is no accident that the choirs of black inner-city churches are festively vested, while those of middle-to-upper congregations look as drab on Sunday as they do in their supermarkets and their offices. Nor does the hispanic fiesta feel a moral obligation to duplicate in its celebration the miserable conditions of everyday life which so many of its celebrants are forced to endure. It takes the grim, pursed lips and the non-sequitur thinking of an Anglo-type to come up with and publicly articulate the notion that if excess and "waste" and frivolity are eliminated from liturgical celebration it will somehow contribute to a reconstruction of the social order. In T. S. Eliot's words, "You must not deny the body."[2]

Of the traditional bearers of the sacred in liturgy the one that is still very operative today is that of the aesthetic. It is through art that the mysterious can be liturgically expressed. The irony is that often the professional artist finds the aesthetic less of a liturgical experience than the untrained and artistically unsophisticated worshiper. The professional has the handicap of looking at the beauty in the liturgy for its own sake. The aesthetic symbol is not automatically a signal of Christian transcendence and good art cannot be equated with good liturgy. But often the artist or the sophisticated worshiper thinks so. In that sense, many professional artists have allowed the aesthetic experience,

2. Robert Hovda, "The Vesting of Liturgical Ministers," *Worship* 54:2 (March 1980) 105.

even the context of worship, to become secularized. An artistic liturgy becomes an artistic experience rather than a liturgical one. This is clear from the fact that so much opposition to liturgical change from the professionals is based on aesthetic rather than a liturgical criteria. The ordinary worshiper, however, who is ignorant of the various interpretations of baroque organ playing, of the intricacies of the sculpturing style of Mestrovic, is closer to the place of art in liturgy because she has found that she prays better when things are done better. For that person the ultimate criterion for art in the liturgy is liturgical. However, prescinding from the possible pitfalls in this area, it is the beauty of worship which most easily assists people to enter into a transcendent experience and allows their own religious experience to come to visibility in the ritual. Thus, the continuing need to make our worship beautiful with the best that art has to offer. And here it is important that contemporary art have equal time with traditional art. As a matter of fact, because worship is a living cultural phenomenon, modern art should receive a preference.

There are other areas of living where more contemporary symbols seem to be growing. They are more difficult to identify as such. But it is possible to point out certain directions of human experience which seem to be providing the matrix for such symbolization. The first would be symbols that express fellowship, sharing, and unity. These should not be limited to the gesture of peace. Certainly, different kinds of gestures would be important here because these are specially human symbols that we are talking about. Thus, human expressions and the use of the body would be important. For instance, singing is a unifying symbol if properly used. An important symbol of unity and sharing is the environment. It is necessary to create an atmosphere where this kind of sharing and unity can exist and be supported. We have not taken seriously the context of the liturgy itself. Human interaction can be inhibited or enhanced by the physical arrangements, the color, and the ordering of the appointments. And so while the human person is very important in this symbolization process, it is how the person is placed, asked to move, situated, and directed in terms of others that makes it possible for the liturgy to be a unifying and sharing experience.

A second area for discovering the sacred today is that of ourselves. Often the excessive personalism of some liturgies is due to an attempt to respond to the mystery that we find in our own depth. Our own beings and bodies are an entrée to the transcendent. Here the call for silence is but one example of the many ways in which the liturgy can become the home where we are comfortable enough to get in touch with ourselves. Those who are acquainted with Eastern forms of prayer or have engaged in Zen will recognize the many techniques and forms that deal with contact with oneself that are available for use in the liturgy if we are but attentive to them. While preaching will continue to be an important way in which we hear the proclamation of God's word in our lives, there is a rich fund of material in breathing exercises, awareness of sensations, fantasizing, and the like which can be conveyors of the word of God in our time.

A third locus of the sacred for the modern men and women is found in an appreciation for the ordinary in human living. This appreciation is really a way of discerning the sacred in the secular. It is being in touch with the religious dimension of ordinary human experience. It is more than simply engaging in the ordinary things of life. The stress is on the appreciative valuation of what one is doing. Such an appreciation does not allow one to define the holy as a distinct area of human experience. The point is to see the secular and the holy in continuity rather than in opposition to each other. The importance for liturgy here is that the celebration of the sacred dimensions of life can make that life more bearable. The ritualization of one's experience can humanize it and make it more available to us in its depth. It is not as if the secular remains as it is and one need only notice its sacredness. The secular, our ordinary lives, must be transformed by the process of humanization that is being brought to expression in liturgical worship. It is in liturgy that we can hopefully perceive, become more appreciative of, the sacred within the secular. It is in this sense that the ordinary becomes the vehicle of the sacred in the liturgy. But because this ordinary must be humanized, must be called to some kind of transformation, this use of the ordinary in worship will mean a change for the ordinary things of our lives. And in that sense the ordinary does not remain ordinary. It becomes stylized. Because the ordinary must communicate a sense of wholeness and transformation, whatever that ordinary may be will take on a less literal character. The words, the clothing, the dance, the music, the gestures, the bread, the wine, the water, the oil, the human beings will be that of our daily lives. They will not be separate in their existence. They will not be assigned special meanings. And yet they will have *some* distance. For instance, the bread should be ordinary bread, not wafers, to communicate the meaning of the sacredness of this eucharistic meal. The use of that which no longer looks like bread is to oversacralize: it is to place a dichotomy between sacred and profane. But the way that ordinary bread is handled, treated, contextualized, received, and so forth should indicate the holy, that bread is about transformation.

These three areas of modern symbolization indicate that if the sacred is to be found, it will be in what is experienced, touched, or felt by people, in what provides them personal meaning, value, and dignity. It is where people come to depth and unity. What this means is that the holy is not located somewhere in the supernatural but in the everyday, the natural, the carnal flesh. The holy is recognized in the person's principles and powers presently at work to maintain human dignity. If the incarnation is more than an historical event, it means that healing, wholeness, and grace come through the flesh. The sacred is that which moves us, touches us, and makes us tremble, in the ordinary rather than in the extraordinary, in the immediate rather than the distant. We must be resensitized to what lies hidden in human flesh. Words and ideas surely have their place, but finding the sacred today means re-incarnating our religious experiences in bodily ways.

2

The People Shout Amen: The Ministry of the Liturgical Assembly

WE, THE WORSHIPING PEOPLE, SHOUT AMEN IN OUR LITURGICAL WOR-ship. The Amen, especially the Great Amen of the eucharistic prayer, is the symbol of community involvement in Christian life and worship. If there were one word that could characterize our experience of a worshiping people, it would be the word Amen. Do we proclaim our Amen as did our Hebrew forebearers when Amen meant that those uttering Amen opened themselves to a relationship of fidelity and truth to the speaker? Does our Amen state our faith in the speaker, bear witness to the integrity of the one to whom we are responding as well as the relevancy of what has been said? Does it mean real commitment to and not merely confirmation of our covenant with God? Is the Amen we sing in our liturgy the Amen of the New Testament where Jesus is identified with Amen? Christ is the paschal doxology to God; he is the divine "Yes" acknowledging and responding as the faithful witness of God. Is the Amen which is Christ the image and paragon of all our Christian responses? Do others see us as a community of Amen? Can our liturgical assemblies be described in the same way that St. Jerome so many years ago described the faith that he found in the city of Rome where he said "the Amen resounds so that it crashes like heavenly thunder and rattles the temples empty of their gods"? Can we identify with St. Augustine's description of the Christian community when he spoke so eloquently:

11

My brothers and sisters:
Your Amen is your signature;
Your Amen is your assent;
Your Amen is your affirmation.

The richness of the simple word, Amen, is a summary statement of the meaning of the liturgical ministry of the whole church. What lies behind this simple word and what makes it possible to speak it with full significance is that we are all celebrants of the liturgy. Just as all who partake in Christian worship are liturgists, some of whom are liturgical specialists, so all who are integrated in the liturgical community are celebrants, although some have been chosen to preside.

We are all liturgists and celebrants because we are all priests. The entire church can be described as priestly because when Christ communicated his mission to the church, he gave it its priestly character. This priestly character of the church is the priestly character of Christ. This is to say that the church cannot have some other purpose than the risen Christ. The church has the same priestly orientation that Christ has. This is the general priesthood that all Christians share in common because of their baptismal entry into the community. It is a priesthood whose purpose is the nurturing of the community at the level of faith.

The very finality of the Christian community is priestly because of Christ's own priestly mission. And the mission of Christ is to establish the kingdom of God. This kingdom is coextensive with the acknowledgement and acceptance of God. And so one can say that Christ's mission is in the direction of establishing a worshiping community. The priesthood of Christ means this: that it is the sacrament of God's gift to us, our acceptance of it and the gift of ourselves to God. Because the church is the sacrament of Christ, the priestly mission of Christ and the sacramentality of the church are the same. This priestly character is more basic than any power to act, even to celebrate the eucharist. The priesthood that we all share as Christians is not similar to some office or function. It is the basic direction and function of the church. We are priestly; we act as priests when we are sacramental, when we, the church, function sacramentally. And we function sacramentally when we give witness to the presence of Christ. The church is called to proclaim Christ's saving love and fidelity through its own loving and faithful concern. This implies that men and women are Christians to the extent that they give themselves in faith and love to Christ and to each other. Through the living sacrifice of their lives they become the sacrament of Christ's own sacrificial offering to all people.

This priesthood of faith-sharing is exercised by some kind of public profession of this faith. That is why the priestly character of the community demands liturgical expression. Each Christian as a priest is called upon and is empowered to profess personal faith in Christian worship. This baptismal priestly character cannot be defined within the parameters of some specific function. It is the all pervasive character of Christian living which conditions one's entire life of faith and grace. The church is priestly through and through, in all its aspects, all its ministries, all its institutions and members. No one aspect or agency of the church has a monopoly on the priesthood. The life of the church is so rich and its priestly character is so manifold that no one ministry, even that of the ordained priesthood, can exhaust it. From this multiplicity springs the diversity of ministries that articulates and keeps alive the manifold aspects of the community's reality.

What, then, can one say about those who are specifically ordained as priests? These special ministers are not more priestly than other Christians, but they are called upon to give special sacramental expression to the paschal mystery so that the community can celebrate more fully its priestly character. It is the priestly character of the whole church which demands a special ordained ministry which is dedicated to liturgical leadership. But liturgical ministry certainly is not the monopoly of the ordained ministry of the church. There is also special affinity between liturgical leadership and the priesthood of the whole community because the liturgy brings that priesthood, that sacramental character of the church, to its highest expression. Special ministry, especially the liturgical special ministry, is an intensification of the common priesthood of all Christians. It flows from the community and its exists for the community.

If we are to be a community of people shouting Amen, then our understanding of the liturgical event must assist us in making this so. One way to do this is to see the liturgy as an act of ministry performed by the assembly of which the presider is a part, but only a part. The liturgy is not primarily a ministerial action done to the community by the ordained clergy. This change of self-understanding on the part of the liturgical assembly is due in large part to a shift in the understanding of ministry in the church which has been taking place since the Second Vatican Council.

The obvious fact is that ministry today is undergoing a global change in its theology and practice. This metamorphosis has spurred many questions and debates concerning the identity and relationship of ordained and non-ordained ministers, the diverse needs of the local churches in serving the needs of the people within different cultural contexts, and the emergence of greater lay participation in the church's mission and ministry. The American church has made its own contribution to this ecclesial phenomenon.

Most writers today contextualize the meaning of ministry along similar lines. In the words of theologian David Power, "The most important question about ministry is the question about the existence and functioning of a Christian community as a whole."[1] Though the church has acknowledged God's presence in the midst of the community, it has been slow to recognize the ministry of the community. But local communities are recognizing and encouraging a multitude of ministries. The church ought to recognize and celebrate those with the gift and willingness to serve in a particular way. The point is that the community ministered to comes before the ministry doing the ministering. Ministry belongs to the whole church before it belongs to any individual member. One cannot have a theology of ministry which is independent of a theology of the church. The various images and concepts we use to speak about the church become ways of describing ministry: mission, communion, sacrament, service, discipleship, and holiness. The kingdom of God is the goal of both church and ministry. If the church exists for the world, so does the ministry.

Seeing ministry in terms of ecclesial life means what St. Paul stressed long ago: there is no ministry in general. People are commissioned for specific tasks to keep church life alive. Both biblical and historical studies indicate that ministry is plural. It

---

1. David Power, *Gifts That Differ* (New York: Pueblo Publishing Company, 1980) 29.

does not exist completely or uniquely in one office such as the priesthood or episcopacy. There are several images of the Christian priest found in the New Testament: 1) the disciple, who is called to leave everything and follow the master; 2) the apostle, who is sent to serve others and preach the Lord Jesus; 3) the presbyter, who is responsible for the pastoral care of others; and 4) the presider at the eucharist, who has the sacramental ministry of the liturgy of the church. No one image adequately explains ministry. No one is the essence of ministry and no minister is expected to have all four characteristics. Just as it is impossible to find one unchanging form of ministry in Scripture, so also in the history of the church there have been several operative models of ministry such as the jurisdictional, the cultic, the pastoral, the prophetic, and the monastic. None exhausts the ministry, none defines it essentially.

Thus, no one gift or task can be identified with the fullness of ministry in the church. We must be careful always to speak of ministry in the plural. The variety of ministries helps the church to become more fully realized in the contemporary world. And so the plurality of ministries exists to build up the community. This means that ministry also includes the roles of leadership and service in the community with the purpose of promoting the Gospel. With many ministers who must work in a complementary fashion, there is always the need for a ministry which oversees and provides for the many ministries. In a view in which the whole church is considered ministerial, ordained and non-ordained ministries must function in an integrated way so it becomes clear that there is only one ministry as there is only one church. What is distinct about ordained ministry is not that it is separated from the laity. Rather, the distinction in the church is between the ministries of service and the community itself. What we have is a priestly community with several ministries at the center, some publicly recognized by ordination and others not.

In 1983, Thomas O'Meara, OP, published his book, *Theology of Ministry*. His definition of ministry, while not brief, has provided one of the best summary statements of the contemporary discussion of ministry. For him ministry is "1) doing something, 2) for the Advent of the Kingdom of God, 3) in public, 4) on behalf of the Christian community, 5) which is a gift received in faith, baptism, or ordination, 6) which is an activity with its own limits and identity within a diversity of ministerial actions."[2]

(1) It is doing something. It is not a state in life with its own kind of spirituality which was a favorite position of F. Olier, the founder of the Sulpicians. Ordained priesthood is not a life style. Ministry in itself says nothing about whether one is to be married or not. Hopefully, both marriage and celibacy can be integrated into the ministry. Ministry is not a sacred office so dear to the heart of the medievalist who tied priesthood to cultic functions. Here history provides us with some clarity. In the early church the commissioning which later came to be known as ordination was connected with community leadership and not liturgical leadership. The one who led the community presided at the eucharist because of that leadership and not because of a kind of absolute ordination in which certain powers are conferred on the ordained. Ministry is action. It is concrete service. This is the reason ministry has undergone so many changes. One example would be the creation, life, and death of the minor orders of lector, porter, exorcist, and acolyte, as well as the subdiaconate: all vital and viable ministries at one time.

(2) This ministerial action is to bring about the kingdom of God. Contemporary theological studies have identified various functions for the ministry: forming community through leadership and prophecy, proclaiming the word through witness and teaching, serving people in their individual needs, bringing God's judgment to real life situations, and enlivening the church as a sacrament. These are but some of the ways to establish this kingdom. There is no disagreement on this point.

(3 & 4) O'Meara's definitional points that ministry be "public" and "on behalf of the Christian community" are healthy reminders that we cannot be reductionistic about ministry. Not everything we do is ministry. Just existing as a Christian should not be identified with Christian ministerial action. Once something means everything, it means nothing. As O'Meara puts it: "When all is ministry, ministry fades away."[3]

(5) In his fifth component of ministry O'Meara points out that ministry is a gift received in faith, baptism, or ordination. Faith

2. Thomas O'Meara, *Theology of Ministry* (New York: Paulist Press, 1983) 136.
3. Ibid. 159.

and baptism are presuppositions for ministry but ministry also refers to a precise gift, a special call. That is why it is public. Ministry in the church needs to be named, designated, and recognized in some way whether by installation, ordination, commissioning or prophetic action. Ministry is a gift which must be tested, verified, and accepted. Thus, the need for a way in which local communities can have more to say about their ministers. Although we are broadening our understanding and experience of ministry, we are not opting for less competence. In fact, as more people are recognized as ministers in the church, especially in terms of what we call lay ministers, probably not a very happy term, we would expect the quality competence to rise.

For instance, educators are ministers of the word inasmuch as they lead students to the mysteries of the world. The true educator helps the rest of us to experience wonder, whether over a piece of modern sculpture, the molecular energy fields which produce solidity, or the memory capabilities of the human brain. Those who do this well ought to be prized by the community. And the poet particularly belongs to the category of minister of the word. The word must be embodied in every time and place, and the poet is particularly well equipped for this task of communication. This ministry has been sorely neglected in recent times and ought to be publicly lauded.

Perhaps our process of selecting ministry candidates has too closely followed academic and business practices. Do those who minister need to be well put together? Would not the effective minister be the one in touch with his or her own pain and suffering? Rather than those who reject failure and self-doubt, would not the best minister know fear and doubt? Our ministers must struggle to communicate the depth of our belief about pain, suffering, and death.

(6) O'Meara's last point is that every individual ministry is limited by the other ministries. No one ministry is the source of the other ministries. Only Christ and the Holy Spirit are that. Ordination refers to permanent and stable ministry. But there are part-time, temporary ministries as well as those which are not attached to office. We are witnessing a virtual explosion of ministry with specialized concerns for social justice, spiritual direction, the sick and marginal Christian. Clearly the various ministries of healing and teaching exemplify this extraordinary

phenomenon in the church: the growth of ministry. Often these specialized ministries have no connection with public office. That is the present fact. My own view is that many of these ministers should be ordained, although not necessarily for liturgical leadership. I see no need to tie ordination to the liturgy, even the eucharist, in some essential way. After all, the former minor orders were authentic ordinations.

We cannot equate the decline in the number of ordained priests to a lack of vocations in the church. Even in the past the larger portion of ministry was done by the unordained, namely by the sisters and brothers of various congregations and orders. Even if we take the simplistic approach of counting heads, we must say that the major portion of ministry has been done by women. There is no lack of vocations to ministry.

In concluding this manner of defining the ministry, what becomes clear is that the specific form and function of ministry is not something given to us by Jesus Christ. It is largely a pastoral matter where ministry concretely changes, depending on need, cultural context, and the historical situation of the church. To say that the sacrament of orders is divinely instituted is not to ascribe something to the actions of Christ at the last supper. It means that the church decides what kind of ministry best meets its need that it continue to proclaim the Gospel with authenticity. On these points of definition of ministry the discussions in the American church parallel those taking place throughout the various Christian communions.

What, then, does this mean for the ministry of the liturgical assembly? It means most fundamentally that the worshiping community is proclaiming something about its existence and function as a Christian church. The various individual ministries, liturgical or otherwise, flow from the liturgical assembly as the expression of the church in its ministry. All cultic ministries, even that of priests and bishops, belong to the ministering community. These special ministries have no meaning apart from the ministry of the church at worship. No one ministry of lector, deacon, bishop, acolyte or whatever can adequately sum up, and certainly not exhaust, this ministry of the church at prayer. Individual special ministers can build up the community only because they find their meaning in the priestly community of the assembled church.

What this shift in the self-understanding of ministerial assembly implies is that the relationship between liturgy and special ministry in the church is a changing one, flowing from differing ways in which Gospel values are incarnated at any particular time. So also, the ordained ministry is not something which is unchanging and immutable in the life of the church. If it is true, as this shift indicates, that the images of church are the images of ministry, then community formation, prophetic witness, and sacramental enlivening become more important than hierarchical position, teaching authority, and spiritual mediatorship. Finally, this shift demands that all public ministry in the church, especially that of liturgical leadership, be verified in a fully human way. It is not a gift which is forced upon others, for such action contradicts the very meaning of gift. Just as the community has a right to have its ministers, so it has the right to decide what areas of its life are in need of ministry. It is not that ministry exists for the church or that the church exists for ministry. They exist for each other. How liturgical ministry is shaped and structured will follow the shape and structure of the liturgical assembly. The people of God shout Amen not to their ordained ministers, but to themselves, as priests and celebrants of the worship of God.

3

The Search for Meaning in the Liturgical Experience

IT IS INCREDIBLY TRITE TO SAY THAT WE STILL LIVE IN A TIME OF change, crisis, and uncertainty. Prosaic as it may sound, we are still in a period where we are moving from certainty to understanding. This is caused not only by theological pluralism, but is further exacerbated by the nuclear conflict and the unresolved tensions in so many parts of this planet. The various kinds of global threats have raised the issue of meaning in an even more critical way. We live in the time of massive symbol change. Hopefully we are moving from one symbol to another. Confronted with massive injustice and world disorder, we ask with further passion such questions as what does it mean to be human? What does it mean to be Christian? What is the value of the traditional Christian symbols? What meaning is to be found in the present symbol switching that is going on in the churches. In one sense we have been renewed; we have gone through a period of transition. Yet, as is painfully obvious, we have not changed. We have lost our certainty of the "good old days" (if there ever were such times) but have not achieved the understanding of the new. Crisis and lack of identity still remain. We have been forced to discard old meanings but that does not mean we have appropriated new ones. In moving away from the identifying and comforting symbols of the past, we have found ourselves no longer able to make use of the old, but have not been able to integrate the new. There is even some question whether these new symbols exist. This transition in symbolic living, which is much larger than church life, is at the heart of the problem of Christian worship today.

What is the matter? The problem is that there is too great a gap between the experience that should be facilitated by our symbols and the symbols themselves. Our response to whatever symbols we employ usually is: What do they mean? Both our cultural, political, and economic symbols, as well as our religious ones which are supposed to structure our human experience, have lost their hold on us when such questioning arises. What we say of both secular and religious symbols applies to liturgical ones in an especially cogent way. We must not be afraid to ask the question of ourselves: How can we again place our Christian symbols, some old and some new, in contact with our basic religious experience? If we do not confront ourselves with this question in the very beginning, all other kinds of reforms, institutional changes, even a re-emphasis on community and prayer life will ultimately be the Pauline brass and tinkling symbol.

The answer to the question of what does it mean to be human in a Christian symbolizing way can only be found in our human experience of transcendence. As Christians we are committed to the fact that meaning comes from God through Jesus Christ. This has been the understanding among Christians since the beginning. The problem is how does this happen? It does not seem to be happening as effectively as it can or should be. In order to grasp how such meaning can be found in our Christian commitment we need to understand the nature of our questioning and what it means to transcend.

The experience of transcendence, whether of God or a work of art or in the act of making love, is an experience that constitutes a question, an existential and practical question. But it is a question which does not contain an answer. Ultimate and radical questioning as is involved, especially in the liturgy, does not contain any one answer. Rather it is the question itself which constitutes an invitation to self-transcendence. In our questioning we pass beyond the limits of any expectation or meaning we have set for ourselves. In our questioning process, in our seeking out what it all means, we climb up and over the limits of our understanding. That is what it means to transcend. In this process every aspect of ourselves is relativized: our accomplishments, our values, our significance, all of it is questioned. In this self-

transcending process by which God can become the transforming force of our lives, we climb up and over the limits which our
ordinary experiences set to our world. To self-transcend means
to strip away every mask of self-deception, to go beyond our
achievements and our failures. Self-transcendence is not self-
abnegation whereby one denies oneself, especially one's bodily
self, to attain some higher spiritual plane. Self-transcendence is
not the same as self-fulfillment where one strives to take care of
one's needs and to develop and grow but without a direction of
moving beyond the limits of oneself. In self-transcendence one
moves beyond oneself but in such a way as not to deny the self
or leave the self behind.

Most of all, self-transcendence means progressive elimination
of any objectifiable God in our lives. We must lose the God of
our past and present as we have understood God to be. In the
final analysis, as in the other areas of theology, the underlying
problem with liturgical theology and the liturgical experience is
the difficulty we have with our God experience. For God is no
thing. This ground of our being cannot be made into an object.
God cannot be reduced to an object of sight or touch or any
other kind of perception. What emerges out of my process of
self-transcendence, my loss of control of myself, my loss of the
empirical ego, the self constituted by my opinions and relationships, is the reality of God. But what emerges is not some object
toward which my prayer can be directed. What emerges in experience is a structure, a dynamism, a horizon out of which and
in terms of which everything else is experienced. It is what Teil-
hard de Chardin means by the divine milieu. It is what happens
when you are in love. Before someone became your loving one,
that person had his or her reality. While you love them, they
have the same reality, but it is changed. Now they live in an
atmosphere, a structure, a horizon of your love and they are
different. But while you experience them differently because of
your love, that love itself is not an object or experience. And so
it is with God. God is the all-permeating reality of everything
else. Whatever way this is described, the point is that God is
not any object, not any kind of thing. It is because this reality
transcends all other reality, that it can be so intimately part of
our human lives. It is deeply immanent in every aspect of our
lives. Love is like that. Because it is no object but the structure

of experience, it is possible to enter most intimately into the being of your lover.

Horizon is the frequent metaphor for understanding self-transcendence. Horizon is that against which reality is seen in a new way. This horizon is not any object and cannot be seen in itself. Rather it forms the background against which everything else is seen. It is the difference between two experiences of the same sculpture: one transformative and life-giving; the other, uncomprehending and rejecting. It is the difference between holding someone in intimacy and holding someone in anger. It is the difference between the water of baptism and the water in the shower. It is the difference between the bread on the shelf in the bakery and the bread in the eucharist. What is important to note is that this transcending experience does not change anything as if some kind of transubstantiation were involved. Water remains water, bread remains bread, and people remain people. The wood or metal of the sculpture receives the same chemical analysis whether as a work of art or a merely physical phenomenon. And yet everything is changed about these elements because with new vision we see these same things in their depth and solidarity. We humanly experience them in a different way. We have been transformed by these experiences. And in these experiences of self-transcendence, we experience God, Transcendence. Self-transcendence renders these realities as epiphanies of God. This is probably closer to what theologians have spoken of as transignification or transfinalization rather than transubstantiation. By experiencing our own transcendence, we come to the transcendence of God. By going through the pathway of ordinary human experience such as the aesthetic experience, the loving touch, the use of bread and water in a religious context, God enters our lives to give us the meaning that will restore authenticity to our liturgical worship.

Thus, to understand the meaning of God in our lives, we must perceive the significance of our own self-transcendence. God is a reality but God is not the object of our vision of experience. In that sense we do not experience God. Finally, God is the personal, historical background, the horizon, the perspective which gives meaning and tone to what is seen. The experience of ourselves as transcendent is a deeply personal experience which gives a particular quality to our vision and actions in the world. And in turn this experience becomes the horizon for our experience of God. There are four main aspects of this experience of ourselves that stand out and identify it as the experience of self-transcendence. These four qualities should be our guidelines in discerning that which can give the meaning to our lives. They are checkpoints against which we can judge ourselves as we move from one symbol system to another. If we possess these qualities, we have some assurance of our own self-transcendence which leads to God, Transcendence. And this experience of self-transcendence should so transform our lives that we are able to function in a healthy way in our liturgical life. This is so because self-transcendence sees human existence as the sacrament of God. Our own transcendent selves become the media of God's self-communication and sacramental disclosure.

New Consciousness. Being conscious tells us that we are in discontinuity with the rest of the world; we are not rocks, trees; we are not other people. Because we are conscious, we can relate to ourselves and we can relate to the whole world on a deeper level than that of mere physical interaction, although it is questionable whether there is such a thing as *mere* physical interaction. But as humans we especially are characterized by our past, present, and future. As conscious beings, the world becomes our world. Because we are conscious, we must confront the world. We must do something about this world. We must inquire into the meaning of this world. What do we mean? This is not just a neutral question. It is a question out of which we must question everything. As beings with consciousness we are very restless beings. We seek *our* meaning, *our* value, *our* truth. This is our process of being more fully human. The truth of the question does not lie in any one answer which stops further questioning, but in the faithfulness with which we seek after our life and in becoming more fully what we can be. It is all a matter of openness to ourselves, to the question we are by being in constant search for our meaning. This is what we mean by being a self-transcending person. We must be in constant search for more of life. This is the new consciousness: not to settle for the comfort of well-being, for a fixed and settled framework for our existence. This is dehumanizing. Raised consciousness will not allow us to let that be the context for our living.

Redemptive Time. This is not chronological or watch time. It is not the measurement of the rate of succession of various physical phenomena. Such is a neutral and impersonal understanding of time. If this is what time means for us, then it becomes a shackle and we are locked into a relentless pattern of change in which we have little significance and over which we exercise almost no control. We all need redemption from such kind of time. Some seek it in a kind of timeless existence in heaven. But this is not what we mean when we speak of ourselves as self-transcending.

Redemptive time is that which we create rather than being made by it. This experience of time is not simply an experience of the past, the present, and the future, but of *our* past, *our* present, and *our* future. It is the experience of constant dialogue with ourselves, of making ourselves what we are. It is chairotic time (from the Greek "chairos" meaning the right, proper, or opportune time) rather than chronological time. It is creative time. It is the time for growthful decision. It is the time which belongs to us because it is made by us as people who are becoming more fully human. It is the kind of time when we are doing something about this world. It is the very personal content of whom we have become and whom we will be. Our time is our experience of our existence. It is the time we get lost in. It is the time of a good conversation where the subject matter takes over. It is the time of good ritual. It is the time of holding your lover in your arms. It is the sacred time of a child caught up in play rather than the clock time of the office worker counting the hours. It is the time of peace and serenity when one's troubles are lifted away rather than the time of anxiety, the time of pressure coming from work duty. In redemptive time we surrender to the sunny beach, the cool mint julep, a celebrative meal, the nude body of a lover, and hopefully, to Christian liturgy where song and gesture take us into the time of the human imagination.

Existential Freedom. This is not the notion or concept of freedom. This the experience of freedom, of liberation. Because of our personal struggles and the mysteries of grace we find that the bonds of fear, compulsions, and tensions, as well as the forces of nature, culture, family, and politics are broken, and we discover ourselves able to move into a new area of existence. We have transcended, we have climbed up and over some of the things that have locked our vision, the predictable patterns of habit and conformity, and all those inner and outer forces that inhibit us from new possibilities and new actualities. The experience of freedom is the experience of new being, of self-transcendence.

While we can gain this freedom through our own struggles, by working at it, the greatest force for freedom, certainly the most common one, is human love. Often freedom is possible because we are more in touch with ourselves, because we take the risk and overcome the unfamiliar. Often freedom is possible through some great pain or suffering. Perhaps it comes through an inspiring person, a traumatic experience, the self-sacrifice of a friend or someone we do not know. But it is the power of love more than anything else which makes us more free, more human, and which calls us forth out of our prisons in which we have walled up our humanity. This experience of freedom is the passing beyond human limits; it is liberation from the fear of going beyond the confines of the known, the familiar, the predictable. We need someone who can make our passage easy. It will be those loving people in our lives who will challenge us to move away from free floating depression, our vague feelings of personal unworthiness, and the doubts about our purpose in life. The one who loves us provides the necessary support when life seems overwhelming and when we become psychologically paralyzed. It is love of father, mother, sister, brother, friend, companion, associate, colleague, husband, wife, or lover which helps us to make the passage into death, that last reality which holds us in its limits, whose terror now prevents us from experiencing freedom and true humanity.

Hope. It is the unity of the three experiences of consciousness, time, and freedom which brings about the experience of hope. Hope equals realism. It is neither pessimistic nor optimistic. It is neither an attitude of mind for which things cannot get any better, nor is it a world view in which things have to get better and better and better. Both positions prejudge the future. In hope we celebrate the future, not determine it. Our experience of hope is found in the emotional and intellectual confidence we have in ourselves. It is really a matter of self-acceptance. When we experience that to be human is meaningful and worthwhile, we are in possession of our own existence, which is our new consciousness; when we create our own time and when we are liberated from the obstacles that keep us from growing in more human spirit, we have real freedom and live in redemptive time. That is hope.

Real hope must be realistic. To the extent that we have been freed from sameness, from the inevitability of the past, to the degree that we have experienced the love of friends and the overcoming of personal paralysis, to that extent we can have hope. But hope faces the future out of the past and present. To hope in a realistic way means to be able to take the past apart and put it back together again out of the liberation we have experienced. We cannot dismiss the past. The question is whether we can do anything about it. The experience of freedom gives us the capacity literally to re-member the past, that is, to break it apart and put it back together again. This gives us a new presence to ourselves. We become people with new possibilities. Only with this experience of liberating hope can we experience ourselves as that which is processing to more being, as a spirit that is absolutely open-ended, a constant open question.

We have evidence of Christian hope even in this era of diminishing expectation. Certain friends, despite the pain in their lives (alcoholism, family turmoil, the collapse of self-purpose), still somehow struggle on, living and resisting the cultural temptation to resignation, acceptance, inevitable self-destruction. Men and women die of cancer with such peace and confidence that it amazes doctors; they are a source of faith for their communities. A family endures the tragic death of one of its younger members with grace and dignity. Every era is tempted in dark moments to consider itself the worst time in earth's history and to despair. Ours is no different, especially with our heightened awareness of global unrest and the malevolent threat of nuclear havoc. Christian hope continues to offer limitless possibilities in our own time.

These four qualities describe the experience of transcendence that gives meaning to our lives as we pass from one symbol system to another. It is important to emphasize again that in the experience of transcendence we do not experience some *thing* but we experience ourselves in a special way. Our vision of ourselves and our world is characterized by the liberating of ourselves as a form of spirit. In our consciousness we experience that we are more than locked into the patterns of physical action and reaction. In our experience of inner time we affirm our transcendence over the brute forces of mere chronology, and we see ourselves as those for whom each moment can be the opportunity for the creation of a history uniquely ours. In our experience of freedom we experience our transcendence over the compulsions and despair of past performance. In our hope we break through the limits of expectations and predictions that would limit our humanity.

But the experience of self-transcendence is not just an individualistic thing. We experience others as sharing our consciousness, time, freedom, and hope. Rather than experiencing people as "out there," we are aware that other people have, like ourselves, an inside to them. We come to relate to them from the inside. It is a matter of shared transcendence. And to the degree that this takes place, there is more communication and a deeper sharing of vision and experience. It can be working together on a common project or it can be a sharing of ideals, or it can be an in-depth sharing in love. And we become aware that to be the kind of human beings that we are called to be, we must be with others who bring us to new life. These others urge us to continue to ask the question of meaning. They assist us in becoming aware of the relativity of our being, in dissolving the images of ourselves, in recognizing the limitation of our autonomy and being comfortable with the relentless burden of natural time and decay. This questioning invites us to seek more humanity, more of ourselves until God emerges. What is revealed is a living God who is not the object of our vision but the ground of our truth and existence. God is the ever receding horizon for our own possibilities. This God is ever new and fresh. Only when our vision, our consciousness, our time, our freedom, and our hope can operate against a background which is seen and experienced as limitless can there ever be that expanding and deepening vision, experience, and action which will make it possible to continue to ask the Christian question in liturgy: What does it mean?

When applying this approach to meaning in our lives to the liturgy, we see it as the celebration of the processes of new consciousness, redemptive time, existential freedom, and Christian hope. Liturgical services seek to promote these contexts for living so that the reality of the living God can emerge more and more within the horizons of human experience. Liturgy is concerned with our being opened to the depths of our human existence and entering into the processes whereby we become more and more human.

The first implication of this kind of reflection is to eliminate any possibility of magic in the consideration of the liturgy. Magic is the projection of our human transcendence upon some exterior principle. Some people still believe that the liturgy can achieve for them what we can only achieve by our own faith, hope, and love—the process of becoming human. The power of the liturgical rite is not magical; it lies in its truth, the truth of the humanity that we bring to it.

The second implication for liturgical theology is the relativizing of the liturgy. It is ritual, but of itself it is not holy. Whatever holiness there is, is the holiness of the people of God. When we endow these human symbols, these human formulations, with the holiness of God we are creating idols.

The third implication deals with Jesus Christ. It may be that Jesus of Nazareth was the perfect religious person, the most self-transcended person of all times. But he has also moved into a new being through his resurrection. Still his humanity is our divine milieu, the center for our humanness and the whole context for our human existence. This humanity, however, is no longer objectifiable any more than is God. Christ can only be the horizon for our human living reality. The reality of the resurrection forms the background of our human vision, experience, and action, and through this resurrection the Spirit of Christ permeates our lives. His Spirit is the challenger who summons us to more life and more vision. Our lives as Christians are dominated by Christ's Spirit (his form of self-transcendence) and what this Spirit reveals is the utterly new possibilities that lie before us. This Spirit can penetrate the center of our lives and transform everything we are from within, changing the most ordinary aspects of our everyday existence to real life. It commands us to newness of life. It is the unlimited possibility of our experiences of limit in a specific tradition of perspective called Christian.

The Christian meaning the liturgy is to convey is the experience that Jesus Christ is alive and is our redeemer. It must create an experienced background for our vision, experience, and action. Out of this transformed vision, experience, and activity we can see Christ in and through the transformed possibilities of our own lives. In the last analysis if God is to be God and if Jesus is to be the Christ in any meaningful way, it will be because we are becoming more and more human.

The fourth implication is the meaning of church and sacrament. The experience that we have of the risen Christ in the context of our own transcendence is a shared experience. And that is what is meant by church. To be the church of Christ means that the shared experience of liberation without our lives is to be and become more and more human. In this sense we can call the church a sacrament.

A sacrament in this context is defined as that which contains and conveys the meaning of Jesus Christ for the depth of humanity. To the degree that the spirit of Jesus, that is, his own self-transcendence, takes over our lives because of our experience of self-transcendence, the reality of God functions in our lives and within the relativity of our human experience. This is what the sacrament contains. The grace of the sacrament, that which comes to expression in the sacrament, is Jesus' own self-transcendence mediated through our self-transcendence.

Sacraments are symbols, that is, they are our self-transcendent experiences rising to visible form. These symbols express the reality of our own concrete human existence and in so doing they are the very being of our humanity. It is obvious that the power of these symbolic actions to bring the human into being depends on their truth. These symbols only more or less bring the human into existence and operation because they cannot produce something that is not there. They are not magic. Their power lies in their truthfulness, that is, in the faithfulness with which we enter into our processes of self-transcendence. The power of any sacramental act in the church depends upon the quality of our consciousness, the extent of our liberation, the innerness of our time, and the depth of our hope. It is pointless to talk about the ever present and unfailing love of God for us in the sacraments in itself. The liturgy has no meaning in human life unless it actually functions with truth in our lives. But we must admit that our lives are not all truth and probably never will be. This means that liturgical life and reality will never be completely true. It is always a question of more of less. But it is the place where we are called to serve one another and the world, making whatever truth in the self-transcending Christ we have visibly available to be shared and communicated to that world.[1]

1. Many of the insights in this essay are from Joseph Powers' *Spirit and Sacrament* (New York: Seabury Press, 1973).

4

The Liturgical Symbol

POPULAR USAGE COVERS BOTH THE CONCEPTS OF SIGN AND SYMBOL. There is a tendency among liturgists and a number of symbologists to distinguish between a sign and a symbol. This distinction can be very helpful in the area of liturgy. Symbols are the building blocks of the liturgy, and good planning finds ways of effectively utilizing these symbols and integrating them into a coherent celebration. But to do so it is necessary to know what the symbolic reality of the liturgy is. Often people call and identify things and actions in the liturgy symbols which are really not symbols at all. They are more sign than symbol. And if one is reluctant to change the symbols of the liturgy, a generally recommendable tendency, this attitude may become problematic for any change in the liturgy, if one thinks that one is dealing with symbols when, in fact, they are actually only signs.

The word "symbol" is of Greek origin. It means "etymologically, something which is so broken that when the two broken halves are put together again those who have them in their possession can recognize one another."[1] "Symbol," for instance, denotes two halves of a broken coin which were exchanged by contracting parties or it could refer to any token used to establish identity such as a soldier's badge or watchword. A symbol is an

1. Gustave Martlet, *The Risen Christ and the Eucharistic World* (New York: Seabury Press, 1976) 18.

agent of unity. It is broken only so that it may unite. It divides a single element so that later it may overcome confusions, misunderstandings, or lack of knowledge. The Greek verb, *sumballein,* means to throw together. The idea of throwing is directed toward bringing something to unity. The word means to assemble, to bring together things which were originally discrete. The Odyssey says of two contestants that when they come together, they "symbolize." Two banks of a river symbolize because they are united by a bridge. To symbolize, then, means to unite, not in the sense of substitution, but in the sense of convergence. A symbol does not simply stand for something else; it is not a substitute. It is the way that one really exists in another. It is the way that the meaning of the music exists in the sounds, the meaning of the painting exists in the paint.

In many ways our daily lives are experiences of symbolizing. We are continually adapting to persons and things. We are looking for ways of incorporating ourselves into our environment. Symbols presuppose the healing of a breach, and so our lives belong to the level of symbol. There is a gap between ourselves and our environment, between ourselves and other people. When we try to gain unity, we are engaging in the symbolic project. Think of the never ending search on our part for the ideal significant other person. The fact that this is a hopeless task does not negate the inner drive that we have for symbolizing. We are symbols when we share in others' lives, when we identify ourselves with them, when we try to establish meaningful and sound relationships with them. There is in a symbolic experience, on the one hand, a sense of hope that there will be completion to one's own life in an achieved unity and, on the other hand, a feeling of anxiety because of the dangers of establishing unity with our world and the people in it who so long for union that they actually threaten it. This anxiety emphasizes that the symbols are not the same as the reality, although it may be the best, if not the only, means to that reality.

"Symbol," today, has taken on a more functional meaning so that it becomes more concerned with substitution than union. What is important in the popular understanding of symbol is not the sharing of persons but the establishing of one's objective identity. "Symbol" for many is like handing in your ticket as you enter the movie theatre which establishes your right to be there, but demands no sharing on the part of the person who receives the ticket. It does not take much insight to realize that the water of baptism and the wafer in the eucharist have been reduced to the equivalent of theatre tickets, even though the reality exists on a transcendent dimension. There are other realities which are often called symbols which relate to things or acts in a way similar to symbols. Food stamps and an invitation card to be presented on arrival are two clear examples. Such things bring together in one sense, but also create distance and separation at the same time. It is important to distinguish these realities which are more properly called signs from authentic symbols. Symbols are objects, relationships, activities, words, gestures, and spatial arrangements which exist in the realm of persons and whose purpose is to establish harmony on the human level and to be the epiphany of the deepest dimensions of life.

To put it another way, a sign is something which stands for an absent reality. Its task is to refer the observer to something other than itself. A billboard or a barber pole are signs. A symbol, on the other hand, is a sensible expression of a present reality. Its task is to make the transcendent (whatever that may be) intersubjectively available. It is to mediate the participation of the observer in that which it reveals. The human body is the primary symbol of the personality. Speech is the symbol of inner experience. Art symbolizes the beautiful. The church is the symbol of Christ. Jesus is the symbol of God. A symbol never simply stands for something else. It is the sensible expression of the transcendent whether that be God, art, or the human personality. It is the focus of revelation both human and divine and of participation in what is revealed in the symbolic process. While it would be confusing to call all symbols religious, still there is a sense in which the directionality of any symbol is toward transcendence.[2]

Symbols cannot be created arbitrarily. Signs can. Symbols are born of life and are not simply the result of human creative imagination as are good billboards. Symbols grow. Symbols are found within the human unconsciousness and are in continuity

2. See Sandra Schneiders, I.H.M., "History and Symbolism in the Fourth Gospel," *Bibliotheca Ephermeridum Theologicarum Lovaniensium* 44, 1975.

with creation itself. We can even distinguish between human symbols and nature symbols, keeping in mind that for a natural thing or event to be symbolic, there must be human beings responding to it. Nature symbols would be such things as darkness, light, water. They are given with creation. The most powerful of these nature symbols have been the most universal, for example, the sun as a symbol of creative power. Jung has pointed to this universality of symbols and sees them as related to the collective unconscious. Danielou argues that "the only acceptable conclusion is that the existence of a common set of symbols in the various religions is due to the parallelism of mental processes" and that "this means that the objective reality of symbols themselves must be common ground as well."[3] In other words, symbols derive from a common experience and a common manner of responding to that experience. These nature symbols signify something by their very being. Smoke signifies fire, ice signifies cold temperature. Traffic lights, however, are arbitrary and belong to the nature signs because they can be changed. Bread and wine mean a meal, and anointing means healing. Specific meanings attached to color are for the most part arbitrary, although there is some evidence of colors being symbols. Green may have an affinity to hope, but it is a derived meaning and perhaps could have a conflicting meaning. In so far as it refers to new trees, leaves, and foliage, there is an element of hope, but to the degree it refers to something like vomit and bodily secretion, its signification becomes confused. Road signs are precisely that. Signs. They give information. Bumper stickers may symbolize an attitude or point of view. They are rarely used for informational purposes. Cheering, booing, smiles, and tears are all symbols. Signs are more distinct from and symbols are more identical to hidden reality.

LITURGICAL SYMBOLS

A good working definition of liturgical symbols would go like this: 1) a sensible reality, 2) which renders present to and 3) involves a person subjectively in 4) a transforming experience

3. Jean Danielou, *Lord of History* (Chicago: Regnery, 1958) 133.

5) of the mystery of transcendence 6) by means of a community. The first five elements of this definition come from Sandra Schneiders.[4]

A Sensible Reality

This is the one area where both sign and symbol are identical. They are both perceptible realities; they are things. The bread, wine, water, bible, cross, words, gestures and these in various combinations constitute the sensible dimension of the liturgical symbol. The importance of the sensible element in the symbol is that it renders the transcendent, which is by nature purely spiritual, intersubjectively available to human beings having bodies. In other words, for one reality to exist in another, there must be a material reality in which the transcendent shines through. In this sense a symbol is made of signs on the level of sensibility. A meal is a symbol, but in order for there to be a real eating and drinking there must be things to be eaten and drunk. In that sense the bread and wine of the eucharist are not the symbols of Christ's presence and redemptive activity. They are signs which make the symbol of the eucharist, the meal, real people eating and drinking, available for us. If bread ceases to be bread and wine ceases to be wine, then how can you have a symbol of the eucharist? There is no perceptible reality for Christ to exist in. At times the way that we have talked and theologized about the bread and wine in the eucharist has been tantamount to making the eucharist only an apparent symbol. That is, in order for Christ to be present through bread and wine, the reality of bread and wine had to disappear leaving only the fiction of bread and wine. If the eucharist is equated with Christ's presence at the parousia, then you no longer have a sacrament. You might have heaven, but surely it would be a non-sacramental reality. A less dramatic example would be the sign of the cross. In the sense we are using these words, the sign of the cross in itself is a sign, but in a context of living worship it can become a symbol. But to the degree that it primarily points back to the historical calvary, it remains on the level of sign.

4. Sandra Schneiders, "Symbolism and the Sacramental Principle in the Fourth Gospel" in *Segni e Sacramenti nel Vangelo di Giovanni, Studia Anselmiana* 66, 1977.

Symbols, then, are concretely composed of signs. In themselves vestments and candles are signs. The lighted candle is a symbol insofar as fire is a natural symbol. In a special liturgical context such as that of the singing of the Exsultet in the Easter Vigil, the candle becomes a human and Christian symbol. Along these same lines, words and people can be understood to be more than signs in the liturgy. The word, for instance, is to be symbolic in the liturgical celebration. The Scriptures as well as the prayers and preaching call the community to a faith response. That faith response is often made in a verbal way. To the degree that the words are a part of the meaning of the rite, a part of the experience of the ritual action, they are symbols and not signs.

The worshipers and their environments are liturgical symbols. The liturgical assembly is the primary liturgical symbol, but the people who make up the assembly live in a symbolic dimension insofar as they move from a faith perspective and make it possible for the transcendent dimension of the community to come to reality. It is for this reason that the recovery of body-language is so important in the liturgy today. Posture, prayer gestures, processions and such symbolic actions as kissing, imposing hands, and sprinkling water are ways in which the individual members of the assembly operate in a symbolic way. In this connection it should be noted that the environment is a symbol. The place of worship, the arts, and the furnishings as well as the musical sounds are all symbolic in character when the liturgical experience is shaped by them. When the assembly prescinds from its environment, the latter is reduced to a sign.

The Symbol Renders Present to

Unlike the sign which merely points to or stands for an absent reality, a reality which is totally other than itself, the symbol renders present the transcendent because it participates in what it represents. A symbol is an epiphany of a present reality, not an indication of an absent one. However, the symbol renders transcendent reality present in a limited and in a sensible way. This introduces an ambiguity into the symbol. It simultaneously reveals and conceals. The symbol is the co-incidence of the human conscious and unconscious life. The piece of music does not say everything about the music, otherwise it would not be necessary nor particularly enjoyable to listen to it again. If one can exhaust a symbol it would not be repeatable except for purely functional reasons. On the other hand, one uses an exit sign when one is looking for a way out, but it is not the kind of thing that one dwells on for its own sake, in the expectation that some deeper insight into human living may emerge. The exit sign does not become *more present.* It is because of this ambiguity regarding symbols, namely, that they both reveal and conceal, that it is not possible to substitute symbols in the liturgy. To substitute symbols would imply that they can be the products of free choice. Such would only be possible if they were constructed of known elements; but because they have a hidden dimension to them, only experimentation can assist one in discovering new symbols as they emerge in any culture.

This has implications for the process of the simplification of rites. It cannot be seen simply as the reduction in symbols or the subtraction of symbolic components. That would be a rationalistic approach to liturgical symbols and would not take into consideration the fact that not all aspects of the symbol are fully known. Often the preference for low-keyed, simple liturgies results in the mutilation of the symbols. Such liturgies can lose much of their multivalent character and so not be able to respond to varied personal situations. Simplification takes place through making things clear and by ordering the service and the symbols in such a way that there is an internal dynamic directing people to pray in a particular way. Often this will mean making additions to enhance the clarification process. No doubt when a liturgy is meant for small assemblies and for everyday, subtraction will take place. But what is subtracted is governed by the goal of clarity and not simply less quantity.

In creating presence, symbols have what Josiah Royce calls "surplus meaning." Whereas a sign must refer specifically to one object, person, or event, a symbol is able to refer to a variety of things at different times and places. For example, water confronts us in many different ways: as cool and refreshing it incarnates the beneficence of creation and as flood or storm it symbolizes malevolent and ultimate threat. Thus, in the Christian context water can easily have the meaning of death and resurrection as when in the early church one was submerged under water as if drowning. Thus, it is important to note that symbols create presence in a context. In the example just mentioned, the context is the Christian faith. Only the believer can find the paschal mystery in the water symbolism. When Jesus walked on this earth as a man, all who passed by could see him, but not everyone could see the glory of God in him. The religious symbol, including Jesus Christ, although sensibly perceptible, is by nature revelatory only to spiritual intuition.

The ambivalence of symbols is partly due to differences in geographical and the cultural environment whence they emerged. The Babylonians stressed water as a symbol of destruction whereas the Egyptians saw water as a symbol of the creativity of nature. The diversity of experience gave rise to symbolic dialects, that is, a usage of symbols which is peculiar to a particular people. Such is the case with Christian liturgy. It is its own symbolic dialect. As dialect, symbols create presence in a restricted way.

A symbol is basically ambiguous and obscure because of its richness. This raises an issue regarding the liturgy. The liturgy is fundamentally symbolic. But it is also concerned with clear articulation. Its purpose is to raise consciousness and remove ambiguity. Is there not some contradiction here? How can that which removes ambiguity be basically symbolic in character when symbols are ambiguous by nature? There is no conflict here because while a symbol is ambiguous because it contains many images and so many levels of meaning, it will be dominated by one image in a given context. For that reason, although it is not possible to explain the meaning of a symbol conceptually, it is still possible to speak of a symbol rationally. Furthermore, the heightened consciousness that symbolic experiences bring about is not to be equated with conceptualization. While there is frequently new consciousness on the intellectual level, the experience of symbols presupposes a corresponding new happening on the level of the unconscious. That is the reason that one cannot always evaluate the impact of any single liturgical celebration on the individual worshiper. It may be a true proclamation/response which has happened but without explicit recognition.

The significance of a symbol is not unlimited. It has both flexibility and constancy. But the multiplicity of signification is bounded by the natural qualities of the symbol. Its parameters are set by it being a sensible reality. The symbol can only reveal what is present in it. Fire cannot symbolize God as cool and refreshing, although it can speak of God as refinement, cleansing, and energizing. The versatility of the symbol is restricted by the nature of the symbol, whether it be water or the human body.

Symbols Involve a Person Subjectively

The symbol, unlike the sign, is not an objective communication. Rather, it reveals by involving the person in a subject-to-subject relationship with transcendence, whatever kind it may be. This characteristic of the symbol has two implications: 1) Unlike the sign which designates the known by means of known or an unambiguous one-to-one correspondence, the symbol leads a person into the unknown by rendering present the mystery of the transcendent which is essentially many faceted. Because the symbol involves a one-to-many relationship it resists translation or explanation. The question: "What does this symbol stand for"?—shows that the questioner takes the symbol for a sign. 2) The symbol does not give objective information; it initiates one into an experience which is open-ended. Thus we have the symbolic character of the gospel parables. You must choose the ending. A symbol cannot be explained because it is not an appeal to the intellect but is a locus of experience.

Symbols operate on the level of the subject and not the object. They do not operate discursively but they work intuitively and directly out of the person's experience of him/herself. The symbol is born in and for an encounter. It is the liminal quality of the symbol that requires that it address the personal and inner area of human sharing. Just as the invitation to human friendship is a liminal experience because it goes beyond one's role and status in life, so the symbol attempts to open up the cracks of human existence, to let the transcendent shine through the interstices of ordinary human experience. Symbols relativize structure, roles, and statuses.

The kind of symbol determines the way in which one can enter the symbolic experience. The level at which one can establish relationships with reality in terms of the symbol is limited by the symbol itself. Thus, when the dominant symbols are those of nature such as light, darkness, fire, water, blood, cross, table, and the like, the level of personal relationship is inhibited. On the other hand, when personal symbols such as father, mother, lover, friend, body, meal are dominant, a truly human relationship with the world becomes possible. Nature symbols do not allow subjectivity full play. This unsatisfactory character of nature symbols is the reason for the tendency to anthropomorphize them, to raise them to the level where the I-Thou dialogue is possible. For example, for fire to become a means of access to a truly human experience, it had to become a god.

The validation of symbols can only take place subjectively. One does not create or destroy symbols by intellectual argument. Their persistence can even appear to be irrational. Symbols are adopted because they answer to our subjective needs and are validated in our experience.

The ability for a symbol to work subjectively is dependent upon the necessary psychic conditions. Symbols do not produce an intersubjective relationship automatically. This has repercussions in such areas as the frequency of liturgical celebrations. What this means is that the desirability of a daily eucharist in those traditions which have it cannot be determined according to theological criteria alone. Ideally in the theological realm, it may be good to recommend daily eucharists, but whether the eucharistic symbols so work psychically is another matter. Because the symbol is the medium point between the psyche and the world, the ultimate criterion for the frequency of liturgical celebration is the worshipers' psychological capability to enter into the symbolic event at any particular time. Can one have a celebration everyday? What kind of celebration can that be? Symbols are tied to human growth. We mut all engage in the symbolization process for psychic health. Symbolization is not an arbitrary project that humans engage in. Thus, the use of symbols must be psychologically healthful and rewarding.

Symbols Involve Persons in a Transforming Experience

The involvement of a person with the transcendent present in the symbol is necessarily a transforming experience. A symbol is never neutral. By nature, the symbol demands commitment as a condition for entering into the revelation of which it is the locus. It opens up the dialogue between transcendence and ourselves. However, the initial commitment which enables one to encounter the transcendent in the symbolic is only the beginning of the relationship of ever deepening commitment which gradually transforms the person. In this way it directs our lives, determines our moral behavior, and brings out our spiritual possibilities. Signs do not call for such commitment. One is not in dialogue with traffic lights. In making love, human bodies are symbols; in sexual manipulation, they are signs.

The result of symbolic activity is the attainment of emotionally experienced meaning. It is the meaning that transforms. At this level of subjectivity mere intellectual construction is insufficient. What exists on the level of signs can leave the knower untouched in his/her being. Assent to a theological proposition is not an existential experience of faith, and correct theology is no criterion for a satisfactory relationship with God. When symbols really work they call us to understand and experience the roots of our existence.

Another way to validate symbols is through their transformative power. Surely the maintenance of a symbol over a long period of time is some indication of the satisfactory nature of that symbol. But the point is that it continues to ring true because it helps to make sense out of human experience. Those symbols which have been most evocative for people are those through which they encounter reality in a meaningful way. Lasting symbols enhance our personhood, create a healthy existence, open up our being. Symbols are discarded which finally turn out to diminish us.

Life giving symbols can become demonic. When a symbol is taken literally, when the sense-object of the symbol is taken as the reality itelf, then the symbol becomes a destructive force. It becomes idolatrous. Idolatry is the elevation of a thing to the level of God, of the identification of the symbol with ultimate reality. This is precisely the feminist critique of biblical and liturgical texts which use masculine denotations of God, such as Father, in an exclusive way. When that happens, the symbol of God, the word, Father, becomes harmful and has ceased to operate as a symbol. We can ask the question of the bread and wine in the eucharist. Much of the older form of benediction of the blessed sacrament was in effect a form of idolatry. If one treats the bread and wine taken out of the context of the meal as if they are the ultimate reality of God, then what happens to the symbol? How can one reality (God or in this case, Christ) exist in another (bread and wine) if there is no bread and wine. If the sensible reality itself is treated as that transcendence which it is assisting people to encounter, then what does it mean to speak of the bread and wine as symbol? And if one cannot speak of them as symbol, how can one refer to them as sacrament? How can you worship a sacrament? Is that not mistaking the sacrament for the reality it is attempting to incarnate? Music's meaning comes through the sounds, but the sounds and the meaning are not reducible to each other. Symbols become false or demonic when one symbolic meaning excludes others or one symbol excludes any other symbol and when the symbol results in the diminishment of the person. An overemphasis on the bread and wine as being equivalent to Christ has excluded the other meanings of bread and wine that these symbols had in the Jewish history out of which Christ was working. It also excluded the liturgical assembly as a symbol of Christ's real eucharistic presence and finally it tended to make the bread and wine and their reception of greater importance than the love and personal relationships that are necessary for the church to be the Body of Christ.

Symbols Involve Persons in the Mystery of the Transcendent

Signs express our understanding of the nature of things. Symbols attempt to go further. They are the language of ultimate reality. They, like any language, are a way that people view the world. They are a way of being in the world. Symbols do not denote things which are already understood, but attempt to grasp the depth of existence. In that sense they seek a subjective appropriation of the transcendent. They go beyond empirical meaning and value. They deal with that which does not meet the eye or ear or other senses. The transcendent may be the reality of any good meal, the personality symbolized by the body, the meaning of darkness and light in human creation, the meaning of a Beethoven sonata or a Picasso painting, or it may be God in one of the religious traditions.

Symbols mediate transcendence as language mediates meaning. Symbolic language operates by taking images derived from the world of sense experience and using them to speak of that which transcends them. Liturgy is a kind of language. The symbols are not simply thrown together arbitrarily, nor is liturgy simply the addition of one symbol after the other due to the vagaries of history and the needs of the era. The liturgy has its words, sentences and paragraphs. The baptismal rite, the eucharistic meal, the Easter Vigil service have an internal dynamic which is reflected in the external ordering of signs. The baptismal rite communicates the meaning of entering a transcendent community through the language of water, oil, light, cloth, and word. The actual language of the eucharist is the ordered eating and drinking by which Christians proclaim who they are in the most explicit way. And the Easter Vigil speaks of the way of salvation in proclaimed paschal mystery, by means of fire, candle, stories of sacred history, baptismal renewal, and eucharistic sharing. It is the symbolic system, the ordering of symbols that brings one into the transcendent mystery. It is not the case that there are some symbols which speak of God in liturgy and some which have other purposes. Nor is liturgy a series of symbols each of which speak of God in Christ independently. The symbols are words that make up the sentences of the paragraph we call liturgy.

Symbols Operate by Means of a Community

Liturgy is the articulation of the spirituality of a community. We are dealing with the ritualization of the relationship of a community with God. Liturgy is never a personal/individualistic affair. Liturgy presupposes community. Thus, any definition of the liturgical symbol must include the concept of community. Thus, any definition of the liturgical symbol must include the concept of community. Liturgy is not simply a complexus of individual symbols which exist by themselves to be utilized at their preference. The symbols that make up the ritual of liturgy belong to a set or a system, and this system lives and takes on meaning in a community. The liturgical symbols reflect the reality of this community and also feed life and vitality and significance into this community. No community—no liturgy; no community—no liturgical symbols.

Salvation comes through community according to the Christian perspective. We cannot find God in Christian liturgy except it be a community happening. The reason that often we do not discover God with reference to community is that the individual worshiper must be first horizontally restored to the community itself. That is, one must be integrated into a larger horizon or context of meaning than oneself, before the transcendent becomes available in symbolic disclosure. If symbols only operate within a certain matrix or context and that matrix is community, then one can only experience what these symbols contain if one is part of that context. One must belong to a transcendent community before the community's symbols can engage one.

This entrance into community, in this case, the liturgical community, is part of the transformative process of the liturgical symbol. Unlike other symbols, one is not transformed by the liturgical symbol working on its own independently as might be the case with aesthetic symbols. By being integrated into a worshiping community, an inner transformation takes place that brings together our individuality and the collectivity of others. We discover community as an integral part of ourselves. In discovering our organic belonging to community, we are now capable of realizing this community in a ritual way. Thus, we become part of the symbolizing process of this community. This has tremendous repercussions for what qualifies one to belong to the liturgical assembly. So often what is happening in contemporary worship is that we have ritual transformation which is being celebrated by an untransformed people.

The liturgical assembly is a symbol because it is *the* manifestation of the church. It effects the presence of the church and Christ in the church. The assembly is the symbol of God calling all together to salvation. It symbolizes the community that God has called to faith and conversion. Because the liturgical community presupposes faith, it also realizes the church as a community of witness. It witnesses to the universal unity of all peoples, as a community in which there is to be no discrimination of persons, a church characterized by concern for the underprivileged and poor. It is a community of protest against narrow ideologies and excessive individualism by its portrayal of the ideal community of faith, truth, and justice. Of all this is the liturgical assembly a symbol.

5

The Meaning of the
Liturgical Community

LITURGY PRESUPPOSES COMMUNITY. THAT IS OUR PRESENT CONVIC-
tion. Few of us now expect that meaningful dialogue homilies,
beautiful slides at the intercessary prayers, graceful dances as
communion meditations, and sung eucharistic prayers, well-proclaimed liturgical texts, warm embraces as the gesture of peace,
well-appointed reconciliation rooms and running water in our
baptistries will create community for us instantaneously as we
make our coffee at breakfast time.

As liturgist Fr. Kenneth Smits, O.F.M. Cap., points out, "the
age of facile creation of Christian community through a renewed
liturgy is over."[1] We now realize the liturgy does not create
community. Rather there is need for catechesis which builds up
to the liturgical celebration. But even catechesis in itself is not
the answer. It has only further uncovered another problem, the
need for conversion. As Smits insightfully remarks, "the limits
of the conversion experience mark the frontiers of religious education and these in turn determine the possibilities inherent in
liturgical expression."[2] In other words, liturgy not only presupposes community, but it must be preceded by a theologically
informed community which has been enlightened and created
by the Gospel.

---

1. Kenneth Smits, "Liturgical Reform in a Cultural Perspective," *Worship* 50:2
(March 1970) 101.
2. Ibid. 102.

But these considerations remain abstract unless we see the meaning of community in American culture. This is not easy to do. Americans relate to one another on a superficial level and do so with ease. In many parts of the U.S. social anonymity is a desideratum. American individuality has a long history and is found in the roots of our nation. And with the present privatization of religion in our country it is not reasonable to expect people to relate to one another in the large anonymous groups which usually characterize our eucharistic celebrations.

There is only the resultant seeking of closer relationships in small intimate groups, in home liturgies, prayer meetings, charismatic celebrations and communities, marriage encounters, cursillos, Better World retreats, faith sharing, and endless other forms of weekend experiences. When community is found, it is found here despite the occasional aberration of reducing the faith dimension to social relationships and varying degrees of friendship.

What is experienced in these groupings is rarely found in our Sunday gatherings. It is as if we were doing something quite different there. And we are. We are still living within an institutionalization of what was at one time a natural rhythm of life: namely, the rural society family gathering once a week to overcome separation from others on the previous days. The weekend which was once the time of leisure and communality has now become the time of escape and struggle to have members of the family become reacquainted. Thus most Catholics choose their Sunday liturgy in terms of convenience rather than in terms of the quality of celebration.

The problem admits of no easy solution. We cannot go on with business as usual, oblivious to the pernicious effect that changing cultural patterns are having on our worship. Nor can we merely capitulate to a kind of "everything everywhere" attitude. In both cases we are not dealing with the problem of community. We are merely suppressing our anxieties about it. Different styles or worship on Sunday, different and more extensive use of ministries, a more intensified development of the humanizing aspects of the liturgy, organization of a specifically liturgical life for segments of the parish according to location, interest, or age grouping will help alleviate the problem of the present Saturday evening or Sunday morning squalor, but Christian community

is too complex a phenomenon to respond to liturgical improve-
ments alone. As Kenneth Smits says, "efforts to work at it from
liturgy alone are doomed to failure."[3]

The fact that community does not take place through the revision of rites is clear in the case of Christian initiation. What
Christian initiation is all about is the entrance into the community
of the faithful. But since there is the lack of experience of real
community among so many Christians at the present time, the
very notion of the liturgical community has become a problem.
This is the reason that all our efforts in the renewal of Christian
initiation should not be centered on the formation and implementation of new rites. Rather, the first consideration should be
given to understanding the meaning of community and especially the Christian community. Methods will have to be devised
whereby the conditions for Christian community can be brought
about if initiation is not to be a meaningless process.

The difficulty of determining the meaning of the liturgical community becomes salient when one ponders the problems which
have emerged in the past several years in conjunction with the
sacrament of reconciliation. The very private form of reconciliation of years past reflected a questionable understanding of
community as applied to church. Only respect for traditional
authority could maintain such a practice during the lengthy period of liturgical history when the liturgical assembly was, for
all religious purposes, in a state of disarray. When such respect
for authority waned, as it has, private confession strikingly de-
creased in practice.

The reconciliation room and the communal penance service
will remove the anonymity of private confession. But even if the
communal penance becomes the paradigm of reconciliation with
the church, we are still left with the more basic problem: the
quest for the meaning of the liturgical assembly.

There seems to have been little in-depth reflection on the
meaning of community. Christians have not come up with the
underlying rationale of community. It is necessary to develop
some theory of community if Christians are to discover the direction they wish to go when building community. What guidelines or criteria are there for authentic community, especially a

3. Ibid. 103.

community which can be called Christian? First we must keep in mind that any developing of these criteria for community must be done in the context that we are 1) Christians who live by the word of God, 2) Americans with our own cultural values, and 3) believers who are influenced by changing views of reality.

First, the word of God. One of the New Testament pictures of community is given to us in Galatians and Ephesians where Paul speaks of Christians gathered by the Spirit to proclaim the power of the life of the Risen One in the community. The characteristics of this community based on the fruits of the Spirit are: unconditional commitment to one another, understanding, patience, goodness, and meekness. This community is a healing, liberating community in the power of the New Life. Love, joy, and peace are the fruits of this commitment to one another in patience, understanding, and the other manifestations of the presence of the Spirit. Other New Testament books speak of community. Matthew does so in terms of mutual support and correction; Acts, as a sharing, celebrating, praying community; and John, as one built on the love which Jesus has shown for us.

It is an image of an adult community, taking freedom and responsibility for one's own and other's lives. Rather than presenting the institutional model which suggests passivity, dependence, and subjection to law, it gives us the image of people actively nourishing one another. Is this just an ideal rarely or never to be attained, an eschatological model? Possibly. It is, however, certainly a theological model for the freedom and life of the Christian community. It is a model of community where the bond is love embodied in concrete action, and that concrete action and that concrete activity are spelled *conversion*.

Joseph Powers, S.J., sums up the biblical concept of a conversion community when he says:

> It is at this level, the level of the pattern of saving life in the community, then, that we speak meaningfully of "conversion" or "transsubstantiation." For what is changed, converted here is the whole of life, the whole of people's vision, experience and capacity for action in the world. The fruits of this kind of mutual engagement and support should show in the lives of love, peace and joy which the Christians are called to live in the unity of the Spirit

(Eph. 4:2). And, if we take Paul's judgment of the Corinthians seriously, it is this conversion of life which changes the meeting of the Christian community into the "Lord's Supper". Without the Christian commitment to one another and the actual engagement in one another's lives, there is no Lord's Supper. There is only the judgment of weakness, weariness and disappointment which lives at the heart of the so-called community. It is the patterns of "converted" (transsubstantiated) life in the community which constituted the basic truth and power of the community's celebration of the Eucharist, its proclamation of the saving reality of the death of the Lord until he comes.[4]

Although much of the picture of Christian community that the New Testament portrays for us was either lost or distorted in the course of the history of the church, in many ways the Second Vatican Council represents a return to that biblical mode of thinking. While the hierarchical form of the church is present in such a document as *Lumen gentium*, this constitution reveals an attempt to return to the deeper communitarian theology of the church. The emphasis is on the people of God and the ministerial function of priests and bishops. Along with *Lumen gentium*, the Constitution on the Sacred Liturgy stresses that it is the whole community that celebrates the eucharist.

The theology of celebration articulated by the Council moves in the same direction as that of the Pauline letters. Not only is the liturgy seen as a foretaste of the heavenly worship, but before one can worship in Christ, one must undergo a conversion. What is primary is not the observance of liturgical law, but that the worshipers participate knowingly, actively, and fruitfully. The conversion that is required for the liturgical assembly is not focussed on the conversion of the elements of a meal but on the lives of the Christians themselves. Vatican II invites us to reflect on the eucharist in a wider context than that bequeathed to us by the post-Tridentine theology.

Second, in attempting to discover the criteria for community, we must remember that we must do so as Americans. What about community from an American perspective? David O'Brien

4. Joseph Powers, "Eucharist: Symbol of Freedom and Community," in *Christian Spirituality in the United States: Independence and Interdependence*, ed., Francis A. Eigo (Villanova, Pa.: The Villanova University Press, 1978) 200.

speaks of the renewal of American Catholicism as coming from the American tradition of self-determination, the idea of the voluntary association and participatory membership. This would demand a more pluralistic, interest-oriented pattern to Catholic communities. They would be formed from the base up rather than being territorially predetermined. It would certainly involve a greater amount of freedom. Theologically, one would add to this a concern for the quality of life in these communities, this in light of the fruits of the Spirit as presented in Galatians 5.

Another characteristic of the community in the American milieu would be a Christological pragmatism. This means that members of the community are seeking the incarnation of faith and grace-given potential in and for the world around us. Such would imply that the validity of the eucharistic community is sanctioned in its day to day living. It would also involve training, personnel, and finances for experimentation and radicalization in temporary structures; it would demand emotional and intellectual openness and freedom. It will mean a pluralism of approaches to the forms of Christian community. It means that the church must be seen in terms of very concrete incarnations of free communities. From a theological point of view, the quality of life in terms of the fruits of the Spirit must be valued to avoid the formation of merely ideological interest groups.

Another quality of American community is the historicity and relativity of any human articulation of faith, whether it be in theology, ritual, or church structures. This would reinforce the necessity of pluralism in ritual, structure, and theology. This means that in something such as any understanding of the eucharist, it must go beyond ritual and face the concrete issue of the quality of life of the Christian community in terms of our understanding of the human today. The recent movement in eucharistic theology from a theology of confection to a theology of celebration is an attempt to make eucharistic theology relevant and fruitful for the church and not remain abstract speculation. The quality of life and freedom in the Christian community, the creativity and vitality with which life is lived and shared is for us, as it was for Paul, the real judgment of the validity of our eucharist. Appeals for more regular attendance at Mass by pope and bishops are fruitless unless they are accompanied by a real effort to involve actively people in the renewal of the whole life of the church. And here it is important to say that appealing for people to return to the church or to get more actively involved is pointless unless we are willing to listen to what they really want of us.

Third, any understanding of the liturgical community must be placed in the context of a perspective of reality that is claiming more and more attention in our country. At the risk of doing grave injustice to this less classical world view, let me sum it up by saying that it is a movement from a view that saw what was important, significant and abiding in reality as that which was unchanging, to now speaking of what is real as in process. Reality is constituted by the network of relationships. Reality is that kind of complex unity which is processive in character and relational in structure. This model for understanding is based on human experience that what is really important in human living changes and that what contemporary persons find of value is usually seen in terms of relationships. As Cardinal Newman put it: "to live is to change and to be perfect is to have changed often."

What this means is that we cannot view the church as static and easily definable. It must be seen as constantly changing and adapting itself because like the rest of reality it is both processive and relational in character. Once one sees the church as the whole community of persons who are related to God in faith in terms of Jesus Christ, the lines which define this church become blurred. To be a member of the church means to be one who is possessed by Christ in such a way that he causes a further becoming of faith in that person. While such a view of church will be less satisfactory, less cleanly defined, less empirically discoverable, still it does take seriously the notion of the pilgrim church where the people are always in the process of creating the church.

This perspective sees the church as an event moving throughout history. Its concrete shape is influenced by the actual make-up of faith of its members and the way in which this faith is articulated in dialogue with the contemporary culture. The church, because it is highly relational, cannot prescind from its environment. This is not to be considered an unhappy turn of events. There is no particular value in mere repetition.

What this means for the liturgical community is that the liturgy is always an event in process. It is not as if the detailed structure of the liturgy of the church was given at one time in history and remains valid until the end of time. Rather, this framework for understanding the church implies that change must be built into the very liturgy itself. Only if that is the case, can one speak of a truly human liturgy. It is certainly true that anthropologically speaking, ritual involves and demands a great deal of repetition, but it is also the case that when Christians ritualize, they are doing much more than the mere reiteration of what Christians have done before them.

As the lines which separate the church from those parts of life which cannot be classified as church are not easily delineated, so in the case of the liturgy. It is not easy to define what is liturgical and what is not. The most public, most visible, most sacramental, most communitarian event of the eucharist is certainly liturgy. Private mediation in the desert would probably not qualify. But what of all the instances between? Many more of these could be considered liturgy than we have thought in the past. Liturgy is not so just because ecclesiastical authority says it is so. Authority does not create truth.

Another point which flows from the insight that liturgy is a processive event is that we cannot presume that there is a basic unchanging objective minimum to the liturgy which is always found whether one can speak of the presence of the community or not. Since liturgy is more than the mere reiteration of the past, it must respond to the present community going beyond that past. The truth of each liturgical celebration is not only rooted in the paschal mystery, it also is something new in terms of the present relationships involved. While it is certainly a celebration of something already present, there is a deepening and a creative advance in the religious experience of the community. This is the case because the spirituality of any liturgical community is a developmental phenomenon called forth by God to the future kingdom. What this perspective has to say about liturgy is that since the Christian community is in process, the liturgy is the way in which this community is maintained in process.

And finally what this view of reality means for liturgy is that the liturgical community is the one which highlights the purpose of Jesus in our lives. Since Jesus is the model of what it means to be human and since the church is the explication of Christ in the world, the praying church is to aid the humanization process. The need for a really human liturgy, for an authentically human liturgical assembly, is demanded by such a task.

With these three background considerations in mind, namely, the biblical picture of community, the specifically American colorings of community, and the more processive and relational view of reality, we can now proceed to consider the conditions necessary for community and for the liturgical community in particular. In this matter, the American philosopher, Josiah Royce, can be of help.

For Royce the only way to achieve human fulfillment is by a sense of community. Community is the first need of humankind. It is our first duty and commandment. This flows from Royce's reflection on the dynamism of the human personality and the human experience of a need for a unifying purpose in life. Royce sees that it is necessary to commit oneself to some outside cause. This commitment which he calls loyalty demands that persons dedicate themselves to the service of other human beings. Thus, the individual needs to engage in community life. But Royce also is aware that any unity that is attained through loyalty can only be partial and fragmentary. However, those who are loyal will be saved by finding their completion in God. His point is simply this, that salvation comes through community.[5]

What in Royce's framework are the main traits of the liturgical community? Presumably they are not essentially different from those which he identifies as qualifying any group of individuals so that they can be constituted a human community. If it is true, as Josiah Royce maintains, that a community is "essentially a product of a time-process," then a community has both a past and a future. This implies that if community is to come into existence as well as be sustained once it has been created, certain conditions must be present. And in the light of Christian faith these criteria become theological. According to Royce the following conditions are necessary for the life of any community. I will attempt to apply these conditions to the liturgical assembly in particular.

5. For an expansion of Royce's idea of community see chapter three in John E. Smith, *The Spirit of American Philosophy* (New York: Oxford University Press, 1963).

(1) *Community presupposes a plurality of individuals who are able and willing to communicate with one another.* If any good human community demands that it be constituted by people able and willing to communicate, then the liturgical community must be composed of members who are highly communicative. Only in that way can the definition of liturgy as the symbolic articulation of the spirituality of the Christian community be fulfilled. To put it simply, spirituality is one's relationship with God which is brought to expression in the relationships that exist among Christians themselves. But if these human and Christian relationships are not to be aberrant and to atrophy, those involved in them must have the ability and the willingness to communicate.

Once the communication is present, one can meaningfully speak of a spirituality of the community. The community's relationship with God, its spirituality, is created in the very symbolic realization of it. Without this there is nothing to ritualize. And when ritual has no inner dynamic to bring to expression, there is no liturgy. Again, the familiar words: liturgy presupposes community.

Here it should be noted that the move to the more person-oriented celebration is one of the happy outcomes of our present liturgical reforms. Such an orientation can only enhance community. Although there are fears expressed that the celebration of the person will lead to a loss of a sense of the transcendent so that we are left only with the techniques of group therapy and encounter sessions (which, after all, are not so bad in comparison with the rigidity and individuality of the previous centuries), it is still possible to give a priority to the sense of God in the personal act of celebration.

(2) The second condition for a human community designated by Royce is *that each individual in the group must use his/her memory and imagination to extend his/her life into the remembered past and projected future.* When one speaks of this kind of anamnesis in regard to the liturgical community, we see how the paschal mystery of Christ is explicated in Christian liturgy. The memory of Christ's death and resurrection is kept alive through the power of memory of the community, which is not simply a commemoration of dead events but one that possesses the Christ of the past in such a way that he is present in its midst. To remember as a community means to extend oneself back into those chief

events of Christ's life as well as to project oneself forward into Christ's presence at the end of time. This second condition for a human community is the foundation of the fact that the liturgical assembly is the remembrance of the past, the explication of the present, and the anticipation of the future.

(3) The third condition is *that the extended past and future selves of the members must include some events which are, for all these selves, identical.* Obviously, here in the liturgical community the events which are identical are all those chief events which the second condition requires be caught up in the community's memory, celebrated in the present and looked forward to in the future. These identical events are the means by which the community is bound together. This union is especially brought to visibility in the eucharist which is an action symbolic of the unity that should exist between the members of the assembly with one another. This unity in the body of Christ must be found in both the local community as well as in the great community of the universal church.

(4) The fourth condition is *that the members of the community must work together in a conscious way to achieve common goals.* This implies that the liturgy must call forth some moral direction in the lives of the worshipers. And here we are not confining ourselves to personal individual morality. Christian life is not circumscribed by the limits of worship and the immediate worshiping community. There must be no such artificial compartmentalization of liturgy and life.

This communal striving for the same goals on the part of the participants of the liturgical community is the psychological and theological basis for the understanding of the relationship between liturgy and culture. This involves both the community's striving to worship in the thought patterns and life style of its own culture as well as taking care that its inculturated worship sits in judgment upon that very culture.

The results of the studies on the anthropology of ritual by the anthropologist, Victor Turner, which so interest liturgists these days, has highlighted the fact that there is a marginal quality about being a Christian. Being marginal means that one stands in judgment of one's cultural values. The "communitas" that Turner speaks of is that underlying reality that one finds when one strips away the statuses and roles that infect our human relationships, preventing us from touching them and ourselves with any depth. Turner maintains that to discover and experience this communitas, this imperceptible reality that gives the life force to community, one must pass through the stages of separation, suspension, and reintegration. In other words, one must be converted. He points up very well that community does not result from catechesis or from the reception of the sacraments. Along the same line the philosophical theologian, Bernard Lonergan, has pointed out that to do theology more is needed than information or experience, or to rephrase it, to do liturgy more is needed than catechesis and liturgical celebrations.

(5) Finally, the fifth condition for community is *that the members be loving and loyal to the other members and especially to the community as a whole.* If this is to be verified in the liturgical community, individual worshipers cannot use the assembly for their own devotional needs. They have a mission to help build up the liturgical community itself. There is no room for the Jesus-and-me mentality in liturgical worship. Rather, salvation is through community, and this is the case because God in Christ comes to visibility in the very union that exists between the members. To the degree that members show forth their love and loyalty to the community, to that degree salvation is shown forth and there is an epiphany of the often imperceptible God.

If Royce is correct that "a community is a group of people who are bound together by the memory of a shared past and by the projection of common hopes for the future,"[6] then the parish should fulfill this definition. Do the inner dynamics of the Sunday liturgy make the members of the parish more aware of their heritage as a Christian community? Does this liturgy enable them to work together more during the week? The eucharist is a memorial of our redemption through Christ's death and resurrection, but a commemoration effective of Christian community now. It is a way that the worshipers share their past. But it should also articulate their common hopes for the future. The Mass is not only memorial, not even primarily memorial. It is an eschatological event, literally taking its significance from the future. The eucharist should then also be a celebration of the very direction into the future of the community.

6. Joseph A. Brachen, "Salvation through Community," *American Ecclesiastical Review* 164:2 (February 1971) 102.

Even more important than this Sunday eucharist, which apparently is not fulfilling the conditions of community set forth by Royce, is the formation of subgroups within the parish bringing people together during the week or on weekends. These may be CCD groups, adult education groups, parish choir, discussion groups, and prayer groups. These groups are important not so much for the work they accomplish for the parish but "also for the heightened sense of community which is thereby fostered among the members of the group."[7] Strange as it may be, the sense of community develops faster when one belongs to several groups at once than when one is exclusively a member of one group. It is obvious that anyone who belongs to many communities, for example, the family, one or more units in the parish, in the civic community, will have the tension resulting from the pull of different communities on his or her life, but the more sophisticated understanding and experience of community which he or she will acquire by belonging to several communities at once will outweigh the disadvantages. A person's function will differ in the various communities.

It should be obvious that the place and attitude of the pastor in the area of community building is paramount. If he jealously guards his authority, then a strong sense of community will develop very slowly, unless one considers everyone united against the pastor as a form of community. However, if he sees his authority as coming in part from the parishioners, he will react more positively toward the formation of small groups in the community. Again, religious communities working in the territory of the local parish can make a great contribution to community building. Certainly, they can be involved with the various subgroups of the parish, being in contact with the lay people. They too must be members of many communities. This may produce some tension, but again it is better to belong to several communities simultaneously and so be required to reconcile the various demands upon one by the several communities than to align oneself with one community exclusively and so become fixated with the single role one has within that community.

Most of all, religious are to communicate the meaning of community life with a certain intensity. This is not the appropriate place to examine the reasons why in the present, religious com-

7. Ibid. 103.

munities are often countersigns. Hopefully, one of the characteristics of the Christian experience in the U.S. will be the concrete exemplification of the idea of community in the lives of
religious men and women.

In developing the meaning of the liturgical community in the
U.S., it is helpful to be aware of Royce's conditions for human
community. But, of course, those conditions apply to all human
communities and we are concerned primarily with the liturgical
assembly.

It is the hope that Royce's five conditions will help make it
possible to realize and actualize the liturgical community as such.
But what makes the liturgical community different from all other
communities? It is too abstract and insufficiently focused to say
that it is the place where the church becomes the church, that
it is the expression as well as the actualization of Christian community, that it is the concrete symbolic clarification of what the
community was, is, and will be.

What makes the liturgical community different is that in it the
spirituality of the community is expressed. Certainly, liturgy
manifests and creates the church, but not any aspect of the church.
It reveals the faith dimension of the church. The rituals, rites,
and prayer formulas are the expressions and forms of the way
the community reveals the faith dimension of the church. When
we speak of the liturgy as the symbolic articulation of the community's spirituality we are not only concerned with the contexts
and conditions of this community, we are also concerned, primarily concerned, with the vision and faith of this community.

But if it is true that liturgy articulates the spirituality of the
Christian community, then what is that spirituality? When we
speak of spirituality we are dealing with the phenomenon of
how we relate to God. And when speaking of communal spirituality, we are dealing with how the community as such relates
to God. And to find out what it means to relate to God either
as an individual or as a community, one must understand and
discover the meaning of the self-image involved. We relate to
God in terms of our self-image. The person, for instance, whose
self-concept is that of someone who is deficient, without value,
inferior, will relate to God differently from those who see themselves as worthwhile and lovable. Our self-image is what in fact
we are becoming. In the ecclesiastical sense, the community

relates to God in terms of its self-image; we can say that its spirituality is its self-image. The liturgy then is a ritualizing attempt to express this self-image.

But how do we discover our self-image? I believe that the community can appropriate its self-image in basically the same way that the individual does. I see this as being accomplished through the process of self-transparency. For ourselves, our self-image comes to visibility when we engage in whatever is helpful for personal development and growth. Often this involves a kind of ritualizing. In the process we gain insight into ourselves and our relationships, and we are more and more in contact with our feelings, our thoughts, and our bodily sensations. True, it takes time for feelings to catch up with insight, but gradually there is that kind of integration which allows for a person to accept oneself, possess oneself in such a way that one is comfortable with one's existence, actually rejoices in it, and discovers that one is truly lovable and capable of love. This is the entrée to the total acceptance, both intellectually and on the feeling level, that God has first loved us. This kind of self-transparency is what brings to expression the kind of self-image by which we relate to God and by which we can speak of our spirituality. I am loving and loved by God.

But what kind of self-image does the church as community have? What is the process of self-transparency that would allow such an image to emerge? I think that the self-image of the Christian community has been obscured and suppressed for many years. The differing models of the church which theologian Avery Dulles speaks of indicates that differing self-images were operative at different times in the history of the church. I believe that the gospel self-image of the community is again surfacing. In the various prayer experiences taking place across the country, people are becoming clear to each other in their faith-dimension. They are letting their Christianity show through. What comes to expression is that they are the people of God in terms of the vision of Christ. This vision impells them to celebrate the event of their being the Christian community, and in liturgical worship they let this vision rise to such explicitness that they place themselves in relationship to this vision.

When this vision is shared we have the kind of self-transparency that is necessary for emergence of the self-image. But what does it mean to share a vision? Is it the exchange of an intellectual understanding such as the teacher in the lecture hall sharing a conceptual framework with the students? I think not. It is more like trusting others because of the way that they are as human beings; it is interacting with them and allowing them to enter your life and they inviting you to enter theirs. This brings about a reciprocity which is mutually revealing and creative of a deepened relationship. The result is union. There is the union of friends, of colleagues, of husband and wife, of co-partners in an enterprise. In all these cases there is some kind of self-transparency, albeit, in different degrees; there is shared vision, there is mutual self-exposure, there is the affirmation of the other and the affirmation of oneself. In all of this complex human interaction there is the emergence of one's self-image.

When one moves from the individual personal dimension to that of the communal, although still personal, aspect, we are dealing with the self-image of the Christian community which is brought about in the kind of self-transparency that goes on in a community. As in the case of the individual, this transparency implies the sharing of a common vision by all the members of that community. Since the liturgical community is Christian, the content of that shared vision must be Jesus Christ himself. He is the primary ingredient of the Christian self-image. This communal self-image is the means by which this community can relate to God. In other words, as in the case of the individual, the community's spirituality is in terms of its communal self-image. *And one can speak of the liturgical assembly as being the place where the self-image of the whole Christian community is raised to the level of explicit communal activity.* This is so because liturgy is the articulation of the spirituality of the community, and liturgy is the communal faithful transparency brought to the level of ritual awareness. This communal self-image by which the community relates to God is composed of the shared vision, the communal faith, and the mutual self-transparency of the members of this community. To put it simply, what is shared, what is believed in common, and what is reciprocally exposed to each other is that Christians have been, are, and will be those who are claimed by Christ as his sign of salvation to the world. And so when Christians do that, when they engage in their spirituality as a community, when they relate to God in terms of the self-image they have as a group, when they share their common vision in a ritualized fashion, they become more the people of God in Christ, they become the church. In their mutual transparency as a community, their own identity is affirmed because in that sharing, that exchange of vision and faith-sharing, Christ rises to visibility and we have that ecclesial reality we call the church. Liturgy in that sense becomes the place where the church becomes the church.

Thus, shared vision means that by such sharing Christians become present to each other. And it is in this mutual becoming present that God comes to expression. Jesus comes to presence when we as Christians share a vision about the significance of life. All of this is celebrated in the human symbolic involvement that we call liturgy.

As a result of this theory we must ask some questions. Can liturgical planning ever be primarily a question of technique? Should it rather be dealing with attempts to facilitate the transparency of the faith aspect of the community? What about the faith of the person who presides at the liturgy? Must he or she attempt to communicate a faith they do not have? Should presiders allow room for the ambiguity of the faith that is found in the worshiping community? Does our present excessively verbal liturgy stand in the way of the emergence of the community's self-image. Does it not rather attempt to impose the way the community is to relate to God? Does the present normative Roman Mass rite really allow for the possibility of self-transparency when used in small groups, or is some other form of ritual necessary there? Do we not misuse ritual by attempting to hide behind it? Are we not afraid that if we engage in faith-sharing we will expose a deficient faith and so turn ritual into a defense mechanism rather than the kind of symbolic and ritual involvement which demands self-exposure?

What then is the liturgical community? It is one founded on the New Testament concept reiterated by Second Vatican Council that community is adult, freeing, nourishing, and calling for personal responsibility. It should embody the American values of self-determination, participation, pluralism, emotional and intellectual openness, and relativity in life and the ways that life is lived. A third important consideration is that these notions must be contextualized in terms of a more process oriented perspective of reality, implying that change is positive and that it is relationality and not some unchanging essence which more adequately describes contemporary religious experience. In all of this the point about the liturgical community is that it is the quality of life of the community more than anything else which makes it true, which validates it as a Christian community.

Ultimately, the liturgical assembly is the place where the spirituality of a Christian community in terms of its self-image, self-transparency, and shared vision can come to ritual expression. If this is to be the case, then the five conditions described by Royce must come into play. They will facilitate the actualization of a Christian community into a liturgical assembly. The degree that Christ comes to expression will be dependent upon the quality of communication between the different members of the community, the effectiveness of the community's memory in recalling the paschal mystery, the union which arises from the common identification with that mystery, the judgment the community renders to its culture, and the extent to which all members devote themselves to this community in building it up so that the church may become the proclamation of God's salvation to the world and in turn becomes each worshiper's way of salvation through community.

6

Models for a Liturgical Theology

LITURGY IS A MYSTERY AND CANNOT BE DEFINED ACCORDING TO VIS-
ible components alone. A definition of the liturgy which would
proceed from clear and univocal concepts is impossible. As with
everything else in the area of faith there are no categories which
exhaustively express the meaning of the liturgy. It is a mystery
of faith and can only be dealt with in terms of symbols, models
and paradigms. But because the liturgy as mystery is a rich and
complex reality, it is possible to speak about it in terms of several
models.

Models by their nature are inadequate. They attempt to clarify
reality in terms of our human experience. No single model can
be used alone. One should not absolutize any particular model
to the detriment of the others. What one model might be obscure
about, another will serve to enlighten. This pluralism of models
is a theological necessity today. For instance, in the last few
decades there have been several operating models to describe
the church that have been popular: mystical body, people of
God, sacrament of Christ and church as servant. The models
change as the church seeks to find its identity in a changing
world. There are obvious limitations to the use of models in
theology but the value of this kind of approach is that it allows
for conversation among the various theological outlooks at a time
when theological pluralism is considered a desideratum.

Needless to say, this shift of paradigms can be very threatening
for some people and they resist such change. Such a shift implies

more than a change of language. It means the adoption of new values, priorities, and commitments. The polarization in the church today should come as no surprise to someone who is aware of the changing models of the church. Tolerance of pluralism is the only solution. No benefit will result from trying to impose any one model as the last word. It is true that one model can function as a unifying focus for a particular theologian's framework of thought. And even in the same theologian, one model will be operative in one area of theology and another model in another area. But the theologian is called to go beyond these images. He/she must use the image in a reflective and critical way and when that takes place, he/she is working with the model theologically. The use of models in theology should emphasize for us that at no time do our concepts and symbols actually capture the infinite that lies behind our liturgical experiences. And since all models have their limitations, the task is to work with several models as complementary.

It is very important to realize that when the liturgy is described in terms of theological models one is talking about it in metaphorical terms. One is using images that have an evocative power. The use of models in a liturgical theology is only an attempt to speak of worship analogously in terms of life experiences. Such images and symbols are able to focus human experience in a new way because they so exceed the powers of abstract thought. These models convey a meaning which is apprehended in a nonconceptual way and which have a transformative effect on the horizons of human life.

Religious Models and Experience

While religious models can influence our attitudes and suggest courses of action their validity is dependent upon their ability to articulate our own religious experience. Certain models of the liturgy no longer are able to thematize our present experience of worship and these models are less helpful now than others. The images of the liturgy which are important today are those which can be found to be deeply rooted in the experience of the worshiping congregation. There is a kind of schizophrenia that takes place when there is such discontinuity between the models we use to talk about liturgy and the way we actually experience it. In a sense the crisis of faith is a crisis of images as Avery

Dulles has so well indicated. He says: "Many traditional images have lost their former hold on people, while the new images have not yet had time to gain their full power . . . Many of us know very little from direct experience about lambs, wolves, sheep, vines, and grapes, or even about kings and patriarchs as they were in biblical times. There is need therefore to supplement these images with others that speak more directly to our contemporaries."[1] We cannot, however, pretend to create these images on the spot. They are born and they die but they cannot be manufactured by committees or individual theologians. Yet these models are indispensable for any liturgical theology.

Some of the models of the liturgy have an exploratory or educative value in that they highlight for us elements and qualities of our worship to which we have not previously averted. Often this will have practical consequences for us which were less pressing at a former time. But there is no way in which one can prove the truth of the models used. One can say that their validity depends upon whether or not they work, whether they are more helpful than some others to articulate what is going on in the worshiping community informed by Christ and the gospel. Liturgy like any area of theology must begin in faith and with the fact that we are dealing with a community of revelation. Because certain models do not describe what is actually going on in certain parishes today does not immediately call into question the usefulness of the model. It may be that such a model is necessary to call those parishes to a "liturgical conversion." The truth of a model depends upon the consequences that follow upon the use of such a model. If a model leads to distortions and abuses on the practical level, then it is judged to be a bad model.

There are more models than the five described here. But the ones I have selected appear to me to be most helpful. It is better to work with a few models in an article of this length and risk some oversimplifications than to cause confusion by multiplying the paradigms of liturgical theology. It should be obvious that what is said of each model does not apply to it exclusively. It is a matter of emphasis and predominant reference.

1. Avery Dulles, *Models of the Church* (Garden City, N.Y.: Doubleday, 1974) 19.

Liturgy as Institution

This view of the liturgy presupposes an ecclesiology which sees the church primarily in terms of its visible structures, its officers and its required procedures. Such a view is more than the affirmation that for the church to accomplish its task for building up the kingdom of God, it is necessary to have some kind of visibility, some leaders and some accepted methods of conducting its business. Rather it is the institutional aspect of the church which is regarded as primary. It is *the* model for understanding the church.

According to this model the church is described in terms of teaching, sanctifying and governing. All three of these tasks are done for the faithful by the leaders of the church, thus identifying these leaders with the church itself. The liturgy in this framework would be seen as something which is primarily done by the clergy for the people. The clergy is the source of grace that flows through the ritual actions. The liturgical celebration is basically a pyramidal event, in which the ordinary worshipers find themselves in a primarily passive position. There is also a clear cut distinction between clergy and faithful in the liturgy itself.

Liturgy here becomes a legalistic consideration. The observance of liturgical regulations takes on paramount importance and the sanctifying power of the sacraments is dependent upon the proper observance of canonical rules. It is important in this model that the test of authentic liturgy be what can be juridically verified. The criteria for the liturgy of the church must be visible as are the standards for membership in the church itself.

This view of the liturgy is basically triumphalistic in character. Those who consider worship primarily as institutional see little need for the liturgy to change. It was perfect from the beginning and any questioning of the significance of any of the structures becomes a threat to the underlying ecclesiology. And so it is only logical that this model which is based on the presupposition that what is essential is unchanging would place a great deal of importance on the institution of the liturgy by Christ. The seven sacraments would be seen as being either directly or indirectly instituted by Christ. And the church must have been brought into existence by Christ with the same fundamental structure that it has today. The liturgy is necessarily hierarchical because that is also of divine institution.

Since theology in this view becomes basically defending what the church has already taught and since there can be no question in this position of any new revelation after the close of the deposit of faith, liturgical theology becomes the attempt to find in the sources of revelation the proof for what the church is saying about the liturgy.

As in the case of the other areas of church life, the chief beneficiaries of liturgy are the members of the church themselves. The sacramental liturgy becomes the source of nourishing graces for those who belong to the "Catholic Church." Other liturgical forms such as the liturgy of the hours are reverenced to the degree that they approach the sacramentality of the specifically seven sacraments. And the purpose of this liturgy is to bring people to heaven, to help them to stay on the straight and narrow path and to stay within the parameters of the Catholic Church so that their salvation can be assured.

In this empirical approach to liturgy a great deal of stress is placed on what is statistically measurable. For instance, baptisms, marriages, anointings, converts and communions are counted. Remember the days when the priest sat in the confessional with his hand counter clicking away as he tallied up the number of penitents. Or how often in the old days did one hear at jubilee celebrations the recounting of how many thousands of Masses Father so-and-so said in his life as a priest.

Limitations of the Institutional Model

Is this view of the liturgy still in existence? Very definitely. It has strong endorsement in official church documents and by the leaders in the church. Certainly, it is still clearly stressed in the document on the liturgy that the church's worship is of divine institution. Many hold on to this view of liturgy because it gives them a sense of stability in an everchanging world. At times these people focus on relatively unimportant aspects of worship such as genuflections and incense because they want to have at least one thing in their life which does not change. The unchanging liturgy gave Catholics a strong sense of identity. The remark was often made that the wonderful thing about the Latin Mass was that one could go anywhere in the world to worship in any Catholic Church and always feel at home.

There are some serious limitations to the juridical model of liturgy. There is little if any New Testament evidence for such an approach to worship. What we find there is more flexible, pluralistic and adapted. The liturgy before the formation of the Roman Rite in the fourth and fifth centuries was a rich and variegated phenomenon. Until the freezing of the Missal by Pius V in 1570 there was considerable diversity in the Roman liturgy itself.

Another problem with this approach is that it reinforced the clericalization of the liturgy. It is no coincidence that as the institutional model of the church gained control, the juridical model of the liturgy became paramount. The history of the liturgy becomes the gradual removing of the liturgy from the people. Fidelity to rubrics becomes more important than the quality of the celebration and attendance at Mass under pain of sin looms larger than the call to authentic worship. The concern over communion in the hand has gone far beyond any regard for worshiping in spirit and in truth. Liturgy can hardly have a prophetic quality about it if the local authorities are preoccupied with the observation of minor liturgical regulations.

This juridical concept of liturgy raises problems for theology. For instance, there is little leeway for the developing of the ecumenical liturgical experience. The problem of intercommunion becomes one of fidelity to the Roman See. This view of liturgy seems to render the liturgical life of other churches (non-Roman) as without content and life. Needless to say, in this approach anything like a charismatic liturgy would be highly suspect. Perhaps, that is the reason why the Catholic Charismatic Movement has gone out of its way to be "law-abiding" in its liturgical celebrations.

Liturgy as Mystery

Odo Casel, the author of the mystery theology approach to liturgy, has been unjustly passed over. The fact is that despite the criticisms about his position, many of the ideas of Odo Casel have been accepted by the document on the liturgy of the Second Vatican Council. This is especially true of his notion of Christ's presence in the liturgy. It is inappropriate for a council of the church to embrace any particular theologian's position, but the sounds of Casel ring through the Constitution on the Sacred Liturgy, especially in Chapter One. For instance in No. 2 the document states: "The liturgy is thus the outstanding means by which the faithful can express in their lives the mystery of Christ." It is a fact that many of Casel's ideas have become part of post-conciliar theology.

Casel defined mystery as a "sacred ritual action in which a saving deed is made present through the rite; the congregation, by performing the rite, takes part in the saving act, and thereby experiences salvation."

The content or meaning of mystery in Casel's thought (and in the framework of those who identify themselves with the mystery-theology approach to liturgy) refers first of all to God himself as he exists in himself and in the things that he has made. Secondly, it refers to Christ, not just the person of Christ but Christ performing his salvific actions, especially his death, resurrection and ascension. Thirdly, mystery means the saving activity of Christ in the church and in the sacraments. This third sense is really the one that is most operative in this liturgical theology. As such the liturgical mystery possesses a sacramental mode of being. It means making present again by a cultic action. The content of this ritualizing is not just the power of the effect of Christ's saving deeds, but these very deeds themselves. It is the presence of historic-nonrecurring actions of salvation, not of some eternal, extra-temporal salvific will nor of an event in heaven. And what is made present is the reality which lies behind the historical actions, not these actions in their historical trappings.

Christ is not separated from his mysteries but is present and active within them. The presence of the risen Christ is not properly speaking the reality made present in the liturgy but is the preliminary condition making possible the presence of what is essential, the saving actions of Christ. It is necessary that Christ *and his saving work* be present in the liturgy because a person only becomes a Christian by participation in this saving activity. Neither the presence of the person of Christ, nor the presence of divine life in him, nor the mere presence of the body and blood are enough. The redeeming work itself must be present. Our particpation in the mystery of salvation demands a real and mystical participation in the life and death of Christ which must be present in the sacramental act. The great breakthrough that Casel made was to move the focus in eucharistic theology away from the presence of Jesus' body and blood to the presence of the redemptive action itself.

Word and Sacraments

The saving action of Christ is not limited to the sacraments. It is communicated by the word of God. Casel says that one should not make too great a distinction between the presence of Christ in the divine office and in the eucharist. He admits a difference but blames late scholasticism for seeing almost nothing in the Mass but the real presence as the effect of transubstantiation. It makes too little of Christ's saving action in the word. For the ancient church there was only one saving action of Christ and this was the ground for the entire liturgy, both word and sacrament. Christ is not divided. Even blessings and consecrations participate in and show forth the mystery of Christ.

How the saving acts of Christ are rendered present is difficult to understand. We can say that the mystery of Christ is incarnated in the mystery of worship which consists of actions performed both by people and by Christ. Salvation becomes visible because the sacramental symbol is visible. The content of the cultic mystery is present as soon as the sign is set forth because there is a necessary connection between the sacramental process and the incarnation. The sacraments are images of Christ full of the reality of his being *and his activity*. The saving work of Christ is objectively present in the sacraments and it exists before the effect itself.

Past historical events can only be rendered present again through the sacramental mode of existence which can only be understood in faith. Just as the mystery of Christ's redemptive work is *sui generis* because it is both supernatural and yet accomplished in time, so the sacramental mode of existence is different from every natural way of existing. The sacramental mode of existence is not the same as the natural or historical way of existing. The exterior rites are performed in time but the content of these cultic actions does not exist in time. There is no question of a repetition of Christ's saving deeds. The act of Christ is one because it is an eternal, supernatural and transtemporal mystery. There is no before and after. Odo Casel did not attempt to explain metaphysically how the mystery of Christ is sacramentally present in the liturgy. It was for him a matter of understanding what a sacrament is and how it differs from other signs.

There is only one mystery although birth, death and resurrection are events different from each other. It is the substance of this mystery in its totality that is rendered present in the cultic acts. And the substance of the liturgical mystery is the *transitus Christi*, the paschal mystery. Since the paschal mystery is the central mystery, Easter is *the* feast. But a liturgy adequate to the whole mystery of salvation requires a liturgical year and liturgical feasts. The Christian liturgy participates in the sacramentalism inherent in the whole life of the church in time. There will be present in every liturgical celebration the mystery of God communicated to people in Jesus Christ. Each liturgy celebrates the real presence of Jesus who came at the end of a period of preparation, the paschal mystery now reconciling people to God in the church, and the prophecy of the kingdom inaugurated in sacramental signs and to be manifested fully in the parousia.

Liturgy as Sacrament

The sacramental model of liturgical theology is presently the one most widely used. It is basically the model that is operative in the Constitution on the Sacred Liturgy, although the institutional model is ever present in that document. This model is the one employed by most Catholic (Eastern and Western) liturgical theologians today. There is a considerable spread of emphasis among these liturgists and there is a variety of ways in which they utilize this method for articulating a liturgical theology. For instance, on one hand, you have Vagaggini with his highly scholastic approach to liturgy and on the other, Broccolo who makes use of the psychological model as an adjunct to the sacramental one. Theologians such as Bouyer, Verheul, Martimort and Dalmais are found somewhere in between. But to the extent that these liturgical theologians attempt to construct any real systematic approach to worship, they work within the rather wide parameters of what is called here the sacramental paradigm.

In this view the church is the primordial sacrament and the liturgy, which at heart is sacramental in the narrow sense, is the expression of the church and is directed toward the building up of the church. We have the Second Vatican Council to thank for the most articulate and official expression of the sacramentality of the church. In the Constitution on the Church we find this: "The Church is a kind of sacrament of intimate union with God and of unity with all mankind; that is, she is a sign and instrument of such union and unity" (art. 1). The Constitution on the Sacred Liturgy says: "The Liturgy is the summit toward which the activity of the Church is directed; at the same time it is the fountain from which all her power flows" (art. 10)). The same document says that the church "reveals herself most clearly when a full complement of God's holy people, united in prayer and in a common liturgical service" join together in worship.

A contemporary understanding of sacramentality as applied to the church and liturgy would be based upon an understanding of the human person as an incarnate reality. Avery Dulles has put the matter as well as anyone. "The structure of human life is therefore symbolic. The body with all its movements and gestures becomes the expression of the human spirit. The spirit comes to be what it is in and through the body. The symbolic expression does not simply signify what previously existed independently of it. Rather, the expression and the realization accompany and support each other. The corporeal expression gives the spiritual act the material support it needs in order to achieve itself; and the spiritual act gives shape and meaning to the corporeal expression."[2] Liturgy according to this model would be seen primarily in terms of this meaning of a sacrament: an outward sign of a spiritual reality, not in the sense that it merely points to something beyond itself, but as an efficacious sign so that it intensifies that which it is bringing to expression. Because of the incarnational structure of the human spirit, we can talk about sacraments conferring what they contain.

Sacraments as Social Symbols

Sacraments are dialogic in character. They are social symbols which allow the experience of God to break through in terms of a human interaction. Sacraments as the encounter with God are not experiences in isolation. They are communal symbols of grace coming to visibility. For this reason we do not baptize ourselves,

2. Ibid. 60.

we do not anoint ourselves and for this reason the so-called individual celebration of the eucharist can only be described as a highly deficient sign. Thus, worship in this model is primarily participative. There is no room for spectators at the liturgy. Sacramentality by its very nature calls for participation. In participating in the sign of the liturgy, the worshipers are actually creating the church and the sacramental sign.

To the extent that this model makes use of such images as body of Christ and people of God it sees the liturgy in the context of the church as community. This emphasizes that what is being brought to sacramental expression is a Spirit filled fellowship of charity and truth. The main focus will not be on the visible institutional structures of the liturgical assembly. A liturgical theology in which these metaphors are prominent would stress the union of grace on the personal level which is made visible through the ministry and the sacraments. The union that exists among the worshipers is that of the graces of the Holy Spirit which make this community more than a purely sociological phenomenon. Worship is not seen primarily in juridical terms but according to a union which is deeper than any merely human union. The purpose of the liturgy is to establish a deep and lasting union between God and Christians. What is celebrated in the liturgy is grace as a communal gift.

The sacramental approach to liturgy then, brings together the institutional and more community oriented approaches. For liturgy to be sacramental it must be visible; it must be incarnated through outward signs. It must be structured. It is more than communal undifferentiated enthusiasm. But it is more than structure. It is event. It is the dynamism of grace realizing itself in coming to visibility. It is the community's spirituality achieving historical tangibility. There is an internal thrust in the spirituality that the liturgy articulates that demands coming to expression. In the actual liturgical celebration this spirituality is not only reflected but also constituted. And this means that something must happen in the lives of the worshipers. They must be transformed by the spirit so that they manifest the biblical gifts of that same Spirit.

This approach does not claim for liturgy a monopoly of the grace of God coming to expression. Grace and salvation are found outside of liturgy. However, it would affirm strongly that liturgy is the clearest articulation of the Christian's experience of God. Christ and the church as sacraments of God's reconciling love for the world imply that liturgy is the unambiguous manifestation of this sacramentality of Christ and the church. Grace is always seeking visibility, and it is most adequately articulated in the liturgical celebrations. God's working in the world outside of the areas under the sphere of influence of the church's liturgy will tend to be more ambiguous in their witnessing character.

This liturgical theology can easily view the worship situation in a much too exalted fashion. References to the heavenly liturgy can make the theology seem too artificial or unrelated to actual liturgical experiences. With this approach liturgy can turn out to be the plaything of aesthetes and the social and ethical dimensions of the liturgical assembly can be underplayed.

There is an inbuilt tension in this model when it stresses the community aspect of worship. There can be a great deal of frustration with the liturgy when it is described in terms of a community celebration. The fact is that the experience of community at most liturgical services is quite deficient. One can so idealize this aspect of the sacramental model that it cannot be found verified any place in human living. It is necessary to be realistic about what can actually be achieved here in terms of this more interpersonal mode. The search for a perfect human community which can adequately celebrate the liturgy is illusory.

Liturgy as Proclamation

Most Protestant and some Catholic liturgical theologians are more at home with understanding the liturgy as an event of the proclamation of the word of God. Liturgy is constituted in the proclamation of the word. It takes place in the very act of proclamation. Proclamation is a linguistic event in which the church is constituted. Sacraments are looked upon as "visible words."

The theology of liturgy which is articulated in terms of proclamation is based upon the fundamental understanding that the relationship of God to the world and to human beings is to be seen in terms of a dialog between the two. God has shared himself in creation and is calling it to union with himself. This dialogic relationship which describes the reality between God and persons presupposes the mutual presence of God and humans to each other.

In this dialog between God and ourselves, it is God who takes the initiative. God speaks first. The basic attitude on our part is to listen. It is necessary to listen if God is to become present to us. God becomes present in God's actual speaking. If the relationship between God and ourselves is one of dialog, then this relationship can only come about through communication. When God speaks and when we listen there is that mutual presence which is so necessary for this dialogic union. The presence of God to us is a human presence; it is a personal presence. But it is a presence brought about through language.

Wherever sharing in someone's life is to take place (and this is what is meant by a dialogic relationship), it is necessary to be adequately present to that person. This is equally true of the dialog between friends, married people or between God and ourselves. This adequate presence comes about through communication. And this communication requires a form of language. In the case of God he is adequately present to us in Jesus Christ. Christ is the form of his communication. Christ is the language of God. He is thus called the Word of God. Not that he says everything about God that there is to say, but that he adequately expresses the reality of God so that this sharing of life, this mutual presence, this union or dialogical relationship can be brought about without excessive difficulty.

To understand how it is that Christ is the Word of God, how he is the one who makes it possible for the dialog between God and ourselves to take place, and why it is that it is the liturgy which becomes the common language of God and his people, it is necessary to know something of the nature of proclamation. What is the meaning of proclamation? Surely, it is more than speaking in a loud voice. It is more than mere talking. One could hardly talk about liturgy as proclamation if to proclaim meant little more than communicating information such as reading a dinner menu to someone who is blind.

The Meaning of Proclamation

Proclamation is language, but not any kind of language. It is not the language of ordinary conversation or of a business transaction. It is more than verbal communication. It is what theologians call a language-event. By that is meant that language has a broader meaning than the words we use. All forms of human communication such as smiles, laughter, music, art, dancing, making love and other non-verbal gestures can be proclamatory. Two persons embracing, kissing, or having sexual intercourse may use the words "I love you." But they need not, and real communication, real proclamation would have taken place without any words at all.

In this wider sense, language becomes the way that human beings communicate and become mutually present. In this sense human presence depends upon language. The human presence brought about through a language event is a personal presence. For instance, if you are in a crowded subway train, there may be a number of people who are physically present to you, especially if they are pushing and shoving you. But it is only when someone speaks or smiles at you that there is a question of human personal presence. At that moment your personal reality has been constituted by language. We live in relation to others to the degree that they are present to us through a language event.

The point of all this is that language creates us because it enables us to relate with others. When this happens we have an event of proclamation. The proclamatory word (which need not be verbal) brings meaning into our lives. It challenges us to make a decision. We can accept or reject this proclamation to us, but in some sense it calls for decision. Whether it is a question of acceptance or rejection, a new relationship is constituted.

This kind of proclamation can be creative of community. The eventful word both depends on the community and is constitutive of community. A community is that group of people who share the same language, who assent to the same proclamation in their lives. The community of the church is that group of individuals who have heard the proclamation of the word of God and who now live according to the vision put forth by that language-event. They are people with the Christian vision and the Christian language, because what they share is Jesus Christ with a certain explicitness. This is so because Christ is for them their eventful word.

Liturgy then can be described as the dialog between God and ourselves because of the place of Christ in the liturgical celebration. When God speaks, proclaims, to us his Word who is Jesus Christ, we have liturgy in the form of the gospel and the sacraments. When we respond to God through the prayer of Christ we have the language of liturgy in terms of praise and thanksgiving. In the liturgy Christ becomes God's most perfect proclamation and at the same time he is our most adequate response. Christ is God's best answer to God's own call and he is also the fullest proclamation of the community.

Christian liturgy, as the community's proclamation, is the articulation of the presence of God in Christ especially in terms of the paschal mystery. Liturgy is the permanent proclamation of the paschal mystery which constitutes and reflects the church. The liturgical assembly is the most explicit expression and manifestation of the Christian life because it lights up what is going on in the rest of Christian living.

This model of liturgical theology has some important implications for the planning process. The liturgical dynamic is one of proclamation and response. The very structure of the liturgy should be designed in terms of the rhythm of proclamations and responses. This will influence the placing of music in the celebration, the use of gestures and the celebrational style of the ministers. In all of the rites, response should follow proclamation. One should not employ several proclamations or several responses in a row. To do so would destroy the rhythm which is so necessary for an enlivened celebration which is supposed to articulate the very rhythm of our lives in a Christian perspective.

Liturgy as Process

The process model for constructing a liturgical theology is developed in the light of the principles of what is called process theology, a specifically American systematic conceptuality for understanding God and the Christian message. This theoretical framework stresses the relationship of God to the world as one of unity rather than separation. God is always at work in the world and the world is the symbol of God, the manifestation of God's presence. This world, the only one we have, is the arena of God's activity and existence.

According to this view there is no possibility that liturgy would be seen as worship of an absent God, or a God who is infinitely separated from this world. Rather it is the liturgy which is the human activity which highlights for us that God is working in and through the world to bring about a greater union with himself.

This view of reality places considerable emphasis on the interrelatedness and interdependence of all reality. Reality is highly relational. This means that the usual dichotomies between God and the world, the church and secular society, Christ and the rest of humanity are broken down and blurred.

Another important component of a process theology is that it is the "becoming" of reality which is stressed. It is process rather than substance, becoming rather than being which are the inclusive categories of understanding reality. God who is intrinsically related to all reality is a God who changes, who is living and yet is perfect. Perfection in this framework does not demand immutability. With such a presupposition, liturgy can never be seen as a finished product. It is an event always in process. It is the constant result of creativity in life and in the actual celebration. The process mode of thinking would eschew anything like an immutable church or an isolated and independent liturgy. The church is a distinctive stream in the general flow of reality. Its purpose is to bring out of concealment the directionality of the total process but it is in no essential way separated from it. Thus, the language and gestures of liturgy would be the language and gestures of today's culture.

God Involved in Life

A process liturgical theology presupposes a God who is very much involved in people's lives. It rejects the God who has no feelings and emotions, who is self-contained and outside of time, a God to whom nothing in the world can really make any difference. The fact is that worship does presuppose a God who is personally concerned with the worshiper's problems and desires. Process theology says that God is so personally involved in this world and with human beings that God is actually affected by what is going on. God is diminished by our sinfulness to the degree that God cannot become the kind of God that God would have become had we not sinned. God is enriched by our contributions as we become more fully human. In this sense the world is constantly changing God. God sees the direction in which God would like the world to go and God tries to lure this world to greater and greater humanization, to greater and more creative things. But God cannot coerce. This position is not pantheistic. God and the world are not reduced to each other. But God is part of the fabric of this world. God and the world are unthinkable without each other.

This view, then, helps us to overcome the kind of conflict we have had between our traditional theology and the prayers of our liturgy. Often our theology said that God could not be affected by what we did, and yet our prayers and hymns presumed otherwise. Liturgy can be seen as that event in the Christian community where we have the clearest and best statement, by means of ritual, of how God is affecting the world and how the world is contributing to God. God does not enter our world through the liturgy, and when we are at worship we are not addressing someone who is outside of the liturgical assembly. God is always there, and because of our ritualizing God rises to visibility for the community which is gathered together, hears the gospel, shows forth its ministry, and shares in the supper of the Lord.

The liturgical experience which is constantly undergoing change is open-ended. The Christ of the liturgy is evolving. There is no immutable, static Christ. He is always in the process of completion. This does not mean that there is no relation between the Christ of the liturgy and the Christ of the past. There is continuity between the Christ of the liturgy and the Christ of the past. There is continuity with the death and resurrection. However, this is continuity and not mere repetition. There is always something of the past in each liturgical event, but there is always something that is novel. In this sense, the direction of the liturgy is more to the future than to the past. It follows that if liturgy is truly to be alive and working, then it is necessary to build change into the structure of worship itself. Christian ritual does not mean to repeat only what Christians have done before.

The liturgy does more than reiterate the past because it responds to the present community and where it is at the present time. Liturgy facilitates the growth of the church by taking into itself what is new in present ecclesial relationships. In that sense liturgy is caused by the future. As the process theologian sees it, God, Jesus Christ, the church, and the sacraments are in the process of becoming, and in this sense the liturgical life is lived from the future. God through Jesus Christ assumes a persuasive posture toward the church in the direction of greater humanization and union with God. Thus the church's sacramental life is to be in a constant process of creative advance.

Sacramental theology is to be viewed as the special moment in the church were the relationality that makes us Christian, our relation to God in Christ, is highlighted and established in a deeper and more unambiguous way. Through the individual sacraments, the event of the church in process continues to be created. Liturgy is the way that the church is maintained in process.

This process liturgical theology can be summarized in the following points: 1) liturgy is a processive-relational event; 2) the God to whom the liturgy is directed is a changing God who so interacts with the world that God is both its creator and is created by it, a world God entices to further growth and enrichment; 3) the liturgy is future-directed, implying that the worshiper, the worshiping community and the mediating Christ are constantly evolving; 4) the Christ who does the worshiping in the liturgy makes it possible for the community to be the paradigm of the relationship of God and the world; 5) the church whose spirituality is articulated ritually in liturgy is an event-always-becoming; and, 6) the sacraments are those special moments in the church's life where its relationship to Christ and to the individual members is so expressed that the liturgy becomes a celebration of salvation by appropriating the past, by relating to the present, and by responding to the allurement of the future.

Conclusion

How is one to evaluate these models? They are not all equally appropriate to a contemporary liturgical theology. Each model must be judged in terms of its basis in scripture and tradition, the degree that it corresponds to modern religious experience, its ability to give the worshipers a sense of mission and identity, how much it fosters Christian virtues and ecumenical dialog and especially how creative it is for theologizing about worship.

The institutional model rightly emphasizes a structured liturgy although it can lead to a rigid preoccupation with rubrics. The mystery model clearly indicates the importance of the liturgical realism of the ritual action in that worship is the prolongation of Christ's work on earth although this approach runs the risk of viewing the liturgical symbol too Platonically and of viewing the presence of Christ (in distinction from his actions) too statically. The sacramental model highlights very well that it is the community at worship which is the primary symbol of God's salvation, but it can also cause an excessively in-house consideration of the liturgy. The proclamation model sees the liturgy as the primordial place of the event of the word of God although there is always the danger of a form of fundamentalism. The process model avoids the ever present temptation to separate liturgy from life, but it does not speak as clearly as do some of the other models of the transcendence of God and the eschatological dimension of the church's worship.

No one model can be the supermodel under which the others are subsumed. The liturgical theologian must work with them all in a complementary fashion. An individual theologian may choose one model as the dominating image if he/she in no way excludes the other models. I do not believe, however, that the institutional model can be taken to be a primary image in a liturgical theology because institutions and structures are subordinate to persons and life. In fact the imperialism of any model in a liturgical theology will be detrimental to that theology because ultimately worship is part of the mystery of Christ and the church.

7

Liturgy as Humanizing
or as Therapeutic

THIS MODEL WHICH CAN BE DESCRIBED AS ONE WHICH IS PHENOME-
nological, that is one that speaks in the language or ordinary
human experience, is an attempt to bracket the metaphysical
approach as such. It is concerned to address that segment of
humanity which no longer finds ontological considerations of
God and liturgy helpful. This model, therefore, can assist the
preacher and the liturgist better than some of the other models
in proclaiming God's word of salvation in terms and concepts
which correspond to the contemporary experience of reality. It
does not demand that the listener first enter into a philosophical
framework in which metaphysical questions of God and worship
would arise. This is not to suggest that the metaphysical approach is wrong, but simply that the Gospel must be made available to those not metaphysically gifted.

This approach is more experientially oriented. The method is
to examine human experience carefully and to find there the
presence of God. It is a method which is similar to the biblical
one where, for instance, we find that the experience of Israel in
the Hebrew scriptures is seen as an organ of divine revelation.
In accordance with the phenomenological approach, the theologian employing this model would try to be sensitive to the
religious experience of other human beings engaged in worship.
This study is not modeled after the empirical sciences such as
in the case of chemistry, but is conducted by the theologian who
goes through his or her own life and that of others to discover

transcendence. In other words, the theologian speaks of God in terms of human life. Often this will mean that the liturgist will examine the high points of human living and see them as entrance ways into understanding and experiencing oneself and ultimately finding God there. This model does not claim that it can prove that the experience of God takes place through human experience. But it does claim that it makes sense in our attempting to understand the relationship of God and the world. Both the gospel and the liturgy help us to read our own history and the history of our community as the place where God is redemptively present. In other words, God is present in the humanization process. Or the humanization process is the history of salvation.

The therapeutic model does not intend to reduce everything to the psychological method. It is not some exaggerated kind of existentialism which would maintain that we are simply what we will to be at any given instance. This model speaks of salvation in terms of humanization because it wishes to use more therapeutic terms. And it wishes to do this out of the conviction that speaking about the experience and worship of God by articulating the human clarification process which leads to personal growth is closer to the worshiper's life than more metaphysical language. It is after all the language of ordinary human experience which will communicate most effectively to the majority of people today. And far from being reductionistic, that is, asserting that everything can be exhaustively described in psychological categories, it is especially concerned to stress that those people, those moments, those events in our daily lives which lead men and women to greater self-knowledge and which enable them to triumph over past patterns and seemingly present inevitabilities are not reducible to the purely human. They are not merely psychological. They are salvational. Gregory Baum has written that God is redemptively present in our humanization.[1] Or to go back further into the history of theology, St.

---

1. See chapter two, "Redemptive Immanence," of his *Man Becoming* (New York: Herder and Herder, 1970). I wish to acknowledge my great debt to this book in the formulation of the therapeutic model of liturgy. It provided me with many of the insights I needed to construct this model. I consider *Man Becoming* to be one of the most significant theological books of our time. It is still relevant, and I recommend it to anyone who is interested in exploring the theological shifts of our times.

Irenaeus puts it this way: "The glory of God is the human person fully alive." In other words, mere humanism is bad humanism. We are always more than what meets the eye or what can be described in the language of the physical and social sciences.

According to this model, the liturgy is important because the acknowledgement of the divine presence in the ordinary or the recognition that the salvational process and the humanizing process cannot be separated on the level of experience is not automatic. Not all Christians recognize that to become a better human being is to become holy, that holiness is inconsistent with psychological fragmentation in the same area of a person's life. So the purpose of the liturgy is to insure that those who publicly confess Jesus Christ will also see that the destructiveness of human life militates against personal and communal salvation and will recognize the need for redemption, a redemption accomplished by entering more fully into the process of becoming a better human being. There is something in all of us that inhibits us from wanting to know the truth and recognizing the evil in our lives and society. The clarification that is involved in dealing with this is assisted by God and because this is so, one can speak of this clarification as being salvational. The liturgy is the event of the community which both brings this clarification to common acceptance and which gives the individual worshiper the permission, the support, and the direction to engage in this clarification process.

As should be obvious, this model of liturgical theology emphasizes the immanence of God. God is not imaged as being outside of human history. In that sense it resembles the process model. But more than that, it does not even image God as objectifiable. God cannot be understood as some kind of object, even a personal one, outside of human existence. In other words, not only does this approach reject the subject-object (I see the tree) model for theologizing about God, it even dispenses with the subject-subject model (the so-called I-Thou approach). These models may be helpful in understanding the people and things of our ordinary experience, but there is a limit to this experience when we come to God. This model claims that it is more helpful to say that God is in my knowledge, but is not the object of my knowledge, that God is present in every act of loving, but is not to be imaged as a lover facing me. This is not to reduce God to humanity, but simply to state that people are more than people.

There is something present in human knowing and loving which cannot be reduced to our understanding of human knowing and loving.

According to this model God and Christ are present everywhere, certainly in the liturgical assembly. As a matter of fact, it is the liturgical community which is the visible symbolization of God. For this reason liturgical prayers are not to be addressed to a God outside of the worshiping people. The fact that it is this group of people assembled for worship which is the concreteness of God at this time should not be contradicted by the preaching, the prayers, the songs, and the various ceremonials. This does not imply that it is necessary to engage in a massive translation process of all the present official liturgical texts. What is more relevant is the context within which the prayers, preaching, readings, and songs function. Words and gestures derive their meaning and communicate their significance in terms of the environment of meaning in which they have been established. For instance, one can still speak of the Father, Son, and Spirit as in the concluding formula of liturgical prayers. But that does not demand adherence to a certain theological system which attempts to speak of this mystery. Rather the trinitarian formula can be understood as God's way of giving Godself to us. The Trinity is a way of talking about God's multiple ways of being present in our own humanization process when God summons us in love to our destiny.

This is simply an example of what this model can do for the liturgical experience. The language of the congregational acclamations, the liturgical readings, and the presidential prayers should be perceived as saying something about human salvation. They are not referring to a God in the abstract, but to a God for us. It cannot be denied, however, that often this is very difficult to do because most of the liturgical texts were composed under the influence of other models. For this reason it is necessary to look to gestures and ceremonies for concrete articulation of the therapeutic in the rituals. This model of liturgical theology more than the others demands that the signs of reverence in the liturgy be concretized in how we show our respect for each other as human beings rather than in showing respect for certain things such as bread, water, statues, crosses, and relics. It is the breaking of the bread, the kiss of peace, the sharing of communion and any movement employed which can communicate power-fully that all this worshipful reference to God is really a message about persons. It brings to visibility God's complete entrance into our process of self-making.

Because God is seen as working therapeutically in all of cre-ation, this model of liturgy more than the others calls for bodily involvement. Salvation is ritually expressed by the worshipers getting in touch with their bodies, senses, imaginations, and sexuality in worship itself. Because it is our relationship to society and our bodies which is broken and becomes the source of our self-destruction, the liturgy will reflect this brokenness and es-trangement. However, worship must also provide the experience of discernment where new ways of being related to the body and the wider physical environment can be found so that this alienation can be overcome.

The phenomenological model is very similar to the process model in describing divine transcendence. God is very much part of history but is never identical with it. As the process model, it does not see God as transcending the world by existing in some superhistorical world in and by self. Rather the thera-peutic model emphasizes the transcendence of God by God being judgment and critique and new life in our personal and com-munal histories. When the liturgy celebrates divine transcend-ence it is not an event of worship offered to some superbeing outside of the Christian assembly; rather, it is a revelation that there is no aspect of human life which is not in need of further redemption, that all of history is under the critique of God who summons it to forgiveness and offers it restoration. One can speak of this divine critique being the salvational aspect of the personal and communal self-analysis which is productive of in-sight and growth. God's transcendence is thus seen in the way that God is therapeutically present to and in the world. God's otherness is in addressing us as judgment, confronting us, mak-ing us face that with which we do not wish to deal, confusing us at times and then enabling us to turn away from the destruc-tive forces in ourselves and in our world and to enter creatively into the future. The divine grace that transcends this world is really the grace of self-transcendence.

One of the purposes of liturgical worship is to give an op-portunity for the Christian to experience God not by focusing psychologically on a divine person, but by calling oneself to submit to the divine critique given in Jesus Christ. The liturgy should move us to test our experiences according to the criterion of whether these actually lead us to greater openness to truth and more availability to love or whether these experiences simply confirm us in our past prejudices and ideologies.

A major problem with this model of liturgical theology is how to understand what it means to speak to God in prayer. This model rejects the idea of God as a substantive being, a subject totally outside of ourselves. God is not even understood on the analogy of a human person. God is not a person who is the object of our worship. An understanding of the nature of God as someone with whom we relate in prayer according to the therapeutic model would tend to speak of God as *personal* rather than as a person. This would mean that when men and women as persons are in touch with the deepest dimensions of their lives, when they are in contact with the divine presence in them that calls them to further growth, they are relating to God. They are praying. This is usually difficult for us to understand or at least to envisage. We are attempting to describe something which goes beyond the subject-subject model in subject-object or subject model language. The closest analogy we have would be the mystical experience where the person praying does not distinguish the self from God. It is like being in an altered state of consciousness. It means that there is no difference experientially between the prayer of the person and the God to whom the person is praying. The experience is one.

What lies behind this approach is the presupposition of many contemporary theologians that it is impossible to speak about God without also speaking about oneself. It is a rejection of theologizing by beginning out there in a thoroughly objectified world—a world which has little to do with our gestalt subjective world. Basically, this means approaching theology through personal story. Story provides the framework in which our past, present, and future are held together. Story gives meaning to our time, and meaningful time allows us to move beyond the present moment. Theology is an attempt to articulate the meaning of our time and our story.

The question which is addressed in this theologizing is: where am I? Not where am I in my external history of how old I am, what is my job, but who or where am I in my internal history where I find my worth and value. Not that my external history is not worth considering. But the point is that it is my internal history which is embodied in my external history. How I act as a minister, how I pray and preach, how I relate to my friends are symbolic expressions of my own self-understanding. And the whole system of my self-understanding emerges from my past, my present circumstances, and my future expectations. Moreover, being a person of faith, I make life decisions in the context of this faith. I live out of a faithful past, in a faith filled present, and toward a faith alluring future. In other words, I try to sort out my life story by illuminating it with the story of Christ. In his story I find my direction for my own decisions which will constitute my story.

When we look at our own stories we find that we are people who move in reference to a number of other human beings and that we do so both internally and externally. We experience ourselves as relational but also as separated. We find that our story is a continual search for meaning and truth. Others are also working out the story of their lives by this same search for meaning. This meaning is brought about by communications with others and with ourselves. Certainly, the love between husband and wife communicated in depth is an example of this emergence of meaning. But the birth of meaning is not restricted to marriage. It is verified wherever true communication takes place.

The means of such communication are listening and giving. One must listen to others through the eyes and ears and touch. But one must also listen to oneself. The other means is giving. To give means involving ourselves through our words and actions. And one must give oneself to oneself as well as to others. The point is that communication takes place when giving and listening are held together so that they become one experience.

It is the story of Jesus which assists us to continue to communicate. When communication fails, as in the case of those who are perceptive of others' faults but not very much aware of their own deficiencies, then something from the story of Christ such as the parable of the person who has a log in her own eye while trying to remove the speck from her sister's eye comes into play. Entering into a relationship with this Jesus story can assist one in listening to oneself, and this allows one to reinterpret one's own story or self-image. By listening and giving oneself to the image of the parable, one can also listen and give oneself to a new image of self. For instance, in the case just mentioned, what may happen is that when someone's irritating fault in a liturgical planning session emerges, I may be less inclined to focus on the person and concentrate more on how I might improve the functioning of the group. The irritating behavior may well pale in significance, and I may discover more meaning for myself by my participation in the group. The therapeutic process is the incorporation of the Christ story into my own life in such a way that I reinterpret myself, reinterpret my internal history so that it makes a difference on the level of my external history. The case of spiritual direction is similar. The purpose of the director is to assist the directees to:

1) listen and give to themselves;
2) discern the story giving meaning to their lives;
3) open up other possible stories.

This becomes clearer when one examines what happens in the therapeutic model of spiritual direction or the directed retreat. In the situation of spiritual direction, the director is called upon to assist the directees in discovering their story. First of all this means that the director will help the directees to listen and give. Part of the spiritual direction process is for the directees to learn how to listen to themselves and to others and to give themselves to themselves and others. On the other side, directors must always listen and give themselves in the situation of direction. If directors cannot hear themselves during the time of direction, they are not really listening to the directees.

Second, in spiritual direction the director will aid the directees in discovering their *own* stories, the stories which are presently giving meaning and direction to their lives. Often this will reveal that the directees have imprisoned themselves in one self-image, one life-story, and this story exercises an imperialism over their internal history and so over the way they act in relationship to others as well as the way they deal with themselves.

Third, the purpose of the spiritual director is to facilitate the discovery of other possible stories. Freedom from an ennervat-

ing, debilitating life story takes place when there are other options. These possibilities will help the directees to relativize the
confining story of their past and present situations. Becoming
comfortable with many stories is one of the results of good spiritual direction. The clarification process, so necessary for the
humanization process which is phenomenologically the same as
the salvific process, is dependent on the reinterpretation of oneself according to a number of viable life-stories. What this therapeutic model presumes is that in actuality all of us are the result
of many stories and that the restriction to one is ultimately both
dehumanizing and a lie.

The point to all of this is that the liturgy should be the place
where people can become involved in the listening-giving relationship with the Christian incorporating story. An incorporating
story is one which makes sense of the failure of our own stories
by including these failures as part of a larger drama. Our stories
which are often filled with these failures are caught up in the
incorporating story of Christianity. In the liturgy we test, we try,
we even play with our relationship to this incorporating story,
the history of salvation. This enables us outside of the liturgy to
take the risk of entering into a relationship with God when it is
offered in those situations of humanization, those humanizing
moments of communication brought about by listening and giving. What the liturgy should help us experience is that Christian
communication is not primarily concerned with the "facts." My
family history, the schools I attended, my degrees and work
experiences are not important when compared with my inten-
tions, values, motives, feelings, and all the components that
make up my internal history. The real meaning of my life is from
that arena and not that of my external history. Only people who
define themselves by the work they do would so rely on their
external history. Rather, it is my internal history which is the
most appropriate vehicle for the revelation of myself to another
and to myself. And if liturgy is the coming to expression, the
revelation of the spirituality of the church, then it is the community's internal history which must be symbolized in ritual as
the best means of bringing about that revelation.

But what kind of liturgy will bring about this revelation through
humanizing communication? Or in other words, what kind of
liturgy allows the Christian incorporating story to function in

our lives? Certainly, not one characterized by informational, objective, external language that puts the worshiper to sleep. By informational language I am not referring to the announcement of the times of the next parish picnic. I refer to the use of obviously religious language which calls attention to itself rather than to its content. Such language can get in the way of communication or be a distraction. It may be that this language is referring to something of deep liturgical significance, but it is the depth which appeals to the intellect more than the whole person. It is not the language of the proclamation model because, while it might be interesting, it does not lead to any kind of decision. One can preach about the redemptive activity of God in the world in terms of creation as described in the Hebrew Scriptures and as fulfilled in the New Testament through God's revelation in Jesus Christ who is now the new creation. Certainly, there is a great deal of depth there. But this is depth of content and not of meaningfulness. Preaching on this topic does not necessarily involve an invitation to various levels of meaning, nor does it demand any involvement on the part of the listener. Often what we experience in the prayers and preaching of the liturgy is language more appropriate to convey information to the theologically schooled than the kind that assists one to participate in God's creative activity. Imparting information takes place in the liturgy but that is not its primary concern.

Liturgy is an invitation to involvement and decision. The language that works best here is the language which is familiar but which turns out to be something other than expected. It has a twist to it which challenges. I would call this kind of language therapeutic. I believe this to be the language of spiritual direction. This kind of language does not work automatically. It works only in the context of the listening-giving mutuality. Such language in the liturgy will draw one into it and will foster communication because of this listening-giving relationship. In the liturgical community this relationship makes it possible for all to have some common ground which can serve as the bridge between the individual members which makes depth communication possible. Our common human experiences certainly serve as a foundation for such communication, but it is also necessary to have explicitly common Christian experiences. Thus the common liturgical language will be that of the Christian incorporating story, a story which has a twist to it.

The therapeutic model is more explicit than the model of proclamation which also calls for this common shared vision by demanding an openness to self and others to engage in the process itself. Incompleteness is a way of life which implies that one must always grow. Withdrawing from a relationship because one finds oneself changing or unwilling to participate in the pain of creative growth is challenged by the therapeutic model. Therapeutic liturgical theology not only moves one away from shriveling relationships, atrophied communication, or ennervating insensitivity, it also provides for the context of gaining new insight. We are free to choose what will be real for us, and this model of liturgical theology indicates that I must be open to perceive reality in such a way that there are other possibilities than I might envision or desire. For instance, what the liturgy of reconciliation should do is create an atmosphere where one can expand one's sense of reality in such a way as to make reconciliation possible. Often in a situation of conflict, reconciliation is difficult because the various people are at opposite poles. Unless there can be an expanded sense of reality there can be no behaviorial change and without such a change no reconciliation is possible. Liturgy according to this model helps me to be open to another option regarding myself or my relationship with others which simply was not present in the beginning. It is not simply substituting one self-image for another. Rather it is expanding one's vision of others and oneself in such a way that previously unperceived levels of reality are now included.

In therapeutic worship I open myself to the possibility that I have not perceived reality in all its fullness, at all of its levels and in terms of all my relationships. Others in the situation of worship have similar insights and hopefully experience a similar openness. As a community we take into our internal history the images of the liturgy which stimulate our imaginations to fantasize on the possibilities of perceiving reality (God and creation) in new ways. We respond by accepting or rejecting this new perception and acting accordingly.

In more individualistic terms what this means is that by having my imagination stimulated by some form of communication, some clarification process, I can stand back from my own perception of reality and play with, fantasize, and entertain new ones. If I am open, I am challenged to decide to live according to these new possibilities. In worship I have freely chosen to place myself in a situation where I am called upon to decide about myself. So the liturgical assemby should find worship the place where it can test various ways of looking at itself and the world. It can project these world-views back into its history and decide whether this different viewpoint is a viable option for itself. If this new possibility makes sense out of the various relationships in which the Christian community is involved, then it can help expand the community's view of reality, and the community will have a better framework out of which to live and work. To use religious language, the revelation of God has been manifested in the liturgy. Of couse, as individuals or as a community we can decide to reject the options. At best this would mean confirming ourselves in our present understanding of reality; at worst it would mean our inability to risk in faith.

The value of this humanizing model of the liturgy is that the worshiping community makes it possible for the worshipers to distance themselves from their own ways of seeing themselves and the world by being stimulated by an incorporating story: the paschal mystery.

What very frequently happens is that antecedent to the liturgy the individual Christians project themselves into their own reality with new options for looking at themselves and others. They try out these new views in their own minds and lives. My experience tells me that often this procedure is what takes place in spiritual direction and on the occasion of a directed retreat, although it is certainly not limited to those situations. The point is that this process, whenever it occurs, allows Christians to change their relationships with others when they gather for worship. What we do in our individual lives therapeutically becomes a "dress rehearsal" for what we will do in the liturgical assembly.

8

The Liberation Model of Liturgical Theology

AS IS WELL KNOWN TO ANYONE WITH EVEN A CASUAL ACQUAINTANCE with liberation theology, it is a new way of theologizing with an emphasis placed on method. This method is that theological reflection is part of the historical process itself. Theology does more than reflect on the world: it is actually an important element in the transformation of the world. Liberation theology assists in the building of the kingdom of God by refusing to distance itself from human struggles for dignity and brotherly and sisterly love. Each of the traditional components of theology is called upon to engage in a new way of "faith seeking understanding."

The way that this theologizing is linked with the world and human beings is through "conscientization." One moves from a low level awareness where problems are avoided, where mythical explanations are accepted, to a critical sensitivity which no longer takes the status quo for granted, is open to new perspectives, enters into problems confrontively, and searches for the real causes of that which holds back the transformation of society.

The present day liberation theology has its roots in the theology of hope that developed in the 1960s. It was influenced by certain salient features of this theology of hope: God is the one who is pulling us into the future; the resurrection of Christ is a sign of the future already present; the death and resurrection of Christ grounds our hope in God; God enters into the very process of the building of God's kingdom; human history is the process of the establishment of this kingdom; the church takes its meaning from the kingdom to be established here and so it exists for the world; and all Christian theology must be political theology.[1]

To summarize, then, in an unfortunately cursory way, liberation theology begins with the commitment to the poor and their attempts to achieve liberation. Priority is given to the gospel injunction to follow Christ in his preaching the Good News to the deprived. All theologies of liberation affirm strongly that salvation is not only outside of human history. It is also found now wherever poverty and injustice are overcome. Thus, if the church is to preach the gospel effectively, it must commit itself to the struggle for justice. The liberation that the church hopes to promote must begin from the experience of the oppressed peoples and from their reflection upon that oppression. Only the poor and the oppressed can provide the solutions to their situation. Theologians can make a contribution to their efforts by rethinking the christian tradition in terms of these oppressed peoples. Theology will of necessity become prophetic and critical of societal structures. Because liberation theology is a method of doing theology, it is not primarily concerned with specific dogmatic considerations. It is an aspect of all of the theological disciplines.

Thus, before fleshing out a model for an approach to liturgical theology from a liberation viewpoint, it is necessary to sketch briefly the way in which some of the central Christian beliefs are understood in a liberation context. The topics only briefly considered here are: God, the kingdom, Christ, the church, the covenanted people, eschatology, and spirituality. The rest of this paper is then devoted to detailing the way liturgy is to be viewed from a liberation perspective. Some of the limitations of this model will be noted. And the paper concludes with a specific problem to exemplify the liberation model of liturgical theology. The problem is that of the relationship between liturgy and politics.

God

What kind of God is presumed in a liberation theology? The primary understanding of God in a liberation model is very sim-

1. Confer L. John Topel, *The Way to Peace* (Maryknoll: Orbis Books, 1979) 148-9.

ilar to the conceptuality of God in the process model. That is, God is very much involved in this world and is a participant in this world's history. God enters into the arena of human activity in a free and gracious way. God is one who, while respecting human freedom, lures the free person to further the cause of society's transformation and human dignity. As in process thought, God needs us but the emphasis is less on the human contribution to God's becoming and more on the human achievement of God's salvific ends.

God is both immanent and transcendent in this model. God is immanent insofar as the kingdom of God is here and because God lives and works and acts in history, in humanization, and in the struggles of the poor and the oppressed. God is transcendent insofar as neither the church nor secular reality are ever a perfect fulfillment of the kingdom. The eschatological dimension cannot be weakened or be de-emphasized in this model.

There is some similarity between the liberation and therapeutic models regarding God. In Segundo's words:

We now realize that God is a continuing inner call within our lives toward authentic solutions; toward solutions that are more difficult, because they do not result from a false, premature synthesis that sacrifices truth to compromise and leaves us calm and satisfied in our mediocrity . . . So God is the unrest in us that does not allow us to be tranquil and content, that keeps plodding us toward the better course that remains ahead of us.

But in the end the transcendence of God is firmly maintained in liberation theology. Segundo continues:

Atheism should continually teach our faith a radical and important lesson: i.e., *God is above and beyond our mediocrity* in the most pure absolute and total value . . . What separates us from the atheist who is seeking sincerely? Nothing . . . God is already present in his soul because he is sincerely seeking a God that is not in league with man's mediocrity and egotism.[2]

2. Juan Luis Segundo, *Our Idea of God* (Maryknoll: Orbis Books, 1974) 181.

The Kingdom of God

The particular formality under which humanity experiences God is in the establishment of God's kingdom. This is where the liberation model finds it Christological centering. The kingdom of God and its implications for justice in the world is found in Christ's preaching. Christ speaking from his own cultural context, perhaps inspired by the Jewish year of Jubilee, sees the kingdom as a time of moral and social transformation. The liberation celebrated by many of Jesus's contemporaries would have been concretized in the cancellation of debts, the freeing of slaves, the welcoming of foreigners, and the restoration of family property. Jesus as a Jew would have interpreted the coming of the kingdom in similar terms.

But the kingdom about which Christ preached goes beyond his own cultural matrix. More than debts are cancelled; there must be a more equitable distribution of goods. More than slaves are to be freed; there must be the abolition of all social barriers. More than domestic justice is required; there must be reform and renewal of all existing institutions, both civil and religious.

However, the concept and realization of the kingdom does not exhaust the meaning of God in this model. This God goes beyond the justice demanded by this kingdom. God is characterized by love. God persuades through love. It is basic to liberation theology that the kingdom of God is now growing in this world and that if Christians are to participate in the founding of that kingdom they must struggle against the various forms of institutionalized injustice. But what has been revealed in the life of Jesus is that he is in charge of setting up this kingdom. We join Christ in that effort. And we do this not by some kind of enlightened legalism or succumbing to human ideologies, but by personal commitment to God by means of a covenant of love in Jesus Christ. It is our entering into Christ's own relationship with God that makes the kingdom a visible reality because it is this relationship of love which creates the human family and brings about Christian salvation, apart from which liberation theology as *theology* makes no sense and the search for justice and freedom loses its evangelical warrant.

Jesus Christ

In the liberation model Christ is the paradigmatic liberator. He makes it possible for humankind to live in communion, free of injustice and oppression because he demolishes sin which is the source of all injustice. The New Testament message is that God loves us in Jesus Christ and that Christ's own death is the model for the kind of love that we must have for one another. It is a love that builds the kingdom of justice because it can only be realized if we share what we have with the poor and if we join the suffering Christ by entering into the struggles of the oppressed. We incarnate the incarnate Christ when we bring justice to those in need.

Christ is the paradigm because in the man, Jesus, we discover what God wants for this world. In Teilhardian fashion, liberation theology sees the whole world converging in Christ. This is true of secular society as well and so even in the political field the incarnation of God's salvation is taking place when political endeavors become the means whereby humankind moves forward to its completion.

Liberation theologians see Jesus as bringing a manifesto for a new humanity. They see this manifesto most clearly expressed in his visit to the synagogue at Nazareth when he read the message from the scroll: "The spirit of the Lord is upon me . . ." (Luke 4:16–21). His whole life was a negation of everything oppressive and a yes to all that would bring about a new age of freedom. His gospel is one of healing and humanization. He is the vindicator of the poor, calling upon those who possess this world's goods to transcend the inhibiting tyranny of private property and to live by an economy of giving.

With Jesus a new spirit has entered human history. It is a spirit which calls for humanizing love and mutual concern. It is a spirit which overcomes fragmentation by creating new bonds. It is this spirit that gives meaning to his community whose mission is to release this new energy in the world. It is the task of his church to foster the new age of humanity.

The Church

The ecclesiology of the liberation model demands more of the church than the communication of sacred doctrine. The church must build up a community of believers who discern the signs of the times; it must promote that which humanizes life for all; it must bring about the unification of the global community in Christ; and it must enable its members to work for these goals. It is called to be a church which engages in cooperative efforts with all the churches to be agents of peace and justice and to be prophetic voices which point out the dangers of dehumaniza- tion. It should inspire concrete initiatives for the transformation of human society according to the ideals of the kingdom of God.

Liberation ecclesiology would see that political responsibility is part of the vocation of being a Christian. Members of the church must go forth and preach the gospel and this in terms of direct action for justice and participation in the advance toward greater freedom for those who are enslaved by economic, polit- ical, and social structures. The special ministers of the church have several duties: building the just Christian community, pre- siding at worship which reflects the demads of justice, proclaim- ing the word of God in a prophetic way, and engaging in activity which changes civil society in the light of the Gospel.

The church is not an institution alongside worldly structures, but is a community within the world which recognizes God's work for humanity, confirms the importance of people to fashion their futures in freedom, protests the pretensions to ultimacy in any human organizations, and suffers with people in the combat against the power of evil. The primary end of the church is not confessional proclamation or cultic celebration, but a discerning reflection on God's presence and promise in the midst of history. This theological model places a strong emphasis on the Pauline notion of "kenosis," and emptying out. The church must re- nounce its claims to honor and power.

More than most of the models, this one sees the church as moving beyond itself to break down barriers. This does not mean that the Christian community can provide remedies for social evils. Rather the church's competence is to keep alive the hope and inspiration for the kingdom and its values. Through its crit- ical stance the church becomes the herald and catalyst of king- dom values. But it must also personalize these values. It cannot be identified with abstractions whether they be peace, justice, reconciliation, or affluence, power, and authority.

Thus, the Christian Church must be part of the renovation of this world. This means that the lines between the church and the world will be less distinct. It is not that the church summons all people to itself. Rather it moves toward the world to embrace it. There is salvation outside the church for wherever human beings enter into the process of liberation, salvation is taking place. All are called to build up the kingdom of God, which is non-religious language means the construction of a just society. But not all are called to belong to that sacrament which is the servant of that kingdom being born in the course of human history.

The Covenanted People

How would one characterize Christians according to the liberation model? They are first of all a covenanted people. Their right to justice in their own lives as well as the challenge that they be justice-oriented people is mandated in terms of their covenant with God. This covenant is made concrete in their commitment to God which must permeate all the levels of their lives: intellectual as well as religious, affective as well as moral. In this way their covenant with God makes visible the kingdom.

Based on this covenant of commitment to God is their covenant with each other. There are two characteristics of being a covenanted people in terms of these human relationships. First, their ethical stance toward their brothers and sisters is the test of the authenticity of their covenant with each other. This moral commitment becomes a sign of the presence of the kingdom. Secondly, this covenant among Christians leads to sharing. It is a sharing with others which is gratuitous, that is based on need and not merit. It is sharing which is unlimited; it is not merely the sharing of material goods but also faith and whatever personal charismatic gifts may be involved.

Covenanted people are those who live by the Sermon on the Mount. They are a leaven for the kingdom rather than narrowly legalistic. They bring peace to themselves so that they can bring peace to others. They are converted to their neighbor. Conversion to the neighbor is a sign of the covenant. What this means for Christians has been summed up by John Topel:

> Real conversion to neighbor demands that we try every non-oppressive means to convert the opponents of justice from their oppressive ways, which oppress themselves, too. Doing to others as you would have them do unto you means that the oppressor must be challenged and converted; that is what we all really desire for ourselves. Choosing nonviolent means of challenging injustice demands more ingenuity and more persistence and more heroism,

but in the long run it will succeed because it cares not only for the victims of oppression but for the persons of the oppressors themselves.[3]

Eschatology

Because the covenant between God and God's people and God's people among themselves is a form of the presence of the kingdom, the liberation model sees the church and salvation in strongly eschatological images. However, unlike some theologies of eschatology, this model not only affirms that the reign of God is among us, although not fully realized, but that Christians are responsible for working for the completion of this kingdom. This inevitably leads into the mission of the church. It is a mission of gratuitous and unrestricted sharing. It is a mission to bring about mutual reconciliation where Christians forgive themselves as well as others.

This model of theology demands the eschatological emphasis since liberation is an unfinished process. Liberation theology stresses the importance of the historical growth of the kingdom. But this kingdom of peace and justice can never be fully achieved or history would come to an end. Liberation theologians do not exclude the possibility of retreat or failure. The liberation process is ever under threat. We are liberated as Christians because we have hope and this hope is founded upon something already present, but not yet completely so. People who are liberated now were oppressed at one time. But there is always the possibility that they may fall into bondage again. No one is free from all oppression and sin. As Leonardo Boff puts it:

> Salvation is not realized in such a way that it freezes history; it keeps the latter open to all the unforeseen possibilities of grace and disgrace. Thus a human being is *oppressus in re, liberatus in spe* oppressed in certain areas of his/her life, but also free through hope . . . So long as human beings live, they stand in need of liberation. They are oppressed and liberated at the same time, and they live in an openended process of liberation.[4]

---

3. Topel, *The Way* 127.
4. Leonardo Boff, *Liberating Grace* (Maryknoll: Orbis Books, 1979) 156–7.

The eschatological dimension reminds us that the freedoms we have won are not definitive. From these freedoms come the possibility for both new freedoms and new oppressions. Both must be recognized. The "not yet" of the future is manifested in the struggle, conflict, and ambiguity that is ever present in human living. But at the same time something new has emerged. There is something "already" achieved. This should be cause for celebration and play. This "already" grounds our Christian hope and makes liturgy a possibility in the midst of so much violence, hatred, destruction, and oppression. It is precisely in this worship, where God is recognized as the one who gives meaning to all human projects, that Christians are designated as missionaries to live in such a way as to liberate people from their oppressors. In liturgical celebrations new freedoms can burst forth into ordinary life in the world.

Spirituality

As with the other models of liturgical theology this one envisions a certain kind of spirituality. It is a spirituality of responsibility. This means that to be a spiritual person is to be one who is building up the kingdom of God in this world rather than preparing for the enjoyment of a kingdom which comes only at the end of this life. Thus, the components of this spirituality necessarily include 1) the conscientization whereby Christians recognize any part they have played in delaying or destroying the kingdom, 2) the covenant whereby they are responsible to each other to live in community in such a way as to make the kingdom more visible, and 3) the mission which calls for the completion of the Christian spirituality by moving beyond the church itself. This is a spirituality which lives in the tension between the vivid religious language of the kingdom and the eschaton and the lived experience of human society where one starts not from theology but the direct oppression of governments, laws, and church.

At the core of any Christian spirituality is conversion. Liberation spirituality is no exception. It centers on conversion to Christ through the neighbor. And the neighbor here is specified as the "oppressed person, the exploited social class, the despised

race, the dominated country."[5] To be converted is to be committed to conscientization of oneself and others. But this is not
the work of a mindless commitment, some kind of enthusiastic
fundamentalism. It is reflective commitment which analyzes the
concrete situation. It is critical commitment which devises a strat-
egy of action.

A spirituality of liberation, while directed toward communion
with God and one's fellow human beings, has a strong element
of the therapeutic in that there is confrontation for the purpose
of change. It is necessary first of all to break down the network
of evil which binds society and ourselves before entering into
real solidarity with each other. And just as conversion is a life-
long process, so is conflict. But the confrontation is not ordered
simply to the destruction of oppressive systems and structures.
Ultimately, it is God who does the confronting, and the strong
image of God who confronts is also that of one who heals.

Liberation spirituality is also not free of conflict because it is
never an individualistic spirituality. Change in structures and
change in oneself cannot be separated. They must go together.
Self-liberation is an essential element in the process of society's
transformation. One cannot simply struggle for others. Such
would tend toward a paternalistic (maternalistic) attitude. Self-
liberation is a form of justice toward oneself. This form of justice
must precede, or at least be concomitant with, justice for others.
Another way of putting this is that one must be in contact with
oneself before one can minister to others. Because there are unconscious motives at work in all of us, there can be unjust structures in our own lives which need to be addressed. There are
aspects of liberation which go beyond the economic, political,
cultural, racial, sexist, and religious. And so being just means
getting in touch with the power to love oneself. Such love leads
to openness of life where we can overcome the fear of the unknown and the yearning for security and other ways in which
we close ourselves to life. Love must overcome fear and com-
placency if one is to let go and respond in action. And so just
as the God of love moves beyond the building of God's kingdom,

5. Gustavo Gutierrez, A Theology of Liberation (Maryknoll: Orbis Books, 1973)
204–5.

the love of self and neighbor must motivate, and therefore transcend, justice for this world.

The Liberation Liturgical Model

As in the case of any theological model, the liberation liturgical model must pervade the other theological areas with its own specific imagery. This means that this model of liturgical theology speaks of the God who is worshiped, of the Christ who does the worshiping, of the church which is brought to expression ritually, of the people who are gathered in a community of worship, of a liturgy that anticipates the future, and of liturgy which articulates the Christian people's relationship with God—this theology speaks of all of these from a liberation perspective.

What does the liberation model mean for the liturgical experience itself? It demands that worship have a strong prophetic vision. Liturgy must be an experience of witnessing both from those who are oppressed and those who bring their expertise to achieve liberation for others. For instance, the Scripture in worship takes on the special character of the prophetic. Through the biblical vision the community interprets itself and challenges its own self-understanding. From this vision emerges the call to bring justice to this world. Furthermore, in order to bring about the kind of prophetic liturgy expected by this model, there must be a greater use of the imagination in worship. The liturgical assembly, then, can become the place where Christians can be empathetic with the sufferings of others because the community through its imagination is able to touch oppression more concretely without the kind of censoring that the mind is so well equipped to do.

The liturgy itself must be an incarnation of justice. The examples here are as obvious in perception as they are difficult in implementation. For instance, liturgy must be a model of how the variety of ministries is acknowledged rather than being an exemplification of hierarchical power. The ritual structures themselves should work against social, economic, age, sex, or class distinctions. Differences are seen as complementary and not divisive. Discrimination in any form has no place in the liturgy. The language will be inclusive. And the roles of the ministry will be open to all. In concrete liturgical preparation, this means team effort, sensitivity to where the community is in its prayer life, and a variety of ways of proclamation: word, gesture, music, silence. The environment of worship itself must be just.

What kind of human response will the liberation liturgy elicit from the worshipers? It will be one which promotes mutuality, that is, an interchange of respect and trust. The members of the assembly will be asked to challenge each other to go beyond their present life style and degree of commitment. It will not concentrate on the dramatic conversion of life, but rather on the victory in the pedestrian forms of injustice in ourselves and in our relationships. Liberation worship becomes the atmosphere of support both for those actually engaged in the social apostolate as well as those seeking justice in their ordinary experiences. To be just to oneself, that is, to be in contact with one's bodily self, to be self-accepting, while bringing justice to others is not a popular idea today. The liturgy can provide the encouragement which will help worshipers avoid the fear and defensiveness to which the apostle is often tempted.

While giving this support, liturgy summons us to be our best selves and becomes the context for discerning what can realistically be any particular Christian's approach to the justice issues of today. Such discernment will never take place unless there is some degree of faith-sharing. For it is the communal experience of the Christian call to build the kingdom *which is never fully built* which must be dominant in the liberation liturgy. Worship provides no recipes or answers for contemporary society's conflicts and debilitating structures. But it does make possible the process in which the individual worshipers touch the fundamental experience of justice, or the lack of it, in their lives and receive the insight or intuition of how, as members of the liturgical community, they are going to act responsibly for building this kingdom.

What liberation liturgical theology keeps in the forefront is that worship is not simply a matter of private devotion. It is more than a way of concretizing one's individual experience of God. Liturgy is outer directed. It is the community gathered, but gathered in and for the world. The eucharist especially shows how liturgy is at the center of one's commitment to social justice. The eucharist is about gift-giving, the giving of oneself for others. The eucharist is the primary sacrament of reconciliation where we ask to be freed from the forces of societal evil which paralyze us. We seek reconciliation with our brothers and sisters which implies commitment to changing the values of an indifferent society. Liturgy is about assembling wherein we acknowledge each other's presence. We affirm the worth of the other worshipers. We face together our world with its intimidations and enslavements.

The proclamation of the word to us is that we have been redeemed, that salvation has come to us. But our response must become in turn a proclamation to others both inside and outside the assembly that we are called to move beyond self-interest and to find ways to be in communion with others. The proclamation of the word frees us only if we respond by proclaiming to others that the justice of God has been made available to them. Our proclamation must be as empowering as was Christ's. His announcement of the saving message was effective in his redemption of the human race. Ours is rendered authoritative when we identify with the poor and the powerless. The liberation liturgy is one which clarifies that the humanization process is also the salvific one. Salvation cannot come apart from human dignity and the unity of all peoples. Just as the eucharistic Christ cannot be confined to the dimensions of the physical bread that is eaten in the liturgical celebration, so the bread of life we receive in the liturgy includes in its meaning our providing bread for the needy and the starving. There is no sacred-secular dichotomy in the liberation liturgical theology. This is not to pretend that there is no experience of opposites for the individual worshiper. It is that opposites such as 1) power/powerlessness, 2) freedom/unfreedom, 3) oppressed/oppressor, 4) sinful/loved unconditionally can be transcended through self-acceptance and sensitivity to others, both of which are ingredients for the wholeness of the individual and of the community. This juxtaposition of opposites can be an impetus for creative insight leading to action. By means of the contemplative, discerning liturgical experience, there can be movement in the worshipers toward their own inner freedom and power as gift to the group, enabling the community to communal freedom, power, and action by overcoming the stasis of compartmentalization of the sacred/profane separation.

Justice, or put negatively, the overcoming of injustice, is achieved through the coming together of opposites. That is what should happen in the liberation liturgy. Male and female, rich and poor, the person and the group, what is and what is not yet, all are united in the liturgical celebration, and so barriers are broken down in a symbolic movement. This is the liminal character of liturgy. In the proclamation of the word this coming together is brought about through shared reflection, conscientization, growth in self-love, and challenge to act. In the sacrament of the eucharist it is through thanksgiving, the union of a meal, and the communion in the paschal event.

The concept and use of power is central to liberation theologies. And so despite the union of opposites which liturgy attempts to create, power must find its proper, that is salvific, place in the liberation model. Power makes us uncomfortable because it has conflicting meanings. For some it signifies the action of the spirit which is plodding for change and conversion aimed at building up the kingdom. For others it signals the force that nations, governments, pressure groups, churches, and individuals use against each other, usually resulting in oppression.

Despite the negative side of power it must be part of the liturgy. Unless the worshipers experience themselves as people of power, they cannot enthusiastically participate; worship cannot have the aspects of play and prophecy without people being empowered in some way. If their self-image is one of being powerless, they will not be able to enter the liturgy in a meaningful way. But what kind of power should people experience in their worship? It is the experience of a God who is simultaneously present and absent. On the one hand, it is the experience of the God within. There is 1) a sense of internal strength and confidence, 2) a sense of determining choices in life, and 3) an ability to influence social processes. On the other hand, it is the experience of powerlessness because of the absence of God. It is 1) not being able to act on one's own behalf, 2) being a cripple, 3) being imprisoned, and 4) seeming to be ultimately unredeemed. And so the power which is celebrated in the Christian liturgical life is real. Like Christian hope it has a foundation. But like that same hope it contains a clear eschatological emphasis of being "anticipated power."

The just liturgy is the prayerful liturgy. Because injustice is so omnipresent and overwhelming, only a sense of transcendence can confront it. Bringing justice to specific situations and identifying the best means for combatting this impenetrable, cosmic sinfulness can result in alienation because the matter is not clearcut. Some rush in messiah-like without much analysis or desire to make distinctions. Others lose hope in face of the magnitude of the situation and withdraw into their private lives. The prayerful liturgy hopes to ensure that God is at the center of our commitment to justice. It relativizes our personal agendas. Prayer can smash the idols of our own egocentricity or self-hatred which is being projected on those oppressed to whom we condescendingly bring our ministry. But the prayerful liturgy also places the justice concerns in the context of Christian hope which is realistic. Such hopes nourish our commitment and allow us to move forward and not become immobilized by the enormity of the problem.

Finally, a liberation model of liturgical theology stresses a dialogue between contemplation and action. Contemplation can result in a liberating and revolutionary vision. Action can actually liberate. The playful aspect of liturgy arises out of contemplation, the prophetic aspect out of action. The kind of contemplation referred to here is the listening to oneself and to others as powerful or powerless. It is shared reflection of the lived experience of power/powerlessness. It is the discernment which is necessary to avoid the over-politicizing of the liturgy, the exaltation of the unexamined life, and the liberator becoming the oppressor. Contemplation means being in contact with the source of power—the God within history, within community, within oneself. In that sense the liberation model incorporates aspects of the process model. The divine power is at work in the world. But this power must act on someone, on something. And so the liberation model takes seriously the interrelatedness of all reality.

As contemplation in liturgy is shared reflection, action is shared doing. The liturgy must be the place where one can respond to oneself in a new way, a freeing way. In worship we must be able to find the call to move away from isolation and individualism. There we should find the strength to empower others to liberate themselves. In that sense the liturgy needs to be an experience of power. It must bring about a passage from a naive world-vision to a new consciousness, from an I/we can't to an I/we can do something about the situation. This consciousness is often lacking in the downpressed and in the downpressers.

This model is similar to the therapeutic one in that it tries to confront people whose psyches have been numbed by their excessive inculturation in their societies. Moving against prior patterns and present intricacies is therapeutic, is salvific, is empowering.

Action flowing from the liturgy can take many forms. It is not simply limited to moving into either the explicit church oriented social apostolate or various civil forms of societal transformation. This must be accompanied by more "in house" changes. For instance, full participation in the liturgy itself is a matter of justice. Other possibilities touching upon the liturgy would be: elimination of clericalism and sexism, full lay ministry, and the multipurpose use of church buildings.

Limitations of the Liberation Liturgical Model

There will ever be two temptations for the worshipers when confronted with the liberation approach to liturgy: to escape the tension between living for others and self-development and growth by either turning prayer into a private form of pietism or by making one's relevance to the world the overriding criterion for the just life. Authentic liturgy should lead to a greater love of humankind, compassion for the poor, sick, and oppressed, while at the same time being a personal, mystical experience. Liturgy should help seekers of justice in this world to keep their ministry in a Christian sense of history where all the work done for justice must be seen in the light of the risen life and the eschaton.

There is always the possibility in this model that liturgy will reinforce the identification of the Christian message with some existing or future social order and that the Gospel will be reduced to a political campaign. The liturgical celebration may deal with the suffering and oppression found in the world, but that does not insure that worship will be an ecclesial event. Experience shows that ritual can become individualistic or pietistic despite the justice concerns of the worshipers.

Specific dangers involved in fashioning liturgies according to this model would be 1) for the oppressors: (a) tokenism, that is, the idea that what is done in liturgy is all that needs be done, and (b) the guilt trip, that is, feeling so guilty that one is drained of all personal power; 2) for the oppressed: (a) fantasy, or the idea that what is experienced in liturgy is already experienced outside of liturgy in daily life; (b) politicizing or the attempt to make liturgy as ritual achieve the righting of societal wrongs, a task which belongs to the larger arena of human living of which worship is but a part; and (c) mobilizing angers in an unproductive way, that is, while these angry feelings must be rendered clear and acceptable, they are too quickly projected onto others and the structures outside of the worshiper. Such projection can lead to a loss of sensitivity for human beings and the human situation. It can even lead to violence. One unfortunate limitation of this model for both the oppressed and the oppressors is that the liturgy becomes too simple and there is no room for wonder, awe, fascination, and mystery because of manipulation for political purposes or because worship is so tightly programmed that there is no space for spontaneity.

Politics and Worship

In order to exemplify how the liberation model of liturgical theology influences and determines worship, one case study is now considered, that of the relationship between politics and liturgy. Often one hears the slogan: "No politics from the pulpit." Is it true in light of the liberation model that we can maintain that politics and liturgy are antithetical? Politics deals with the art and science of government. It is concerned with the state and its activities. It lives in the collective life of a people and in their social relations. Since the political aspect of life is so all pervasive, it seems impossible to avoid it in liturgy. It embraces the economic, social, and cultural areas of human living. It is constitutive of society. It is that special form of social activity that deals with power and the regulation of public affairs. Can worship prescind from these major areas of life?

The Christian faith must be political if religion is not to be simply a marginal sectarian experience. If belief in God is not political, religious confession is irrelevant or trivialized. How people live their lives, how governments act, how laws are enacted all reveal societal values. It is precisely these values about which ritual is concerned. Even the value of establishing the just kingdom of God demands that worship be related to politics. J. G. Davies says:

> To suppose that worship has nothing to do with politics, when politics covers so much of our daily life, is to declare that worship is largely irrelevant to everyday living. To suppose that neither worship nor politics has anything to do with morals is absurd. But because worship is tied up with values that should guide us in our daily lives, it has a direct bearing on politics.[6]

Christianity is eschatological in its very essence. But the eschaton is not simply a far distant reality, it is also on the way. It has begun. To pray "your kingdom come" demands working for that kingdom at the present time. This future toward which the Christian community is directed must be anticipated in worship. And the kingdom of God is achieved through obeying Jesus' injunction to "love your neighbor as yourself." This love of neighbor is not some kind of sentimental global abstraction of affectivity. It must be concretized in specific relationships which are based on the principle of love. That means that this principle needs to be embodied in the political arena. The call of the Sermon on the Mount to give a cup of water to the thirsty needs contemporary translation. It is to be found in responsible societal action. Love of neighbor cannot be separated from the political task as if they were two separate areas of reality. Neighborly love must also pervade our worship. Loving God by loving one's neighbor is what gives substance to both politics and worship. Justice and equality are not simply the concerns of the politician. They must be hallmarks of the life of the worshiper. And accordingly, liturgy has no monopoly on community and the celebration of life. These should also be made possible because of political activity.

Few would quarrel with the idea that governments should rule justly and that laws should promote human equity and freedom. But many, some liberation thinkers especially, would claim, following what they think some of the Hebrew prophets

6. J. G. Davies, *New Perspectives on Worship Today* (London: SCM Press, Ltd., 1978) 78.

were saying, that justice must precede cult. While injustice exists upon the earth, worship and prayer are not possible. This position cannot be easily refuted since it has a logic which is convincing. In a society where one finds both rich and poor and where the rich are rich at the cost of the poor, common worship for the two groups becomes problematic. If liturgy really brought people together, could the rich and poor really worship in the same celebration? It takes place today because our present liturgical structures support and sometimes even encourage anonymity. There is no confrontation between the two groups. But this is hypocrisy. And so a man like Camilo Torres could say:

> I have stopped offering mass to live out the love for my neighbor in the temporal, economic, and social orders. When my neighbor no longer has anything against me, and when the revolution has been completed, then I will offer mass again.[7]

However, it does not appear that one must come to that conclusion. It seems to presume rather naively that a state of perfect justice can be achieved in the course of human history. If we expect a completely realized eschaton before worshiping, then we shall never worship again. Also while the oppressors may be engaging in inauthentic worship, why deprive the oppressed of what may be the most effective form of articulating the meaning of their lives? In fact, oppressed peoples do want worship. One need only recall the centrality of worship for American blacks in their long history of suffering and inhumanity. Those who require justice first and then worship may be confined by a narrow view of God which separates the God of worship from the God who is compassionate and suffering with God's creation in this world. We cannot presume that God cannot be found within unjust structures because God has so distanced Godself from them.

It was the political structures of his time which caused Christ's suffering and death. That suffering of Christ is called to mind in Christian liturgy. Such memorializing or anamnesis should challenge the contemporary counterparts of those structures.

7. J. A. Garcia and C. R. Calle, eds., *Camilo Torres, Priest and Revolutionary* (New York: Sheed and Ward, 1968) 72.

Moreover, all Christian worship celebrates the God who is all powerful. This implies the destruction of any power idols that could be in competition with God. The power of politics must be subordinated to bringing about the power of God as it is manifested in a just society. If the primary liturgical acclamation is "Jesus is Lord," then perforce liturgy must sit in judgment on the powers of this world. And because the Lordship of Jesus must be translated into service it does not seem possible to maintain a dichotomy between politics and worship.

What is it that we celebrate in worship? In traditional religious language it is "salvation." For liberation theologians salvation and liberation are synonymous. Worship celebrates freedom. Davies puts it this way:

> The eucharist is the celebration of freedom because it is the feast of redemption and of the resurrection of Christ whereby the power of death was broken and all that is death dealing was brought under judgment. To be liberated is to know indeed what the resurrection from the dead is all about.[8]

This freedom eucharistically celebrated refers to the salvation that takes place when there is the struggle against the exploitation of peoples, against political oppression, against the alienation of one person from another, and against despair in personal life. As Christians we must worship so that all the possibilities of the liberating God can be opened up to us. If we really believe that Christ has freed us, but do not give praise and thanks for that, we are less than honest. We also deprive ourselves of an imaginative source from which we can envision new forms of justice and new ways of living humanly.

The close connection that should exist between liturgy and politics must be concretized in the matter of the rites themselves. The words and ceremonies must be an enfleshment of this relationship. For instance, because of the abstract and universal language of so much of our liturgy, it tends to depreciate historical specificity. And yet freedom does not live in theories but in the actual lives of people. For this reason the liturgy should move us into our individual processes. Making worship concrete

8. Davies, *New Perspectives* 85.

is not easy. In order to avoid simply proclaiming a universal but ineffective love for all, some manipulate worship by having it espouse certain kinds of political activity. In order to avoid this kind of manipulation, the liturgy must be carefully planned with involvement from the participants. A good touchstone for determining whether ritual manipulates or not, is the degree to which differences of opinion are possible in the same service.

Hard questions must be asked of our worship in terms of the political dimension. Does it really assist us in being for others? Does it really bring about interactions between the members of the worshiping assembly? Is worship an experience of liberation for us? We must do more in worship than assert, sing, and proclaim freedom. We must feel it in the method of our worship. Liberation is not a completely future reality. It must be experienced in the liturgy as a foretaste of future freedom. Liturgy anticipates the future when it erases the present divisions of society and becomes a symbol of what human beings are capable of in terms of loving each other. It is a sign not of a world which is apolitical, but one which shares a common purpose with politics: justice and equality for all. Davies puts the relationship of worship and politics this way:

> The eucharist is a political act because it in its turn makes a statement about human nature and about the principles and ground work of human interrelatedness. So it speaks of equality, of concern for reconciliation that is the opposite of individual and social alienation. It is intended to be an embodiment and expression of efficacious love and therefore of justice in terms of freedom and material welfare. But to proclaim these things is vain unless there is a consistent effort to have them actualized in society at large and this requires their embodiment in a political programme.[9]

Questions continue to arise: can the worshipers find freedom in a fixed liturgy where all the details are predetermined and where the presider not only presides but dominates? In what way can confession in the Christian service call for repentance from the sins committed in the economic and social spheres? Can the homily proclaim the Gospel if it does not produce the

9. Ibid. 89.

feeling of discontent brought about by the discrepancy between the demands of the Gospel and what is actually taking place in society? Does our liturgical praying commit us to bring about that for which we pray? Does our act of communing by means of bread and wine imply the fair distribution of resources? Does the fellowship of liturgy take its meaning from our solidarity with all the people of this world, especially the poor and hungry? Davies indicates the direction in which these questions can receive a positive answer:

> Worship and politics are two ways of acting in God's world and they interpenetrate one another. Worship can provide guidelines for political action, while politics can put into effect that love which is at the centre of the eucharist . . . Worship can foster a vision of the Kingdom of God, of human interrelatedness, and then political involvement is needed to further the process of making that vision a reality.[10]

10. Ibid. 95–6.

9

Liturgy as Proclamation

IT IS MY STRONG CONVICTION ARRIVED AT THROUGH A GREAT DEAL of experience in liturgical planning that all attempts to revive worship today or to make liturgy a meaningful part of the whole effort of the pastoral renewal of the church must presuppose an adequate theoretical foundation. In other words, there must be a clear and well-defined liturgical theology underlying one's adaptation and inculturation of the liturgy. One cannot continue to introduce new forms of worship, exploit the mass media in different sacramental situations, engage in more personalistic encounters à la the various group sensitivity methods and the like without a solid theological underpinning. Invariably, this lack of an adequate liturgical theology will lead to new distortions and aberrations. All the balloons in the world, all the smiling priests in the country, all the warm embraces at the kiss of peace will not make a liturgy be what it should be: the place where the church becomes the church.

What is a theology of worship? It is a theology of how the church becomes church. We cannot speak about liturgy until we know what it means to be church. If it is correct to say, as liturgical theologians do, that the liturgy reflects and constitutes the church, that is, worship expresses and actualizes here and now in a concrete symbolic situation the nature of what the Christian community was, is and will be, then those who work in liturgy must know what they are trying to reflect, what they are trying to actualize and constitute. The liturgical planner must have a firm understanding that what the liturgy does is to show what the church is and at the same time to help the church to become more church. The purpose of liturgical worship is to direct the church to its present task of being that clear and un-ambiguous sign of what God is up to in the world and to urge the church forward to the shape that it must have at the end of time.

Because the liturgy reflects the reality of the communal Chris-tian experience and is also the self-constructive activity of the church, it cannot be separated from the community. Liturgy presupposes community. If there is no real community, there is no liturgy. But it does more than bring to expression and create the Christian community's experience. It is the articulation of the spirituality of that community.[1] Worship manifests and deep-ens the faith dimension of the church. Rites and ritual formulas express and form the spirituality of the community. Liturgy deals with the vision of a community, the conditions of a community, and the faith of a community.

But what is that spirituality of the church that the liturgy brings to visibility and intensifies? The meaning of this spirituality is basically the Christian community's relationship with God. But in order to get at the meaning of that relationship it is important to note that people relate to others and so to God in terms of their self-image. For instance, those who see themselves as worthwhile and as being loved will relate to God differently from those who see themselves as hateful and without value. Thus, we can say that the church's spirituality is its self-image of who it is. Since our self-image is what we are in fact becoming, liturgy is, then, the expression of what the church is actually becoming.

But how do we know what the self-image of the church is? We know it through the process of self-transparency. For in-stance, we experience this transparency in the prayer groups that are springing up around the country. In these, people let themselves become clear to each other in their faith dimension. They show each other what makes them Christians. And what makes them Christians is becoming the people of God in terms

1. Some of the ideas in this section have been put forth by Gerard T. Broccolo in his article, "A Theology of Worship," published by Liturgy Training Pub-lications, 1800 North Hermitage Avenue, Chicago, IL 60622-1101.

of the vision of Jesus Christ. People who share this vision want to celebrate it. It is in liturgical celebration that they let this vision become transparent and thereby place themselves in relationship to this vision.

Self-transparency means shared vision. For instance, we all know people in our lives whom we are inclined to trust because of the way that they conduct themselves, interact with others and allow what is going on inside of them to come through to us. The natural tendency is to reciprocate by opening up our own interiority and letting them enter more deeply into our lives. This brings about union whether it be that of a good working relationship with your mail carrier or whether it be that of a deep love between two friends. In either case, for there to be reciprocity, there must be transparency, there must be some shared vision. And through this mutual self-exposure, one affirms one's self-identity, one's self-image.

The self-image of the Christian community is brought about by the self-transparency of that community. And that transparency is the sharing of a common vision by all the members of that community. And the vision they share is the risen Christ himself. This Christian vision is the primary ingredient of the Christian self-image. It is by means of this communal self-image that the community relates to God. In other words, its spirituality is in terms of this self-image. And since liturgy is the articulation of the community's spirituality and since liturgy is this communal faith-transparency brought to the level of ritual awareness, the Christian liturgical assembly is the self-image of the whole Christian community raised to the level of explicit communal activity. Liturgy, then, is the articulation of the spirituality of the Christian community because it ritualizes in communal symbolic activity the self-image of the same community. This group self-image is constituted by the shared vision, the communal faith, and the mutual self-transparency of the members of this community. And what they share, believe in common and reciprocally expose to each other is that they have been, are and will be the people of God in the risen Christ. This kind of intersubjective action that goes on in the human dynamic of faith-sharing brings about the ecclesial reality that we call the church. As Christians expose their relationship to God and to other people in a ritualized situation they become more what they are;

they become more the people of God. They assert more and more their self-identity, an identity that is founded on the resurrected Christ.

What this means on the pastoral level is that liturgy should never be primarily a question of the techniques of liturgical planning but should always refer to the transparency of the faith aspect of the community. The fundamental criterion of liturgical planning is the facilitation of the faith dimension of a particular community. What does this say about the faith of the president of the assembly? Must he/she assume more than he/she actually has? Does not the need for transparency argue for the necessity of non-verbal forms of communication? Can the present normative Roman Rite allow for sufficient transparency in small groups? Can we continue to hide behind ritual, afraid to expose the deficient faith that may be there, when true symbolic and ritual involvement means self-exposure?

The importance of shared vision among Christians is that such sharing allows them to be present to one another. It is in their mutual self-transparency that God comes to visibility. And when what is shared is belief in the resurrected Lord, it is Jesus Christ who comes to presence. Presence to one another through shared vision means being present to the world. There are those in that world who claim there is no ultimate meaning to life. We proclaim there is meaning for us. Because we share the vision of life's significance, suddenly the world is confronted with a group of persons filled with hope. Our prophetic witness to the world is achieved by the authenticity of our vision. If we forget our vision after the celebration, our liturgy is inauthentic.

Liturgy must be more than the cementing of a fragmented group into unity, however. It must manifest that human history is the progressive movement by God revealing God's own intersubjective dynamic with the world. Thus, lying behind contemporary liturgical theology is the basic notion that creation itself is revelatory of God's salvific activity. The whole world is a sacrament in this sense. The purpose of Jesus Christ is to clarify for us that what God is doing by utilizing all creation for the purpose of ultimate union is not uncharacteristic of God. God is very much in character in drawing all people to Godself through their becoming more fully human. Jesus Christ is not unique because he alone brings salvation. He is unique because he is the chief exemplification of what God is all about, namely, that salvation is achieved through the world and people becoming what they should be. Jesus was the paradigm of God. By his life of love and goodness and especially by his great sacrifice on the cross and his victorious resurrection he made it clear that all forms of love, goodness, sacrifice, and resurrection are salvific. In this sense, Jesus is the great sacrament of God.

And so too with the church. The church is a sign or sacrament. It is to Jesus Christ what Christ is to God. The church is the clear and unambiguous sign of what Christ is all about. It has no monopoly on salvation. But it is a witness to meaning, to the fact that Christ has stated in his redemptive activity that God is working in the world wherever the world is becoming more and more what it should be. This is another way of saying that the church is the sign of the incarnational activity of Christ in the world. The world must deal with a group of people who believe, who find in their transparent sharing all that makes their lives significant. It is in this sense that the church is a sacrament. But this does not mean that the church or the church's liturgy has any monopoly on achieving union with God. It is the world rather than the church which is the primary place of salvation. The church is not the usual place of salvation. It is the focus of that salvation which is taking place through the whole process of this world's becoming. Rather, the church is the extraordinary place where salvation takes place. Most people have not been saved through the church, most are not being saved through the church, and there is little hope that most people will be saved through the church. The church is that symbol of what Christ is all about, but clearly and explicitly so.

What we have said about Christ and the church can be said about the liturgy. What Christ is to God, the church is to Christ and the liturgy is to the church. The liturgy is the unambiguous articulation of what it means to be church. Just like the church, but more specifically, the liturgy remembers and celebrates the great things that God works in our lives. Just as the church is the focus of Christ's meaning and activity, so the liturgy is the focal point for the action of the Christian community. The liturgy is the clearest statement that can be made about the church. Not that the majority of us are most Christian in the liturgy. I suspect that the opposite is the real situation, but it is in the liturgical assembly that something is done which can have no other meaning but church. Other good Christian activity such as social work can certainly be redemptive, but it can also be understood in such a way that it does not clearly say something about how God is drawing the whole world by the attracting power of all-encompassing love. For instance, Christians working in the inner city are doing something which certainly can bring them to God and salvation. But that aspect of their work may not be uppermost in their minds. Nor would it necessarily be interpreted by the people with whom they are working. Many would understand what they are doing as purely good human activity. They themselves could lose their sensitivity to the transcendent dimension of their work. In brief, the liturgy is the Christian community's *proclamation* to the world about its own meaning: that all men and women can be brought to union with God by becoming better people. The liturgy is the proclamation of Christ and Christ is the proclamation of God.

But what is it that we mean by the word *proclamation* when applied to the liturgy? Surely we mean more than speaking in stentorian tones. It must be more than merely talking. Proclamation would have little connection with our liturgical experiences if it only meant giving information as one does in verbal communication. No, proclamation is much more than that. Proclamation is language, but not any kind of language. It is certainly more than the usual language we speak every day. It is what theologians call a language-event. In order to understand what we mean by liturgy as proclamation we must first analyze what is meant by language-event, how this concept applies to our understanding of liturgy, and finally what are some of the practical results that flow from this definition of Christian worship.

Language is more than the words we use. It is part of our existence and reality. We live in a world of meaning which has been given to us by language. And by language I mean not only words, but all forms of human communication such as gestures, movements of the face, music, art, dance, and inflicting violence as well as making love. Language, in this broad sense, is the way in which human beings communicate and become present to one another. If there were no language, there would be no human presence and if there were no human presence, you could not talk about reality. If you are standing next to someone in a

crowded bus, you might well be physically present to him, especially if he has his elbows in your back. But you are not personally and humanly present to him until you turn around and
say something. There is a sense in which our *personal* reality is
constituted by language. We live in relation to others to the
degree that they are present to us and they have revealed themselves in language to us and we to them. We could not live if
there were no language (in the broad sense). Just imagine how
empty our lives are when even one kind of language is missing.
The inability to talk or see is obvious in its limitations, but suppose that there were no kissing in human activity. There would
be one entire aspect of human affectivity which could never come
to presence: that dimension of human love which can never be
communicated in words, even poetry, or in some other form of
human touch or symbolic involvement.

When we speak of proclamation as language, whether it be
verbal, visual, or tactile, we are concerned with proclamatory
speaking. Proclamatory speaking is a way of pointing. This
pointing allows us to bring meaning into the foreground. By
speaking, we detach and connect meanings; we analyze and
synthesize. Proclamatory speaking permits the one who is pointing to go beyond the limits of time and space. The speaking
word is the creative word. It changes reality. It helps constitute
our relationships. Our world is constituted by the assembly of
words and persons and things that have meaning for us.[2]

In the musical, *The Man from La Mancha*, the knight-errant
encounters the local whore, Aldonza, at an inn which for him,
of course, is a castle. He sees her as a lady and so gives her a
name representing that ideal, Dulcinea. The old man amuses
Aldonza but she is also caught up short and calls him her greatest
tormentor because he has shown her what she might have been.
This is painful. At the end as our hero lies dying, Aldonza and
Sancho arrive on the scene. A bystander challenges her for wanting to comfort the old man. The people call her Aldonza. "My
name," she says, "is Dulcinea."

2. In this section dealing with the idea of liturgy as language-event I am
indebted to Gabe Huck who has developed this idea in chapter three of his
very helpful, but all too brief, book, *Liturgy Needs Community Needs Liturgy*
(New York: Paulist Press, 1973) 44ff. I have referred to some of his examples
because they are so persuasive.

It was not just a sound that changed Aldonza to Dulcinea. It was the faith and the vision of the knight-errant. Not that the word was unimportant. It was everything since what happened could not have taken place without the word. The word was more than the communication of information. It challenged Aldonza to a new vision of reality.

This calls to mind the biblical union of word and action. G. Van der Leeuw in his *Religion: Its Essence and Manifestation* says:

> Whoever speaks, therefore, not only employs an expressive symbol but goes forth out of himself, and the word that he lets fall decides the matter. Even if I merely say "Good Morning" to someone I must emerge from my isolation, place myself before him and allow some proportion of my potency to pass over into his life, for good or evil. . . The word, then, is a decisive factor; whoever utters words sets power into motion.[3]

In his *The Phenomenology of Language*, Rémy Kwant speaks of words as a way of "pointing." When we point at someone with our hands or nod in his or her direction, that person has a meaning he or she would not have without the pointing. Kwant says that our culture does not look kindly on people who point toward the infirmity of the cripple. "If they do it anyhow, his deformity begins to exist in a new and more striking way both for himself and for others. Pointing raises a meaning out of its relative concealment."[4]

Kwant uses the distinction between the speaking word and the spoken word. Ordinarily we use spoken words, but when we are creative and challenging we use speaking words. In the march on Washington in August of 1963 when Martin Luther King, Jr. gave his "I have a Dream" speech, these words articulated a vision that the hearer had to make a decision about. This was a case of the "speaking word." What King meant by what he said would not have been real in the same way for those who heard him had he not spoken in the way he did.

3. G. Van der Leeuw, *Religion: Its Essence and Manifestation* (New York: Harper & Row, 1963) 403–5.

4. Rémy Kwant, *The Phenomonology of Language* (Pittsburgh: Duquesne University Press, 1965) 62.

In this way words can take on special importance in the human community. They depend on the community and yet the community lives by them. A community is formed when people can assent to the "speaking word." They share what is expressed in the speaking word. This word itself comes from within the community and is not an external force. However, since communities are not just groups of people who get together often, but are composed of those who share a common vision and a common language, it may not be possible today for the speaking word to be effective on the parish level. It may be that we will have to look for more natural groupings which have common understandings for friendship and joint endeavors.

The fact is that we all live in community and as members of some kind of community we all live in some language context and tradition. Most of us live in many communities (family, club, church) and so live in many language contexts. Some time ago, in a liturgy in St. Ignatius Church in San Francisco, the presider of the Mass during the breaking of the bread used the words of Jesus as recorded by St. John: "Your fathers ate the manna in the desert and they are dead; but this is the bread that comes down from heaven, so that a man may eat it and not die." In the congregation was a young Jewish man who happened in on the liturgy that day. Later in the sacristy he protested that the presider had disparaged his people, that he had implied that the Jews were spiritually dead. We tried to explain to him that in the context the words did not carry that meaning. It was a good example of what it means to live in a language tradition where the same word takes on meanings it would not have in a different tradition or context.

Language, then, creates us in some sense. It enables us to relate personally with others. One is related to persons by speaking to them. One remains in relation to them only if they answer. And because one is made up of all the relationships that one has, one is made by language, by bodily, symbolic activity. After all, the speaking word is directed to what makes us persons, to our rational, responsible, deciding center. The word mediates meaning which must be understood, judged, accepted, or rejected in a free decision. All this is performed by men and women as persons. We are asked to listen but we are free to decline. In either case one sets up new relationships. When someone actively pursues my friendship I can either respond positively or with indifference. In either case I have disposed myself to reality in a new way: in one case I have the new relationship of loving friendship and in the other the lack of this relationship, or something worse such as a relationship of enmity.

When this speaking causes confusion in the listener, when it demands change, when it sets up new relationships, it is called a language-event. This is what Jesus did, especially in the parables. He invited people to share in bold alternatives. For those who accepted this new language, there was a new community. The word *event* is a happy one in this case because it refers to something that affects the whole person and not just the intellectual and verbal part of our being.

Not all language, of course, is eventful. Language is event when, as in the case of Jesus referring to God as his Father, it touches the deepest dimension of people's lives. And when this was the case with those who heard Jesus, they entered into a new community, a community that could only stay alive if that language continued to be eventful for them and for others as it originally was. Today when we call God our loving Mother, we have a language-event because it places us in a situation which is different from those who do not call God such. They who hear the word Mother applied to God cannot do otherwise than decide whether or not they wish to have this new relationship. They either accept or reject it. If they accept, then they enter into a new community that forms around this word and assents to the relationships implied. This new community shares a language which then becomes their language and their way of relating to others who use the same language and which thus creates a new world in which they live. This is not the case where the spoken word does not set up new relationships and so is not a language-event or proclamation. For instance, if I tell you that I am wearing nylon underwear, this would not be a proclamation since it does not demand any decision from you. It is not a question of your either rejecting or accepting that fact. I am merely giving information. Proclamation, rather, is the kind of communication that creates reality for the hearer. It means giving alternatives, demanding decisions, and requiring responses. And depending on how people respond to that language-event, their lives will be different in terms of new relationships.

"I love you" is an obvious example of proclamation. My life is different because of the people I love and who love me. Our realities are different because of the relationships. Saying "I love you" makes a difference regarding these relationships. Making the love explicit moves people out of the neutral area. A decision is demanded that makes the relationships different. They become more inevitable, more definitive, more committed. In that sense, an expression of love is not *merely* a celebration of something already present. In the proclamation itself we are actually going beyond the love present in the relationship up to that time.

What does all this mean for liturgy and liturgical planning? It means that liturgy is basically a language, but a language which is more than words. Liturgy is a language-event and because it is that, one can affirm that liturgical worship is primarily a situation of proclamation and response. This primordial and unchanging structure of the liturgy must be respected in the process of liturgical planning. The following are certain basic statements representing in summary form a theology of the liturgy as proclamation.

(1) The purpose of God and the people is that there be a union of the two, that there be a sharing of God's creative love with persons and that they become part of the reality of God by means of response. This presupposes the mutual presence of God and persons to each other. In other words, the relationship between God and people is one of dialogue.

(2) In this dialogue God speaks first: the fundamental attitude of persons is that of listening. God becomes present in speaking. Our experience of God is one of communication. God becomes personally and humanly present to us in language.

(3) To share in someone's life even through communication, one must be adequately present. God is adequately present to us in Jesus Christ. That is why Jesus is the Word of God, or God's language. Jesus doesn't say everything about God, but he says enough to bring about the sharing, the union without excessive difficulty. In that sense God is adequately present in him.

(4) The Word of God has been definitively proclaimed by God. We need but recall it. Our recall is done in language since language answers language. Our response is liturgy. Liturgy is, then, the common language of God and God's people. When

God speaks to us the Word which is Jesus Christ, we have liturgy in the form of the Gospel and the sacraments. When the Christian community responds to God in praise and thanksgiving, we have the language of liturgy. But the liturgical dynamic is not simply one of God's proclamation to us and our response. Christ is seen as the subject of the liturgy rather than the object of worship. In the liturgy Christ is the chief liturgist offering worship to God to which we are joined by him. Thus, we can say that in liturgical worship Christ is God's most adequate response. Moreover, since God is in Christ, Jesus becomes God's best answer to God's own call and at the same time Christ is the community's fullest proclamation of itself.

(5) Liturgy, then, is a situation of proclamation and response. God's proclamation of love to those who believe in the Son constitutes the body of Christ. The church is created when the word is received in faith. The proclamation of the word of God by the worshiping people also constitutes the church. In the liturgy both Christ and community proclaim and respond. This proclamation and response structure must find many levels of expression in the liturgical assembly.

(6) As the community's proclamation, Christian liturgy is the articulation and intensification of the presence of God and in particular in terms of the paschal mystery of Christ: the death, resurrection, and exaltation of Jesus. Liturgy is the permanent proclamation of the paschal mystery which constitutes and reflects the church. The liturgical assembly is the most explicit expression and manifestation of the Christian life because it lights up what is going on in the rest of Christian living.

But God is not only present in the liturgy, but wherever people respond to the deepest impulses of nature, wherever they are brought out of isolation to speak a common language. The difference with liturgy is that in the liturgical assembly we can *name* the one who brings us out of silence into existence and call that one by name.

(7) Although liturgy is proclamation, that is, a kind of communication that creates reality for the hearer because it gives alternatives, demands decisions, requires response, makes new relationships and so is a language-event, this does not mean that there must be a new explicit proclamation and response in every liturgy in which one is participating. Most of the real procla-

mations of God in our lives probably happen outside of liturgy, on occasions when we are confronted with reality in such a way that we are required to be decisive. One thinks for example of the challenging people with whom one works and the various opportunities for growth that happen along each day. But what the liturgy does in relation to those moments of proclamation in our lives is to both affirm and remember the past ones and to anticipate those that will come. Liturgical worship commemorates the past proclamations of God in human living as well as makes one sensitive to those that will enter at some future time. We first encounter the grace of God in human living. In the liturgy this grace is celebrated. Liturgy is an explication of God summoning us at the very center of our lives where we discern God's presence and the call to us to create our future.

In conclusion I can only reiterate what I had said in the beginning. The best liturgical adaptation and planning takes place in the context of an adequate liturgical theology. I have tried to indicate the general outlines of a liturgical theology that can serve this purpose. Only with this kind of a theoretical foundation can liturgical planning achieve its final end, namely, that the liturgy be the proclamation of the body of Christ in our own time.

The following chart is an attempt to concretize the theology of liturgy as proclamation just articulated. While the application is limited to the liturgy of the Mass, the principle that all liturgy is structured according to a proclamation/response pattern is valid for all services of worship. Close examination of the chart will show that not all elements of the present normative Roman Rite fit well into this proclamation/response pattern. It is my conviction that this in no way challenges my point that the unchanging structure of all liturgy is proclamation/response. My opinion is that where there is a sense of artificiality in the application of this principle or obvious conflict between the structure of the Roman Rite and this structural principle, the fault lies with the rite. We do not have a perfect liturgy of the eucharist in the Roman Church. There are still elements in the rite which are misplaced or which should be eliminated entirely. One obvious example is that of the so-called penitential rite which as a unit is really a response. But to what is it a response? There is no preceding proclamation. This rite would better be placed after the reading of the word of God. Despite these limitations, however, I feel that this chart is a helpful guideline for liturgical planning and a concrete reflection of the liturgical theology developed in this article.

LITURGY AS PROCLAMATION

LITURGY OF WORD
P

LITURGY OF EUCHARIST
R

Entrance Song	R	Preparation Prayers	P
Greeting	P	Blessed be God forever	R
Amen	R	Prayer over gifts	P
Confession	P	Amen	R
Lord, have mercy	R	Dialog before Preface	P & R
Glory to God	R	Preface	P
Opening Prayer	P	Holy Holy Holy	R
Amen	R	Eucharistic Prayer	P
First Reading	P	Eucharistic Acclamation	R
Responsorial Psalm	R	Great Amen	R
Second Reading	P	Introduction	P
Silence	R	Lord's Prayer	R
Alleluia/Gospel/Homily	P	Embolism	P
Creed	R	Doxology	R
Universal Prayer	R	Prayer for peace	P
		Amen	R
P: Proclamation		Greeting of peace	P
R: Response		And also with you	R
		Gesture of peace	P
		Gesture of response	R
		Fraction Rite	P
		Lamb of God	R
		This is the Lamb of God	P
		Lord, I am not worthy	R
		The Body of Christ	P
		Amen	R
		Communion Song/Silence	R
		Post Communion Prayer	P
		Amen	R
		Greeting	P
		And also with you	R
		Blessing	P
		Amen	R
		Dismissal	P
		Thanks be to God	R
		Closing Song	R

10

Planning and Adapting the Liturgy

THERE ARE FEW NEAR ABSOLUTES IN LITURGY, BUT ONE OF THEM IS that successful liturgies must be well planned. Liturgical planning is hard work based upon clear theological principles of worship plus all the creativity that those doing the planning can muster. Theology without imagination remains sterile and abstract. Creativity without theological understanding is headed for a distortion of the Christian experience. Besides an adequate liturgical theology and some basic creative talent, the liturgical planner must know what planning is. To put it simply, liturgical planning is liturgical adaptation. But what does it mean to adapt the liturgy? It is first necessary to understand what liturgical adapatation is not.

Liturgical adaptation is not the same thing as play. Merely to move the furniture around is hardly to plan the liturgy. One does not adapt the liturgy by passing out balloons although such activity might well be part of a creative liturgy. Presiders who so conduct themselves through the service that you never know what they are going to do next is not adapting liturgy. All of this is play, and bad play at that.

Liturgical adaptation is not the same thing as innovation. By being innovative here I mean that the local community does its own thing following the presumption that it has the ability to discover new ways of saying and doing what is understood to be worship. This is frequently the stance of those who are engaged in the misnomer, underground liturgies.

Despite what many people think, liturgical adaptation is not the same thing as liturgical experimentation. Experimentation with the liturgy has a very definite meaning and it should not be confused with attempts to adapt worship to the contemporary situation. Many people, especially priests and bishops, seem to think that every time a small prayer in the liturgy is changed we have a case of experimenting with the liturgy. We do not. The word "experiment" has a technical meaning here. It signifies an operation undertaken to discover some unknown principle or effect. It is a disciplined means of discovering something, but something which is not yet known. It is more than just testing.

To test something means to try out a preconceived idea to determine the advantages and difficulties of its implementation. But in testing one knows what one wishes to accomplish. It is not a question of discovering something new. The goal or end product is clear. It is a matter of determining which concrete means will bring about this product. For instance, an attempt to make the Roman Rite relevant to small children would demand a certain amount of testing. But the final product would still be the Roman Rite. In experimentation the end product itself is not known. We need to experiment to find the liturgies of the future, but this is more than simply testing out certain means to bring about this new liturgy. We do not really know what the liturgy of the future will look like. Testing, then, is the method of adapting the liturgy. It is necessary to test if one is going to plan well.

Hopefully, we can look forward in the future to situations of real liturgical experimentation in the Christian community. At the present time we do not really have any official ones. When we finally obtain full ecclesiastical approval for such centers, three criteria will have to be met in order to have authentic liturgical experimentation at them. The experimentation must be 1) historically founded, 2) theologically reasoned, and 3) pastorally relevant.

Historically founded means that since the liturgical life takes place in a tradition and not in a vacuum, experimenters must have a considerable knowledge of the past. This is necessary not only to avoid the mistakes of the past, but also because all great liturgies grew historically. They were not instantaneously composed by people or committees. Growth takes place in history.

Theologically reasoned means that all the experimentation must

be measured in the light of the faith commitment of the worshiping people. But this faith commitment must be one of an
informed response to the Gospel. To have a properly informed
response to the Gospel, it is necessary to take account of recent
theological emphases.

Experimentation can be fun but irrelevant. Pastorally relevant
experimentation must reflect the experience of the worshiper
and it must speak to that experience. Just because something is
true does not make it meaningful. Nor is something of pastoral
help just because ecclesiastical authority says it is. Authority does
not create truth.

Liturgical experimentation is an attempt to achieve a liturgy
that can move and inspire without manipulation. Such a liturgy
will have the power and the capacity to enter the deeper regions
of human experience and touch the hearts of people who look
for more than mere entertainment when they go to worship. If
this end of experimentation is to be achieved, then a pre-existent
faith community is required where true experimentation can take
place. The real method of liturgical experimentation is not to
construct new services, but to set up an atmosphere where new
rites can grow.

Liturgical adaptation, then, must not be confused with play
or innovation. It must also be distinguished from liturgical experimentation as liturgists define it. Rather, adaptation is fundamentally the changing of a standard model so that it becomes
more appropriate to a particular situation. Liturgical adaptation
means to change the standard model of the Roman Rite in such
a way that it responds to the particular Christian community
using it. To adapt the liturgy for lively contemporary celebration
is inevitably to particularize, concretize, and localize both its
content and its forms. This is what adaptation is: moving from
the general to the particular, from the abstract to the concrete,
from the universal to the local. Adaptation seeks only to find
and use forms which we can experience as authentic and meaningful at a particular time and in a particular place. For abstract
and general and universal liturgy is not good liturgy because it
is not human liturgy. Good liturgy is always alive, immediate,
and particular because what is human is always vibrant, concrete, and specific. The best liturgy is that which is most truly
human.

Now that we know something of the nature of liturgical planning, let us turn to the principles governing this planning. There are several general principles that cover all liturgical planning in all situations. There are also three main principles which guide the planning in the concrete. Let us take up the general principles first.

(1) Our liturgical tradition does not work by magic. There is no automatic assurance that the performance of a sacrament will communicate the meaning tradition has given it. Does the pouring of water in the sacrament of baptism really symbolize for us the death and rising of Jesus and of our new birth in him? Planners must try to make the present symbols of the liturgy more transparent. The correction here is not to substitute something for the water but to heighten the consciousness of water in its meaning of death and resurrection.

(2) Greater transparency does not mean giving the symbol a new meaning. One does not create symbols on the spot. This would distort the symbol and deprive the community of its meaning. A good example of reading a meaning into a symbol which it should not have is the idea that the eucharist is a sacrifice because one sees the blessing of the bread and wine as a symbolic slaying of a victim. What should be stressed is that when sacrifice is seen in a less restricted way, a meal as symbolic activity can be understood as sacrificial.

When modern planners introduce such forms as visuals, dance, mime, or poetry to enhance the traditional symbols, they must be concerned that the original meaning still be there.

(3) We must be careful that we do not condemn ancient symbols as irrelevant when what we really mean is that it is not easy for us to experience anything by means of symbols. Our technological age has trained us to look at things pragmatically. It is difficult to appreciate things if one is manipulating them. It may be that the ecological crisis will call us back to a more human experience of things. The sign of the water in baptism will only have meaning for those who have some sense of wonder of rivers and rain.

(4) The traditional meanings of symbols are related to certain liturgical structures of which the planner must be aware. There is no point in starting from scratch when there is something to be gained from existing structures. In liturgical planning as op-

posed to liturgical experimentation, only the historic structure of the liturgy should be used. It is not to be idolized, but it is to be honored.

The three principles which influence directly and concretely the process of liturgical planning are: 1) the rhythm of the liturgy must be respected; 2) the proper hierarchy of the structural elements of the liturgy must be maintained; and 3) the musical elements of the liturgy must be integrated in accordance with both the proper rhythm of the liturgy and the structure of the elements which make up the service. Let us take each principle and apply it to liturgical planning. I shall restrict my remarks to the Roman eucharistic liturgy.

THE RHYTHM OF THE LITURGY

The one unchanging structure of Christian liturgy is that it be proclamation and response. The entire liturgy can be divided into a series of proclamations and responses. The proclamations are moments of tension. By tension, I do not mean psychological anxiety, but greater active involvement and attention. The responses are moments of relaxation. By relaxation I do not mean pure passivity, but times when participation is more in terms of receptivity.

The rhythm of the liturgy is the flow of proclamation to response to proclamation to response and so forth. If the service is a series of proclamations or a row of responses, the rhythm is broken, a necessary rhythm which is founded theologically on the idea that the liturgy is proclamation-response.

Turning to the liturgy of the word we find that the rhythm is established by the readings as proclamations and the various forms of responses which follow these readings. The gospel is the high point of the liturgy of the word. When we analyze this part of the eucharist in detail we see that we can start with an upbeat or with a low keyed entrance, depending on what kind of celebration it is. Daily liturgies during Lent will tend to start on a quiet level while Easter Sunday with a rousing hymn will begin on a higher plane. The entire entrance rite: the greeting, the penitential rite, the Glory to God and the opening prayer are all on a medium plane because they are not important parts of the rite. The first reading is a rhythmic elevation while the responsorial psalm is a moment of relaxation. The second reading is another movement to a high point equal to that of the first reading, while the silence which should follow this reading is definitely a response which is relaxed and low on the rhythmic scale. The Alleluia is the beginning of the rise toward the gospel proclamation. The Alleluia is very important for preparing for the gospel. It makes the gospel the high point of the liturgy of the word. People should stand during the singing of it. It is not a response, a moment of relaxation. It should culminate into the gospel. I have witnessed many successful celebrations where this was the case. The gospel literally grew out of the Alleluia. Often the reason that the gospel does not build is that everything is relaxed until the presider says: "The Lord be with you." There is no build-up. On the other hand, I remember one church in which I was examining the liturgy how the people sang a rousing black spiritual as a gospel acclamation. It grew in intensity. We were all keyed-up for the gospel proclamation. But when the presider came to the lectern to read the gospel, instead of launching into the reading in a dramatic way, he changed the entire mood by telling the congregation to be seated while he read the text meditatively. It was like a strong wind suddenly dying. The liturgy lost its momentum and went dead. The repetition of the gospel acclamation after the proclamation of the gospel can highlight the intimate connection between the gospel acclamation and the gospel itself.

The homily can be considered a response to the gospel and so the beginning of the moment of relaxation which follows the gospel proclamation. However, I prefer to keep the gospel and homily together as one unit and consider both the high point of this section of the eucharist liturgy. The Creed and universal prayers are certainly moments of relaxation in the liturgy in so far as they are response to the gospel. There are problems here. With the Creed and universal prayers together it appears that we have two responses following each other. And so we do. The best solution is to remove the Creed from the eucharistic liturgy for the most part, at least in its present form, and restore it to the baptismal rite where it belongs.

The eucharistic part of the liturgy is characterized by two major high points: the eucharistic prayer and the fraction/communion part of the service. This second half of the liturgy begins with the preparation of the gifts, at one time erroneously called the offertory. This presentation should be seen as a transition from the liturgy of the word to what follows. It is low in terms of rhythm. It is not the time for a great deal of activity or lively music. It is a moment of quiet response. With the prayer over the gifts the ascent toward the eucharistic prayer begins. This prayer with its Holy, Holy, Holy, acclamation and doxology is to the liturgy of the eucharist what the Alleluia/gospel is to the liturgy of the word. It is the verbal highpoint of the second part of the liturgy, whereas the fraction/communion rite is more symbolic in terms of bodily activity.

The Lord's Prayer, when spoken, is the beginning of the rhythmic descent after the eucharistic prayer. When it is sung, it tends to maintain the rhythmic level of this prayer. The embolism or the prayer following the Our Father and the doxology "For the Kingdom, the Power" are parts of the downward trend of the eucharistic liturgy's rhythmic pattern. The greeting of peace can be considered a moderate upsurge, the actual gesture being a response to the prayer for peace. The difficulty is that since the kiss of peace usually involves more spontaneity than the rest of the liturgy, it interrupts the flow from the eucharistic prayer to the communion rite. For this reason the kiss of peace would be more appropriately placed at the end of the liturgy of the word. It is more than a greeting. It is an act of reconciliation and whether it be a handshake or full body embrace, it should be the response to the readings or a prayer for reconciliation.

One of the greatest deficiencies in our present Roman Rite and one that makes planning difficult is the lack of a real rite of the breaking of the bread. The first name the eucharist had was the breaking of the bread. It is what the eucharistic service is called in scripture. The symbolism of the one loaf being shared by many is a rich one in terms of our belonging to the one body of Christ. However, as long as we do not use real bread in the eucharist there is little hope for the restoration of this rite. Once we use bread that is really bread and not something that requires an act of faith that it is actually bread or something which can be distinguished from fish food, the fraction will return. The breaking of the bread can be considered a separate proclamation which would have its own kind of response such as silence, reading or singing, especially the Lamb of God.

Silence after communion is a rhythmic point of relaxation. The same can be said about some kind of meditation music at this time. The prayer after communion, the blessing, the dismissal, and the closing song may be on a scale of gradual ascendency if there is a desire to end the liturgy on a high note such as on the occasion of a feast when one concludes with a spirited hymn. One can also close in a low keyed fashion. Then the final prayer, blessing and dismissal would be on the medium part of the rhythmic scale such as the entrance rite at the beginning of the liturgy.

The use of a scale which diagrams the rhythm of the liturgy of the word and the eucharist is not an attempt to impose an *a priori* structure on all liturgical services. It is a helpful model to keep in mind when making concrete decisions regarding the elements of the liturgy. Basically, it is a psychological chart which reflects the reactions of the worshiper in a successful liturgical celebration. But it is a psychological pattern which aptly and adequately reflects the theology underlying the liturgy. It is the idea of liturgy as proclamation/response translated to the psychological level.

STRUCTURAL ELEMENTS OF THE LITURGY

The second principle that governs liturgical adaptation in the area of particulars is that the various structural elements of the liturgy must be maintained in their proper order. Basically, this means that primary elements should remain primary and secondary elements should remain secondary. The point is that not everything in the liturgy's structure is of equal importance. Important parts should be emphasized. Those of lesser importance should not be stressed to the disadvantage of those which are more important.

In the first half of the liturgy, there is an entrance rite and a service of the word. The entrance rite consists of the entrance song to the opening prayer included. The service of the word begins with the first reading and concludes with the general intercessions. The entrance rite is secondary; the service of the word is the important or primary section of this part of the liturgy. That means that the entrance song, the greeting, the penitential rite, the Glory to God and the prayer should not be so exaggerated in content by means of additions or music as to overshadow the service of the word. The readings and the response to the readings should clearly delineate the liturgy of the word. For instance we should not so inflate the penitential rite that it takes away from the first reading. As I will indicate shortly, the proper arrangement of the elements has great repercussions for the positioning of music in the liturgical service.

One of the major problems with the liturgy of the word is the position of the penitential rite. It is more in the nature of a response than a proclamation. But to what is it a response? There is no proclamation which precedes it. It more appropriately belongs at some other part of the liturgy of the word such as after one of the readings or immediately at the end of the liturgy of the word itself.

Another difficulty is the nature of the rite itself. Although called a penitential rite, it is really not a rite for the forgiveness of sins. Rather it is a rite for proclaiming Christ under his reconciling aspect. The Lord Have Mercy originally was not a plea for the forgiveness of sins but a proclamation of intercession borrowed from the secular context of the shout which greeted the emperor as he rode by in public ceremonies. It is not necessary nor even recommended that the petitions always deal with the forgiveness of sins. Probably, there is no way in which we can now avoid turning this into a rite of forgiveness, but a knowledge of the original meaning of this rite might help prevent turning it into a substitute for sacramental reconciliation.

In the second half of the liturgy there are two subordinate sections: the preparatory rite and the dismissal rite. The primary segment of this part of the liturgy is the eucharistic rite proper which begins with the preface and ends with the prayer after communion. It is evident that the preparation of gifts, the prayer at the time of the presentation of the gifts and the prayer over the gifts should not in any way be detrimental to the centrality of the eucharistic prayer which immediately follows. Lengthy so-called offertory processions are not in order. There is no reason why the collection cannot be brought from the midst of the congregation at this time to indicate the people's response to the liturgy of the word, but the preparation rite should be done in such a way as to avoid the impression that there are two offerings in the eucharist: one of bread and wine and another of Christ our Lord. The official Roman liturgical documents no longer call this part of the liturgy the offertory. The real offering of the eucharist is articulated in the eucharistic prayer and is symbolically reenacted in the meal. There is no theological or historical reason why there should be an offering of bread and wine in the eucharist. There was none either at the Last Supper or on Calvary. And to place an offering of material gifts immediately before the expression of the offering of Calvary is not only redundant, it also tends to de-emphasize the latter offering. This section of the liturgy is devoted to the preparation of bread and wine, elements necessary for the meal, and nothing more should be made of it. It is the setting of the table.

In most of the liturgical churches today the offertory procession has been revived, although this is not based upon good theological principles. Often the bread and wine are associated with the offering of money and other items. As a response to the liturgy of the word the collection is quite legitimate, but because the eucharistic prayer so closely follows, there is a tendency to imply that we must also offer to God our gifts of bread and wine before they can be consecrated and given back to us. Often there is involved a kind of pelagianism in which it is necessary to give to God what is of ourselves before God gives God to us.

There is a basic confusion in so closely relating the gifts of bread and wine with the money collection. In examining the practice of the primitive church and the thought of the Fathers of the church, what is clear is that the bread and wine are representative of God as a gift to us rather than of our gift to God. The designers of the new Roman Rite would have preferred that this part of the liturgy clearly speak of the preparation of the table rather than of the offering of bread and wine. But compromise prevailed. Nevertheless, the present rubrics clearly indicate the proper directionality of the rite. The confusion centers around mixing too closely our gifts of money and other articles such as food and clothing and God's gift to us in the bread and wine. The practice of the Eastern Churches is enlightening here.

The collection of money is taken at the end of the service or after the Our Father to indicate that the liturgy is primarily God's proclamation in our lives to which we can respond. The practice of mixing gifts with *the* gifts misleads us into considering ourselves as the givers of bread and wine rather than as the receivers of gifts from God. Our position inthe eucharist should be as those who receive. What we offer in the eucharist is our thanksgiving. We ritualize this in offering the collection of various elements such as money. But God offers God to us in Jesus Christ and this is symbolized by the bread and wine. Our offering is consequent upon the eucharist and not antecedent to it. The older idea of offertory implied that we must first offer God the raw material before there can be any eucharist.

Although the present practice of the offertory procession may be an opportunity for congregational participation, one must ask whether it is instilling a questionable theological position. The preparation rite is not the preparing of our gifts for God but rather getting ready God's gifts to us. Historically, in both East and West the gifts of bread and wine were placed in the sanctuary before the service began. They were placed on the credence table and were not associated with the congregation. The bread and wine are given. They are there by God's initiative. Wherever the bread and wine are placed, they should be so positioned as to avoid identification with the congregation. If a procession takes place, it should be that of the entrance of the gifts representing God's initiative in our worship. This may be done by the more elaborate kind of entrance as found in the Eastern liturgies or it may be the simple transfer of the elements to the altar table from the credance table or the presider's sepping from the chair to the table upon which the elements are already placed. The point is that what is said liturgically is that it is God who has called us as church into being by the gifts of word and the bread and wine. If there is a prayer over the gifts, it should be about thanksgiving. It is the first act of eucharist and should not center upon the bread and wine as our offering. The preparation rite is but part of the eucharistic rite insofar as it is thanksgiving rather than offering.

Nor should the greeting, blessing, dismissal, and final song which compose the dismissal rite be lengthened in any way to derogate from what has immediately preceded.

What is of primary importance in this part of the liturgy is the eucharistic prayer and the communion service. It is here that one should expend one's musical efforts. It is in this section of the eucharist that great care should be placed on the manner of proclamation and ritual involvement not only by the presider but by the congregation as well.

MUSICAL ELEMENTS IN THE LITURGY

The third principle so important in the matter of planning the actual liturgical service has to do with the musical elements themselves. Apart from bodily gesture, music more than anything else can be the best instrument for maintaining a theologically founded rhythm in the liturgy as well as sustaining the right order of elements of which the rite is structured. This third principle is implemented in light of the previous two.

The most important musical parts of the liturgy of the word are the responsorial psalm and the gospel acclamation. They are at the heart of the service of the word. The responsorial psalm was meant to be sung. It is difficult to do it well when it is recited. If it is not feasible to sing the responsorial song, it is better to substitute some song which can be done by the congregation or to respond with a prolonged period of silence. The gospel acclamation which also was only intended for singing is necessary for the proper build-up to the gospel and should never be recited. These two elements are more important in the overall musical picture of the liturgy than even the entrance song. Yet how often is there an entrance hymn without any other music during the liturgy of the word! The opening hymn, while greatly desirable, is of secondary importance as is the Lord, Have Mercy and the Glory to God in the Highest. At times purely instrumental music might be more appropriate in the beginning. The opening prayer could be sung but that is of minor importance. All these secondary elements might be appropriately sung when there is a considerable amount of singing in the entire service. But they should not be over emphasized by singing them and not singing the primary parts of the liturgy. To do so would lengthen the entrance rite. If it takes you ten minutes to enter a thirty minute liturgy there is definitely something wrong.

Neither the preparatory nor dismissal rites of the eucharistic liturgy should be so embellished musically that the eucharistic prayer pales in comparison. Of the possibilities for ritual action during the preparation of gifts, silence, instrumental music and a motet by the choir are preferable. The congregation might sing, but it should neither be the dominant musical number nor should it be about offering bread and wine. The presider might sing the prayer over the gifts but that is of minor importance.

In the dismissal rite the blessing and dismissal could be sung, but this is of little importance. It would be artificial unless done in a liturgy in which everything that could be sung is sung, and there is nothing wrong with having those liturgies occasionally. The final song is important if there is really a recessional, but it is still secondary. There is nothing so silly as standing around and singing an exit song. It was meant to accompany a procession. If there is no procession, then perhaps something instrumental would be more appropriate.

I cannot stress too strongly that the primary musical elements of the eucharistic rite proper are: the preface (if the presider can sing), the Holy, Holy, Holy, the Eucharistic Acclamation, the Great Amen, the Lamb of God, and the communion song. Care should be taken that when there is singing in the liturgy these parts are usually sung. The acclamations during the eucharistic prayer do much to make this the high point that it should be. The communion song should usually be sung during communion as a processional. Occasionally it can be placed after communion as a meditation song, although the song after communion is best done by the choir.

The Lord's Prayer can be sung to enhance the celebration but it is of secondary importance. In the Roman Rite, the doxology: "For the kingdom, the power, etc.," should really be sung whenever the Lord's Prayer is. The embolism prayer, "Deliver us, Lord, from evil," is an unfortunate interruption of the flow of the Lord's Prayer. The post-comunion prayer can be sung, but it is of minor importance.

The significant point regarding this third principle is that in its implementation it is also bringing into play the other two principles. The music should follow the rhythm of the liturgy and it should be guided by the structure of the liturgy. On the other hand, music can make real the nature of the liturgy as proclamation and response. If music is incorrectly used, the rhythm and the structure of the liturgy can be obscured. I have found that liturgies that have proved unsuccessful were frequently guilty of this kind of distortion of this rhythm and hierarchy of structure.

To put it in another way, the days of the "four hymn Mass" should be behind us. The reason the four hymn liturgy came into existence was that, during the time when the liturgy was still in Latin, attempts were made to put the singing of English hymns in the service. The regulation was that you could not sing at those times which would involve covering over the voice of the priest when he was reading and praying aloud. The logical places for singing were at the beginning, the so-called offertory, the communion, and the recessional. When Mass was put into English, the four hymns were kept in the same place. This is quite unfortunate since of the four, only the communion song is of primary importance. The other three are of secondary significance.

Liturgy planning then, as opposed to liturgical experimentation, is built on the four general and three specific principles I have just elaborated. But there is much more to planning the church's worship than I have referred to. For instance, I have said nothing about how liturgy planning must (1) be group work, (2) require an atmosphere of freedom and encouragement, (3) require continuing education and ritual experience, (4) involve budget and search for resources and talent, and finally (5) call for acceptance and approval by the assembly.

Ultimately, I suppose, all these principles and guidelines of liturgical planning can be summed up in the question: "What can put the flesh and blood of life on the bones of our liturgical theology? What does it mean in the concrete?" What all of us as liturgical planners have to do is to take the theory seriously, meditate on it, struggle with it, and try to find the forms in which it can take practical shape and develop appropriate and workable procedures for planning liturgical celebrations.

Liturgy of the Word

Liturgy of the Eucharist

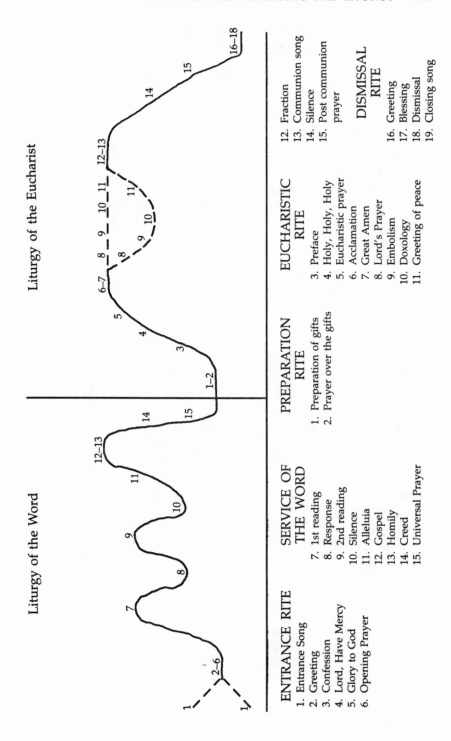

ENTRANCE RITE
1. Entrance Song
2. Greeting
3. Confession
4. Lord, Have Mercy
5. Glory to God
6. Opening Prayer

SERVICE OF
THE WORD
7. 1st reading
8. Response
9. 2nd reading
10. Silence
11. Alleluia
12. Gospel
13. Homily
14. Creed
15. Universal Prayer

PREPARATION
RITE
1. Preparation of gifts
2. Prayer over the gifts

EUCHARISTIC
RITE
3. Preface
4. Holy, Holy, Holy
5. Eucharistic prayer
6. Acclamation
7. Great Amen
8. Lord's Prayer
9. Embolism
10. Doxology
11. Greeting of peace

12. Fraction
13. Communion song
14. Silence
15. Post communion
   prayer

DISMISSAL
RITE
16. Greeting
17. Blessing
18. Dismissal
19. Closing song

STRUCTURAL ELEMENTS IN THE EUCHARISTIC LITURGY

PRIMARY   SECONDARY

Liturgy of the Word

Service of the Word: Entrance Rite:

Epistle   Entrance Song (2)
Responsorial psalm (1)   Greeting (3)
Gospel Acclamation (1)   Penitential Rite (2)
Gospel   Lord, have mercy (2)
Homily   Glory to God (2)
Creed (3)   Prayer (3)
Universal Prayer (2)

Liturgy of the Eucharist

The Eucharistic Rite: Preparatory Rite:

Preface (1)   Presentation (2)
Holy, Holy, Holy (1)   Presidential prayers
Anaphora (1)   Lavabo
Eucharistic Acclamation (1)   Prayer over gifts (3)
Amen (1)
Lord's Prayer (2)   Dismissal Rite:
Embolism (2)
Doxology (2)   Greeting (3)
Prayer of Peace   Blessing (3)
Invitation to Peace (3)   Dismissal (3)
Gesture of Peace   Final Song (2)
Fraction
Lamb of God/Fraction
   song (1)
Communion
Silence
Communion Song (1)
Post-communion prayer (3)

N.B. Elements which should be sung in order of importance:

1—primary importance
2—secondary importance
3—minor importance

11

Planning the Components of the Liturgy

AS WITH OTHER HUMAN SOCIAL EVENTS, ANY KIND OF RITUAL, whether with children or adults, needs a clearly defined beginning and end. But the opening should not be identified with an entrance. One has an entrance when either the whole or part of the congregation or the leaders of worship move from one place to another. Not all liturgies have entrances, but all have openings.

The Opening or Assembling
The beginning of a liturgy should wake up the worshiper psychologically. This does not necessarily imply that the president enter on a trapeze, but it does demand that people be brought together by eliciting from them a sense of oneness and inducing some kind of group consciousness. This can be done by music, gesture and the spoken word. Songs, the greeting of the leader, welcoming gestures, prayer: these are all acceptable ways of beginning a rite. Vocal prayer in the beginning should be brief, otherwise one gets the impression that the congregation is in for a rather wordy liturgy.

The opening part of the liturgy is to present challenges to the congregation to have the advertence, deliberateness, and receptivity which is required for good worship. This cannot be done by verbose opening prayers or pedagogical opening remarks. The important point is not to give people a great deal of information about the scriptural readings, but to invite them to pray about something in particular. The difficulty of the use of the thematic approach to the liturgy is that it tends to be too conceptual in character. And one does not celebrate ideas or persons, but events. And yet simply to ask people to pray without giving any kind of direction to their prayers is tantamount to an invitation to distraction. Whatever is done at the beginning of the liturgy, the congregation should get one simple message: what we are about to do is prayer.

Usually, during the church year the group consciousness established at the beginning will be characterized by brightness, exuberance, and festivity. The greatest impediment to such feelings in the Roman Catholic Rite is the fact that it invariably opens with a penitential rite. When a confession of sin rite is part of a liturgy, it should not be at the beginning. The Gospel and so the liturgy is primarily one of joy, acceptance, and concern. In our ritual greeting we should first become aware of the benevolence of the Gospel before we are judged by it. And the challenge of the Good News does not imply a rite of reconciliation as the most appropriate response. Penance and reconciliation are not the function of the assembling of the liturgy. And even the Roman Rite hints at this by the fact that the penitential rite is not a ritual of forgiveness of sins but of proclaiming Christ under his reconciling aspects.

Proclaiming the Word

The proclamation of the word usually comes early in the celebration because the covenant of faith is initiated by God and not by ourselves. All prayer is in the nature of a response, and the liturgy should reflect this. Those who feel compelled to put preparation rites of purification before hearing the word of God should ask themselves if there is not a lingering Pelagianism still present in their spirituality. The covenant of faith that we live by is a covenant of a community. The proclamation of the Scriptures is the community coming to expression in a speaking-way. The words of the Gospel are an articulation of a corporate faith. And so the dominant concern of the worshiper during the proclamation of the words should not be: what does this text mean to me, but rather: how does this text help this community to interpret itself. The word is proclaimed so that the community can be challenged to greater self-understanding.

The normative word for us is the biblical word. And what is ordinarily read in the liturgy should be the scriptural word. But the Bible is not the only avenue of God's word in our lives, and so judicious use of non-scriptural readings should be employed. They can enhance the communicative value of the Bible. It is really questionable whether the mere reading of scriptural texts constitutes a sufficient proclamation of salvation for there to be a real response in terms of liturgy. We may all be spiritually Semites, but I doubt that such affinity extends to our language and categories of understanding. The liturgy of the hours always contained non-biblical readings. More readings can add to the verbosity of present liturgies, and so there is a need to investigate the visual and dramatic arts as methods of communication which can be more totally involving. Films, cartoons, dance, mime, drama, and slides are all appropriate ways of communicating the word if they are integrated into the liturgy in such a way that the worshipers do not get the impression that they are experiencing an interruption in worship for a multi-media event.

Part of the actual proclamation, whether by hearing or seeing, is a receptive silence. Lengthy periods of silence are not helpful for children but even adults unless warned of an up-coming silence are apt to feel uncomfortable. Silence should be part of every liturgy as it does much to add to the contemplative dimension of the liturgy which has been lost. This dimension will not be retrieved by a movement toward an emphasis on the individual. The only kind of contemplation that is appropriate for worship is the contemplation of the worshiping community. Silence is not simply the absence of sound, but it is a presence. Silence does not just happen or come unannounced in the liturgy. Worship should rhythmically terminate in silence at different times. Silence becomes the freedom from self-assertion, an attitude of receptivity toward God, and a willingness to let anything that we are contemplating have its full self and value.

And finally, the most obvious form of proclamation is the homily. The liturgical homily has its own integral structure. It is a commentary on the actual texts read in this particular liturgy. It is addressed to the people actually present and it has a eucharistic character. Anything else is a sermon. The incongruity of choosing a scriptural snippet or some favorite text which is not part of the celebration should be so obvious as to need no further comment. A homily is not addressed to the world in general or to the people who are not present, which is frequently the case with a scolding sermon. A homily is eucharistic in character if it is directed to the building up of a particular community. It should not be isolated in the ritual, surrounded by signs of the cross and "God Bless Us." Nor should it be the kind of preaching which incites the congregation to leave immediately to engage in some meaningful activity. It is a call to community, a community wishing to break bread and share wine.

Since the word that we preach is never our word but God's, homilists must be sensitive to avoid imposing their understandings of the gospel on the hearers. It is not necessary to give the impression that preachers do not know what they are talking about, or that everything is arbitrary, or that pluralism means that it is not possible to conclude anything about everything. But it does mean that dogmatic preaching is destructive of the liturgical experience. As homilists we must leave psychological room for the hearers to experience doubt. If a member of the congregation is having difficulty grasping something in the faith, this should be seen more as a possible movement to greater commitment rather than the next step to leaving the church. A preacher who despite personal ambiguities and uncertainties gives the impression that everything is clear and that it should be clear can instill guilt feelings in the hearers and cause them to suppress their doubts with the possibility of very real damage to their faith in the future. The way for these people to move into a greater faith commitment is by actually feeling these doubts without a sense of guilt. They must have the space to do this and the good homilist provides such space.

And a concluding remark about the so-called dialogue homily. It is important for homilists to note that even during a dialogue homily they are still presiding at the worship. Homilists do begin the dialogue with the congregation, but they must also ensure that it does not become a flight into the abstract, an exercise in banality, or the opportunity for the members of the congregation to engage in group therapy without expense. Homilists must know when to terminate these dialogue homilies. They must keep the dialogue prayerful.

Praying

The question that arises here is the direction of the stylized form of prayer. It is erroneous to say that liturgical prayer is addressed to God and so not to the people. That prayer is addressed to God is undeniable. But by being addressed to God, it is also addressed to people. Otherwise we would not speak at all in the liturgy, and our use of language and symbols could only be classified as idolatrous. Also, if one thinks that liturgical prayer is addressed only to God, then there is little concern for whether people hear and respond, whether they are touched or moved, whether they find that the prayers resonate with their problems and concerns.

Theologically, one could defend that all liturgical prayer is addressed to the congregation, even those whose texts refer to the Father such as the eucharistic prayer or the Lord's Prayer, in that God is brought to expression in a special way in the liturgical assembly since we are dealing with an incarnate reality of God present in the community. But even prescinding from the theological considerations, it is important from a ritual viewpoint not to give the impression that prayers are addressed outside of the parameters of the rite, that is, to some being outside of the assembly. If some experience takes the worshiper outside of the ritual, then the person is not meeting God in terms of the rite. A person may be having a non-liturgical experience of God which is commendable, but it is not necessary to get involved in the liturgical structure for this experience. Also, prayers which take the worshipers out of or beyond their present symbolic experience make it difficult for the community to be built up in terms of common symbolic experiences.

Very intimately connected with the direction of prayer styles is the symbolic power of the spoken word. Often our liturgies are not the best examples of how the spoken word can be a physical action by which people can become involved in the transcendent. As symbols, the prayers of the liturgy are alive and human. They are interpersonal happenings. Due to historical circumstances the focus of the ritual prayer acts in the liturgy was altered from the living assembly of persons to the things of the liturgy such as the elements of bread and wine. This also meant that often prayer was addressed to God out there. What is the point of using human language to speak to things or to an absent God?

Confessing

The confession of sins may have an occasional place in the liturgy. But I do not consider it an essential part of the service. Those Christian traditions which have turned their liturgical services into penitential rites will have to examine their tradition with a certain openness to see whether such a practice is really communicating Gospel values in a balanced way. When confession rites are employed they should be part of the prayer response to the proclaimed word of God.

In making suggestions to liturgy planners, it is easier to indicate what not to do. Adolescents might use this experience profitably once in awhile, but for younger children we should wait until there is some evidence of problems in this area. It must always be borne in mind that the liturgical celebration of the forgiveness of sins presumes the ability to understand the ecclesial and social dimensions of sinfulness. An experience of personal sin alone does not qualify one for involvement in a liturgical act of reconciliation with God. In general one should avoid in the rite anything that increases or further distorts guilt. As in the sacrament of reconciliation, the emphasis in the eucharist should always be on the proclamation of God's forgiveness which has been granted in Jesus Christ. Worship is praise to God who accepts us as we are at the present moment. Calling sinful an action which is not clearly a defect in loving has no place in our public confession of sin.

We do not realize sufficiently that it is the eucharist which is the primary sacrament of reconciliation. There are certain ritual words and actions which especially emphasize this. The penitential rite, although often in the wrong place, does stress this aspect of the liturgy. The kiss of peace is a gesture of reconciliation in that it is a sign of hope for unity. The Lord's Prayer and the fraction rite are also reconciling rites: one eschatological and the other in terms of belonging to the one body. There are sufficient components in the liturgy, such as parts of the eucharistic prayer, which highlight this reconciling power that it seems unnecessary to make any additions. Certainly, turning the penitential rite into the sacrament of reconciliation or having the sacraments of reconciliation and eucharist together in the same service seems to be a distortion.

Preparation of the Gifts

The most important thing to remember here is that we are talking about God's gifts to us and not our gifts to God. Our gifts to God have already been offered by the time we arrive at this portion of the liturgy (unless we are dealing with the Eastern Rites and liturgies of the word without eucharist). Today our gift response to the liturgy usually takes place at the end of the liturgy of the word except in the Eastern Rites where it more appropriately takes place at the conclusion of the liturgy. The collection of money is the usual form, and this should be clearly seen as the congregation's response to the liturgy of the word.

Theologically and historically, however, the bread and wine are symbols of God's gifts to us. This is clearly seen in the Eastern Rites where the bread and wine move out of the sanctuary into the congregation and then return to the sanctuary. Keeping in mind that the real articulation of offering on the part of the congregation in the eucharistic celebration comes in the eucharistic prayer (an offering which is really Christ's offering), we must handle the preparation rite so that it creates the proper atmosphere for this eucharistic prayer. The preparation rite is not about offering but is a presentation of bread and wine as symbols of God's special presence in our midst. It is more thanksgiving than offering, but even here it should not diminish the eucharistic prayer which is the great prayer of thanksgiving. It is best to see this part of the liturgy as the setting of the table with the symbols of God's love for us. Our present practices of lengthy offeratory processions, of connecting the money collections with the bread and wine, of making this period a time for dance, mime, and other imaginative ventures to stress the giving of ourselves to God is to be regretted because it detracts from the centrality of the bread and wine as symbols of God's gift to us in the eucharist. So much catechesis for children dealing with this part of the liturgy inculcates the idea that we must make ourselves the givers before we can be the receivers. Present practices scream out that we are engaging in some kind of gift-exchange process with God so reminiscent of the medieval times. More energy should be spent on making the collection of money communicate a care on the part of the community for those in need whether near or far and less on self-service and self-preservation. What should be clear to the congregation is that what is taking place in the preparation of gifts is the first of the four eucharistic actions that Scripture gives us: taking (blessing, breaking, giving).

Eucharistizing

The gesture of giving thanks, while not primarily directed to objects, is nonetheless a blessing of bread and wine because the act of praise places them more clearly into the context of God's love and the gift of God to us. The idea of a sacrifice of praise and thanksgiving which is what this part of the liturgy is all about is difficult for the ordinary Christian to grasp and, I suspect, is beyond the comprehension of most adolescents. One should not turn it into an attempt at choral reading by the whole group under the mistaken idea that this will declericalize the liturgy. Such choral reading obscures the structure and purpose of this prayer. The idea of proclamation is greatly diminished when the entire congregation recites this prayer together. Apart from the fact that it is not a good idea to ask prolonged choral reading from an untrained group, such a practice ignores the distinction of roles in the liturgy as well as the rhythm of proclamation/response. There are other ways of asserting the priesthood of all besides choosing the prayer in which the liturgical presidency has its clearest function. Dialogic eucharistic prayers help somewhat to alleviate some of the concerns about the importance of the celebrating community at this time.

Communion

This action of eating and drinking is both natural and necessary at this time in the liturgy. For this reason this part is very easy to make accessible to children. Whatever is done in this part of the service three points should be remembered. 1) This ritual must stress sharing common food as an expression of care, love, and solidarity. The single loaf and cup can help here, and a real fraction rite will enhance the communicative value of this liturgical component. 2) The rite must convey reverence for the eucharist. We should avoid a fetish mentality when dealing with the eucharistic elements, but on the other hand we should not be cavalier about the remains of bread and wine after the eucharistic meal. What would you think of your dinner guests if they went around picking up all the crumbs after the dessert? Or what would you think of someone who takes a piece of your birthday cake and feeds it to her dog? The greatest eucharistic reverence, of course, is the kind of respect we have for each other as persons. Of what value is a great concern for some crumbs if you find it difficult to offer your neighbor the kiss of peace? 3) Communion should always be tied into the mission of the church. The eucharist is supposed to be a sign of commitment to the welfare of the world. Often it is helpful for some of the missionary concerns of the parish to be explicated at this time. What does this say about the kind of thanksgiving at communion time that we might have? The thanks we offer here is not so much that Jesus has come to me, but that he has come for the world.

Dismissal

A definite conclusion is as important as a definite opening. A president of the assembly should not try to recapitulate the liturgy in the dismissal unless that can be done briefly. All that is needed is a final quick orientation toward God, community, and mission. If some other group activity follows the liturgy, the president can gather the people around him and lead them out.

*   *   *   *

Since a major concern of all liturgical planning is to avoid stressing the weaknesses of any particular rite and to reinforce the rite's particular strengths, it is helpful to compare the present Roman eucharistic liturgy with what had been originally intended by those who revised the rite. The original normative Mass underwent some changes in the four years that intervened between its first presentation in 1965 and its final publication in 1969. The point is that in its original form the normative Mass manifested fewer weaknesses than does the present rite. A few examples from the original version follow.

Introductory Rites. These were originally extremely slight. The ministers enter to the opening song. Before going to the seat the priest blesses himself with the sign of the cross in silence after reverencing the altar, kisses the altar or uses some other appropriate sign (incensation is optional), greets the people with the apostolic greeting; they respond. There is an optional word of introduction, then either the *Kyrie* or the *Gloria,* and the opening prayer. The *Kyrie* is understood here as an acclamation rather than a petition; the *Gloria* could have been relocated, but was retained here with the intention of reducing its frequency. The value of this arrangement is that it eliminates the sign of the cross which gives us two greetings, and it removes the penitential rite which is not a confession of sins and is now in the wrong place. The 1969 version is the first time that a public penitential rite with formal absolution was put in the Roman eucharistic liturgy. The former *Confiteor* was considered a private prayer. In the present rite the *Kyrie* is never omitted, even when the *Gloria* is sung, thus obscuring its character as an acclamation.

Liturgy of the Word. In the 1965 version a reader reads the first reading; there is no "thanks be to God," but rather the response is a psalm (responsorial as we now have it); the second reading is proclaimed without response; the Alleluia introduces the gospel; there is the option of lights and candles, the book is reverenced, and the acclamation may be repeated; there is the homily, the profession of faith (Nicene or Apostles') and the general intercessions. In general, most of the problems were solved in both the 1965 and 1969 versions, but the question of the creed was not left open. Since the eucharistic prayer is the profession of faith in the eucharist, the creed would have been better removed.

Preparation of Gifts. The 1965 version has the bringing forward of the elements and their ritualized placing on the table. The eucharistic liturgy begins with the washing of the hands (the experts saw this ritual as the beginning action of the eucharistic rite proper). The ministers prepare the altar, the celebrant or deacon receives the gifts, and the priest places the elements on the table. There are two prayers that the priest says silently: "As this bread was scattered and then gathered and made one, so may your Church be gathered into your Kingdom. Glory to you, O God, forever"; and "Wisdom has built a house for herself, she has mixed her wine, she has set her table. Glory to you, O God, forever." The priest then silently says the old prayer, "In the spirit of humility" and then can incense the bread and wine, but not the altar and people. The prayer over the gifts is said. There are still many difficulties with this rite, but it had a certain simplicity. It was presentation by means of preparation and placing of the gifts. The only prayer aloud was the prayer over the gifts. In the 1969 rite, however, it becomes more confusing. The washing of the hands is placed after the presentation and incensation; formulas for the washing of the priest's hands and preparation of cup were inserted from the old rite. Two new prayers were composed for the presentation of the bread and cup; and the "Pray, my brothers and sisters" was reinserted. The rite is too complicated, more so than that of the old Latin Mass. It is questionable whether there should be any washing of the hands, even with the idea of beginning a special action. There seems to be no reason for a prayer when putting water into wine. There is no point to having any of the private prayers of the priest. The *Orate, fratres* formula is too complicated. The two newly composed prayers infringe on the character of the eucharistic prayer.

The Eucharistic Prayer. In general there were no significant changes between the two versions.

Communion Rite. The 1965 rite begins with the Lord's Prayer, the embolism, and the doxology. Then follows the gesture of peace, the breaking of the bread, and the mingling of the bread in the wine accompanied by the Lamb of God and a single prayer of the priest. Communion is accompanied by song. There is an option for a distinct hymn, psalm, or prayers of praise after communion. The vessels are cleansed at the credence table or this task is postponed until the eucharist is over. The eucharistic rite concludes with a post communion prayer. This rite could have been cleaned up by suppressing the commingling, by moving the kiss of peace to a position before the presentation of the gifts, and by suppressing the private prayers. In the 1969 rite the prayer to the Lord Jesus for peace was made a public prayer as an invitation to the gesture of peace.

Concluding Rites. In the 1965 version the liturgy ended with some time for announcements, a greeting and response, a dismissal, and a final blessing. Options for the blessing were the common trinitarian one, the prayer over the people, or the so-called Aaronitic one. There were few changes in the 1969 version except that the blessing was placed before the dismissal.

Hopefully, future reforms of the normative liturgy will incorporate many of the suggestions of the 1965 rite. It was clearer and less complicated than that of 1969. I heartily concur with Frederick R. McManus who has called for a reconsideration of the Roman rite of the eucharist as given to us by the liturgy Consilium of the Second Vatican Council. The details of the 1965 rite recorded above are related in his article in *Worship*[1] which concludes with these significant words: "It is a matter of some hope that we can be instructed by the work done in the mid-sixties and undertake the study that will guide future liturgical growth, perhaps inspired a little by the genius of the Roman rite."[2]

1. Frederick R. McManus, "The Genius of the Roman Rite Revisited," *Worship* 54:4 (July 1980) 360–78.
2. Ibid. 378.

12

Challenges for Worshiping Today

THE MODERN LITURGICAL MOVEMENT CAME TO A CLIMACTIC MOMENT in 1963 with the publication of the Constitution on the Sacred Liturgy of the Second Vatican Council. Although it emerged out of a council of Roman Catholic bishops, it has served as both the watershed and the charter document of the liturgical renewal programs of most of the Christian churches. And while there are concrete differences in the forms of implementation among these churches, there is also widespread agreement about the principles enunciated in this document. Surveys of Catholics show that a large majority favor the changes initiated by this document, although an intense, disenchanted, articulate, and often noisy minority continue to oppose them. The statistics would be about the same in the Anglican and Protestant Churches.

A great deal has been accomplished in the last twenty years during which the churches have been concerned about the ways in which the major liturgies of Western Christianity can be restructured so that they more clearly reflect the patterns of the normative worship of the early church, as well as be reformed so that they respond more obviously to the religious experience of contemporary Christians. There are the visible changes in the phenomenon of Christian worship: a more wholesome balance between the proclamation of the word and the celebration of the eucharist; the recovery of the central spirituality of the church through an understanding of the church year as a symbolic and not an historical process; a convergence of the rites and texts of the major liturgical services of Catholics, Anglicans, and Protestants by means of a common (almost) three year lectionary; by very similar structures for the rituals of the sacraments; and a more integrated theology of worship and theology of the church, both theoretically by defining worship as the expression and creator of the church and practically by identifying the liturgical assembly as the primary symbol of God's presence for Christians. Many more detailed achievements could be registered as we come to a major turning point in the liturgical renewal of our own time.

We are in the midst of what might be called the fourth phase of the modern liturgical movement. A few words will help situate today's challenges to worship in the context of this larger liturgical reform. The contemporary liturgical movement has been largely a Western phenomenon. Its beginnings are found in the Romantic movement of the early nineteenth century which proved to be a rich seed bed for the kind of liturgical consciousness-raising needed to recover the tradition of the church. And a recovery was needed. The post-Enlightenment and the post-French Revolutionary Church was one which found itself without a worshiping center. From the Middle Ages to the nineteenth century, despite the best efforts of the protestant reformers of the sixteenth century and later, there was a growing marginalization of the liturgy whether it was the unintelligibility of the Latin Rite or the overintellectualilzation of so much Protestant worship. The attempt to bring liturgy back to the center of Christian living began in the monasteries of Europe where scholars sought for the meaning of the church's worship in their historical, aesthetic, and archeological studies. They were not interested in reform, but they did begin the recovery of a lost tradition.

The second phase began at the beginning of this century and lasted until the Second World War. It was a time of taking what those monks had mined and bringing it to the level of seminary training and parish life. This task was only moderately successful. Priests and ministers began to express more interest in this somewhat esoteric topic. The major visible changes were more participation in Roman Catholic parishes and a greater attention to the aesthetic demands of worship in Protestant communities.

One could characterize this time, albeit somewhat modestly, as the transmission of the tradition.

The third phase extended from the Second World War to the early sixties, especially to the time of the Second Vatican Council. It was a time of quickening of interest in the liturgy by most of the churches. The various programs for renewal received increasing official church approval and groups of liturgical scholars made numerous suggestions for changes in the practice of worship. Many of these suggestions found their implementation in church documents as the Constitution on the Sacred Liturgy of the Second Vatican Council. It was not long before the major denominations increased the momentum of their liturgical programs so that most of these churches are now on an even keel in terms of the renewal of worship.

The present period, the fourth phase, is one characterized by implementation, that is, taking these reformed rites and making them live in actual practice, as well as by adaptation, that is, taking the Roman Rite and making it applicable for certain situations as for children, and by experimentation, that is, seeking liturgical forms which we do not yet have but which would better respond to the needs of individual cultures. Some attempts have been made as in India, Japan, and Indonesia. But for the most part very little true liturgical experimentation is going on anywhere. In fact, the institutional church is becoming increasingly cautious about further liturgical change, not to mention more drastic experimentation. The next step is the greater use of imagination in the liturgy. The reason why so many involved with liturgical renewal are moving toward the imaginative is that implementation is often done in a lifeless manner, adaptation has been infected with a new kind of rubricism, and experimentation has often been more productive of fear and regression than new liturgical experiences. We still have more of a new library than a new liturgy.

Yet it is important to affirm what has been accomplished. One way to do this is to look at the platform of the liturgical movement of the past and see how well the positions and ideas came into reality. There are six major emphases of the modern liturgical movement.

(1) *A return to the Scriptures.* This has provided us with more readings and a revised lectionary. The Bible is allowed to bear

its own witness within a liturgical context more clearly than before. It is not simply a matter of more readings. There is a plan to the lectionaries which makes it necessary to know if this is the year of Matthew or of Mark. Biblical theology is more in evidence, not only through preaching or homilizing, but through the introduction of eschatological and pneumatological themes in other parts of the liturgy. There is a greater consciousness that the word is proclamatory, that it creates us in its proclamation, that the meaning of any individual scriptural text is not what it meant to the author or to the listener of the past, but to us today, that the Gospel lives in its present proclamation. For instance, the meaning of the Johannine text "unless you eat my flesh and drink my blood, you shall not have life in you" is not about the scandalized Jews and followers of Jesus who turned away, but about our present involvement with the eucharist and the demands it makes on us. The text is more about social justice than it is about real presence.

There is now a more wholistic sense to the liturgical readings. They are a way that the community understands itself, comes to consciousness about itself. The biblical material is not there to make moralizing remarks about the Bible. This more wholistic sense does not divide the person into spirit and matter. This very biblical understanding of the person is beginning to pervade our liturgical celebrations in that the word is addressed to the whole person and not simply to the intellect. And the presupposition of the liturgy of the word is that salvation comes through community.

Finally, the biblical understanding of memorial now predominates in the theology of the liturgy. Liturgy is not primarily a looking to a past event, the holy sacrifice of the Mass and its relationship to the cross. Liturgy lives out of the future; it is an anticipation of what life is to be like when we live in union with God through Christ. To recall or to give thanks in the liturgy means to become involved with the present resurrected humanity of Christ. There is something really going on in baptism, in anointing, and in the other liturgical rites which makes it possible to encounter the only Jesus Christ there is, the one who, although he is mutually present to the whole world, is not yet fully present in that world.

(2) *Recovery of the experience of the early church.* Here there has

been a considerable return to the sources. Probably the most obvious example of early church influence on liturgy today is the process of the Christian initiation of adults, the RCIA. Here we are presented with a public process of conversion structured by liturgical celebrations. The implications are enormous for church life because it presents a model for parish renewal, and it challenges reigning understandings of conversion as something happening instantaneously. Remember the old days when we could fall into mortal sin in a flash and just as quickly be restored to the state of grace. To move from sin to grace is conversion. But it takes time. Conversion is not primarily intellectual, nor can it be reduced to accepting the content of the faith. The RCIA is not simply a more elaborate way of handling converts. It calls into question certain ideas of what it means to sin and what it means to be saved. The RCIA also helps to recover the meaning of the liturgical year, especially the Lenten and Easter seasons. It casts a helpful light on the sacrament of reconciliation as the experience of the baptized church which is accompanying the catechumens on their journey of entrance into the Christian community. It highlights the fact that any individual parish is rarely a faith unity or a community theologically speaking, but is rather a kind of sociological umbrella under which are found faith groups and unattached as well as attached individuals. Thus the need for small faith groups to join with the catechumens in their process.

Study of the anaphoras (canons) of the patristic period has helped shape our present eucharistic prayers. In the Roman Rite Eucharistic Prayer II is based on the prayer of Hippolytus, an early church leader, which in effect was a basic outline used for the presider's improvisation. Its value is its connection with the mentality and spirit of the primitive church. The shortcoming is that it is presently overused (abused?) in churches today. How can you pray an outline? Eucharistic Prayer III turns to Gallican (French) and Spanish sources and Eucharistic Prayer IV to the ancient Eastern liturgies. Despite so many problems surrounding the eucharistic prayer which prevent it from being a central experience for the worshiper, for example, its manner of proclamation by incompetent presiders, its verbosity, and its still being too dominated by a moment of consecration, the recovery of this tradition has introduced a pluralism into an area that appeared untouchable and unchanging. The continual introduction of additional prayers is an attempt to attend to cultural differences in the larger church.

The liturgy of the hours and what we hope for it has been influenced by early church studies. The liturgical hours are still too monastic, at least in feeling and spirituality if not also in structure, especially in terms of the number of psalms. The centrality of morning and evening prayer we owe to the early church as we do the recovery of the cathedral office. Unlike the monastic office, the cathedral style pays greater attention to public morning and evening prayers and is more oriented to spontaneous and locally concerned kinds of praying. It is less psalmodic in structure.

This return to the sources has helped Roman Catholics realize that all sacramental activity is in response to the word of God and that the eucharist cannot bear the burden of all of one's worship life. It has meant for Anglicans and Protestants a renewed interest in the festive character of the eucharist and the eucharistic prayer as praise and thanksgiving. This has resulted in more frequent eucharistic celebrations as well as a less funereal character to the service of Holy Communion or the Lord's Supper.

(3) *A more wholesome ecclesiology.* The liturgical movement is at base an ecclesiological renewal. The rites of initiation bring out that the whole people is priestly. All are priests. Some are ordained for special ministry, one of which is presiding at worship. The liturgical assembly as symbol of the local church is the primary eucharistic symbol. Bread and wine are not. There is greater participation in the liturgy, and the isolation of the priest at his altar and the minister in her pulpit have given way to the notion and hopefully the experience of the president in the midst of the assembly. Church as God's family, church as symbol of how God is working in the world, wherever good human community is found, has stressed the ministry of each member of the community. Ministry is no longer seen as the domain of the ordained, and the plurality of ministries is to find its reflection in the diversification of roles in the worshiping situation.

Perhaps the most significant contribution of the close relationship between church and worship in our present time is the matter of social justice. Christian witness and discipleship are increasingly found in the ways the rituals are implemented. To take but one example, the sacrament of anointing is no longer the final rite prior to death, but is a celebration of the greater pastoral care that should surround the sick, the elderly, and the disabled. It ritualizes the power of these people's lives who are often pushed to the margins of our society. Happily, our theologies of the church again recognize a necessary pluralism and have added a horizontal imagery to an almost exclusively hierarchical model of the liturgy. And naturally, a people of God equal before God makes the use of inclusive language in the liturgy a necessity. The feminist critique of Scripture and liturgy which invites us to examine our very images of prayer will bring about more revolutionary changes than the mere restructuring of ritual. Studies on liturgical implementation indicate one thing: people as a whole are more and more claiming ownership of their worship.

(4) *The ecumenical dimension of worship.* The euphoria of the earlier years of the ecumenical movement has long gone, and some have questioned whether or not it is dead. I believe that ecumenicity is more a matter of daily living rather than high celebrations. So much is taken for granted in the matter of exchange among the Christian churches, although institutionally we Christians still act as separate communities. And perhaps this is the best way, realistically speaking. Church unity is probably best modeled after the pattern of differing rites or religious orders in the same church.

What is significant for liturgy is the convergence in the liturgical reforms of the various communions. For in the mind of the ordinary Christian the fact that the Lutheran and Catholic eucharists resemble each other will have more effect than agreements which are reported in the several volumes of the various dialogues among the denominations. There is much to be thankful for in the way that the lectionaries and rituals of the various churches are the results of common consultation. Recently the Consultation on Common Texts, an ecumenical venture, has put forth a revised lectionary. Its use would bring the major churches into even closer harmony regarding the biblical readings in the liturgy.

Probably more important than any specific liturgical agreement is the change of attitude wherein denominational differences no longer have the rigidity and intensity they once had. When I was young, Catholics talked about the sinfulness of going to Protestant church services, and if one did go, one needed to remain passive throughout. If nothing else has happened ecumenically, there is less arrogance all the way around.

Finally, at a recent ecumenical liturgical meeting several issues were identified as the work of the next decades: a) making liturgy wholly inclusive in language and ritual; b) letting the central symbols stand as central; c) increasing beauty in worship; d) connecting liturgical renewal to social justice; e) calling the baptized into more faithful communion; f) continuing to shape and renew Christian liturgy to balance the universal with the particular, the historic with the contemporary, the tradition of the first world with the contributions of the third.

(5) *Symbolism.* To recover the fullness of the sign has always been a major point with those committed to liturgical reform. And much has been achieved here. A more generous anointing with oil, a greater experience of water in baptism, the extension of the cup to all; these are all taken for granted, if not always put into practice. We still have trouble using real bread in the liturgy, but this is not a liturgical problem. It is a question of institutional control. Ritual is a form of control and the institutional church is very much aware of this. Why should any worldwide organization as the Roman Catholic Church be so concerned about bread?

What is far more significant for worship in the long run is that today's liturgical students and facilitators are much more conscious of the studies of anthropologists, the work of modern artists, and the writers and philosophers of symbolism. How symbols operate and grow, the difference between a symbol which sets up a situation of encounter and a sign which points away from itself to an absent reality (symbol = meal; sign = exit or no smoking); all these are the concerns of these studies. In the Catholic liturgy this attention to symbols has facilitated the removal of minor ceremonials that stood in the way of the needed clarity of the central symbolic actions. At least we know that symbols are human events. Sacramental symbols are not things; they are gestures or actions. You do not store symbols in your sacristy closet. The unlit paschal candle is just that, an unlit paschal candle. When it is lit, then it functions, as does fire, as a natural symbol. Surrounded by a worshiping community, the paschal candle is a symbol of Christ because it is part of a larger event of Christians doing their symbolizing, engaging in their specific Christian gestures.

(6) *Liturgy and culture.* This final plank of the liturgical movement's platform is the area where there is still the most to achieve. Up to the present, the liturgical reforms have been for a universal church and have been put together by experts known more for their sense of history, theology, and pastoral practice than for attention to national and ethnic differences. Still, there have been accomodations for national churches. We have comparatively few adaptations of the normative rites, at least when compared to such countries as India or Indonesia. The question that is ever present in this area is how far should the Christian community accomodate itself to the varying socio-psychological patterns of communication and behavior that are found in all cultures. Cultural adaptation, or more precisely, experimentation, has been accepted in principle, based on the Christian understanding of the goodness of creation and the Christian life as incarnational. The Directory for Masses with Children is seen as a major effort in adapting the liturgy. But it is, in fact, still the Roman Rite. Inculturation, where the faith encounters another culture and takes root in that culture and is communicated and celebrated in that culture, is really something else. If we are to have American liturgies, we will need to do more than adapt the Roman Rite. Faith communities of differing kinds need the official encouragement of the church to develop rites that best articulate their religious experiences. This task has only begun. But of all the affirmations of the liturgical movement, it is the most radical and the most future directed. As the other five elements of the platform of the liturgical movement achieve some kind of fulfillment, this sixth one will become increasingly important. Of all liturgical renewal, it is the most exciting.

Although it cannot be denied that the churches have met the challenges of implementation of the liturgical revisions to a considerable degree, it must be also admitted that there are still major areas where such implementation has not been as successful. A review of a few of these will demonstrate this point.

(1) *Preaching needs to improve.* In fact, although we might not always think so, it has improved if we make comparisons with

the kind of preaching that took place over twenty years ago when it often had little to do with the biblical readings and was mostly a matter of moral exhortation and doctrinal indoctrination. The lectionary dictates a certain change in that it prevents the choosing of one's favorite texts repeatedly or the choosing of no texts at all. Even our most inept homilists usually try to make something of the readings. At no time in history have so many homiletic aids been available. They do some good, although the dependence on them is sometimes unhealthy. As a former consultant for one of those homily programs, I am aware that there are times when the canned homily is literally read by the presider. Some do not even change the examples.

For the Catholic homilist it is often a matter of acquiring more and better preaching skills. There is no substitute for the occasional clergy workshop in celebrational style. Too many priests are unaware of how they appear and how they communicate. There is no alternative to listening to a tape of one's homily or looking fully and honestly into a full-length mirror. But beyond technique, there needs to be greater sensitivity to the meaning of the homily in a liturgical setting. It is not the same as giving a sermon. A homily opens up some of the Scriptures that are read, helps the assembly understand itself in terms of these readings, and leads the people into the eucharistic part of the service. Often I am asked by priests in workshops about the possibility of this kind of homilizing since the Sunday homily is the only time they have a chance to instruct the faithful. I always ask: What would you like to communicate that does not already flow out of the Scriptures? Most are too embarrassed to answer. Responses to this question reveal a great deal about any priest's view of Christianity. What needs to be noted here is that liturgy is primarily about community formation, not individual conversion. The presumption should be that most of the people who come to church on Sunday are leading good lives. If they are not, I doubt that the liturgy will make any difference. If it did, we would already have these converted congregations. Of course, the issue that remains hidden here is: what does it mean to be a *good* Christian?

Homilizing is as much a ritual experience as any other part of the liturgy? The point is that preaching should facilitate people's prayer as a group. The use of the imagination, stories, and images are ways of bringing this about. The whole liturgy should preach or proclaim. After the environment, the music, and the other gestures of the liturgy have been planned, then the homily can be prepared. In that way it can fill in where the rest of the liturgy may fail. But how often is liturgical planning made equivalent to preparing the sermon!

Today's problem with preaching is found at both extremes. Sometimes it can be too episodic, the sharing of one's story, but over and over again. Or when there is a change in the message (translation: whatever is bothering the preacher), it is done with but a nod to the Scriptures read. The other extreme is the so-called preaching of the faith. This often means the fairly narrow interpretation of the theological affirmations, whether from the creed or from church authorities, without a great deal of nuance. My own perhaps jaundiced view is that preaching would be vastly improved if more homilists had something to say.

(2) *Greater integration of the word proclaimed and the music sung.* This is essential in order to release the power of the ritual. We have more singing, more hymn booklets, more guitars, and some cantors, but in still far too many places the four hymn Mass is in place as is the Protestant arbitrary use of hymns for the structure of the service. The Mass is four hymned if there is singing only at the beginning, the so-called offertory, the communion, and at the end. This approach gained acceptance prior to the Second Vatican Council when singing was not permitted in the Latin Mass if it covered over the voice of the presider. But even when there is singing at other parts of the liturgy, the four hymn mentality can prevail when secondary elements in the rite such as the opening, closing, and presentation of gifts are highlighted to the detriment of the primary parts of the liturgy.

Naturally, we need to use the style of music suitable to the congregation, but that does not mean people cannot get used to and enjoy different kinds of music. They do it all the time via T.V. and radio. It is not clear that music of the most artistic kind is automatically the best kind for liturgy. The great philosopher of art, Susanne Langer, makes the point that a very good poetic text may be more difficult to set to music than one which is less poetic. Good poetry become competitive with the music. In fact, the music of the style exemplified by the St. Louis Jesuits and others did become extremely popular. They responded to some intuited need in the country. We continually need to find ways for the congregation to express itself musically as part of the liturgy itself. Music should be more than a background experience as seen in the Catholic practice of singing only two verses of a hymn because that is as long as the procession lasts. Why not play instrumental music on the way in and put one's music efforts and energies on the *Gloria* or the various acclamations? Better to sing only the gospel Alleluia with attention and care than to do the opening rite with a couple of verses and then have the rest of the liturgy become a purely verbal and one-dimensional experience.

We must continue to look for styles of congregational singing that move the congregation away from books. Some places make effective use of projection for the texts, and I have seen this artfully and unobtrusively done. The music of Taizé from France, highly repetitious but still very beautiful, is becoming increasingly popular because it can be employed with one's hands free. Fuller use of responsorial singing should grow. But I doubt that the integration of liturgy and music, where the parts of the liturgy are not only sung but where the liturgy becomes a musical experience, will succeed without music being accepted as an important ministry in the church. The restoration of the minister called cantor is, I believe, the single most necessary item for achieving a musical liturgy. A cantor is more than a song leader, a choir director, or the head of the folk group. The cantor performs a diaconal role, singing parts of the liturgy as well as leading the congregation. The choir director would best be another person. The cantor should be trained, commissioned, vested, function publicly, and be paid.

(3) *Enlarging the sacramental experience.* We have spent a great deal of effort on implementing the eucharistic rite and rightly so. We are giving more attention to the other sacraments, but this has been more in the way of ritual reform than it has been in the extension of people's liturgical lives outside of the rites themselves. The possible exception is the Rite of Christian Initiation of Adults (RCIA). With the continuing shortage of priests, collaboration with the unordained in all possible ways is essential if people are to have better experiences of the other sacraments. Here it is not so much a matter of dealing with the parish as a whole, but of providing good experiences for groups in the par-

ish. Such groups would include: those involved in infant baptism preparation, confirmation groups, those participating in the RCIA, and those who belong to the various service organizations. They must all become praying groups and faith-sharing situations. The people will need encouragement from the clergy and parish ministers. The general principle that the priest should not do anything that others can do is a good working principle if it is properly understood. If it reduces the priest to a mere sacramental functionary, then ultimately this principle is counter-productive. The priest should see him/herself primarily as the one who motivates the others in ministry, not someone who has a special power others do not have. The shortage of priests in some churches is not the only impediment to the enlarging of the sacramental experience. It is also due to a reluctance on the part of the clergy to let go, to relinquish control.

In bringing about a more comprehensive sacramental life in the church, it is important to find out who is actually praying in the parish and then enlist them in forming communitites. In one sense it is still meaningful to work with the people who wish to be ministered to. Those who want to go their own way will survive on their own or will dissociate, which may be preferable. The question should never be: But are the people ready for this? But rather: Are there some who are ready? The whole church has never moved at the same rate in every place. If you cannot find any apostolically committed people in your parish, perhaps you are not looking in the correct place. If your parish is nearly one hundred percent uncommitted, it should die. It is a countersign. Hard as it may be to accept, the purpose of the church is not salvation of the individual as individual. God saves people as individuals outside the church. In the church our salvation comes through community, a community which proclaims, however weakly, the value of the Gospel.

(4) *Other major challenges.* Other tasks that still lie before us would include the need for healing those hurt by change or the lack of it, by poor preparation, and by misguided enthusiasm. Catechetical efforts must be continued and the proper preparation of prayer leaders must be strengthened. The place of the arts in the liturgy requires more attention, more acceptance, and more money. Often parish priests tell me that people will not come to special classes offered by the parish, such as scripture

or theology classes. No doubt this is true. But that is like asking them to come back to school for more information. They need different experiences so that they will seek the kind of enlightenment that comes from catechetical efforts. Content or input should be part of a larger program. I have given talks in parishes where what I did was but part of a larger initiation of adults or lay ministry training program. In one parish I was asked to speak on confirmation. In that parish the teenagers with their parents had to request confirmation. When I met with them, I had an interested audience.

As mentioned earlier, the second task of this present phase of the liturgical movement is adaptation. Although our efforts have been mainly focused on implementation, there have been some advances made in adapting the liturgy. Many of the ecumenical changes are forms of adaptation. Some churches have turned their attention to liturgies with or for children. There is continual concern about local needs in regard to weddings, funerals, and the adult catechumentate. In general, the adaptations that have been made have been successful. But there is still a lack of fulfillment in this area. It is important not to confuse liturgical adaptation with inculturation. The latter, as already noted, is more experimental and radical in the issues it raises for Christian worship. Adaptation differs from inculturation in that adaptation is concerned with making changes in the liturgy in order for the rite to operate more effectively in diverse circumstances. This is primarily a pastoral consideration as when the official rites of the church are adapted for children, adolescents, the elderly, or when there is need because of a different place of worship, as liturgies in homes or out in the open air. Liturgical adaptation has proceeded cautiously and liturgical experimentation has received little institutional approval. One of the reasons for this hesitancy in these areas is that both demand considerable creativity on the part of the community and its members. Creativity is but another way of speaking about the need to recover the place of the imagination in the liturgical experience and in the process of liturgical reform.

Many liturgical scholars have in the last decade insisted that the next stage of liturgical renewal calls for the recovery of the religious imagination. Patrick Collins in his book, *More Than Meets the Eye*, makes a cogent case for the need for a new liturgical dynamic, one in which the human imagination can bring about a new way of experiencing one's relationship with God in community in worship. A proper liturgical dynamic is more than correct rubrics, readings well-proclaimed, and music tastefully done. Rather, it refers to the feel one has when all the elements of the liturgy fit together. It means that there is direction to the worship and not just one thing after another, liturgical snippets, as it were. The worshipers feel there is movement from the beginning to the end and this movement flows into their lives. A liturgical dynamic refers to a general sense of what community worship should be, what motivates it, what it hopes to effect in people. The majority of worshipers could not articulate this dynamic, but they notice when it is not there. They become bored and the worship is perfunctory.

Most of us would agree that we must continue to do our historical research in the area of liturgy, that we must not slow down in the revision of our liturgical books, that catechesis is never to be an optional choice. But there are many who have concluded, and I believe quite rightly, that these efforts alone will not achieve the main purpose of the modern liturgical movement, that is, to make worship central to Christian living. So many of our liturgical reforms have been textual, so many of them done according to a primarily rational mode. Historical understanding and scientific precisions have bequeathed to us a new library, but hardly a new liturgy. Our brilliant efforts at historical work, our quite successful attempts to extricate a theology from the living rites themselves, and our very helpful methods of making the liturgical tradition pastorally applicable deserve a laudatory affirmation. But they are not enough. More is needed if we are to see the world anew in our experience of worship. Thus the need for creativity and the application of the imagination to this area of church life.

What is creativity? It is not the brilliant idea. It is not artistic creations, such as dance, music, and drama, which are situated in the context of worship. It is not the same as the aesthetic dimension to human life. Rather, liturgical creativity is a form of human interchange. A creative person may be an artist, but need not be. And in the matter of liturgy, the creative liturgist will often not be an artist. But this person will be the one who engages in the kind of human interchange whereby one's own perspectives change. This person will become aware of one's own experiences and that of others through communication and then will seek to find images that will embody the values of these perspectives. The sharing here is more than a sharing of ideas. It is a sharing of values. Often liturgical planners share great ideas, but this is more akin to the sharing of recipes.

The creative person about whom we are speaking is one who looks for the values in any area of liturgical life and ritual, assembles images that incarnate these values, integrates these values and images in one's personality, and comes up with an expanded appreciation of the world. A creative person is one who can see possibilities where another cannot. For people whose consciousness (and unconsciousness) remains untransformed, there is lacking a richness of quality, and so a narrow range of possibilities exists. For those whose imaginative life is wider, possibilities occur which previously did not exist. For example, I work with many professional artists, especially dancers, in the planning and adapting of liturgies. Although I am not a choreographer, I can often make a number of choreographic suggestions which the expert dancer might not see, whereas the dancer could put these into practice in a way that I cannot.

The kind of liturgical adaptation requiring the creative liturgical planner whose world has been expanded because this person was open to new perspectives and personally integrated them is done in community. If you and I expand our appreciable world, then our communities can grow in a healthy, noncompetitive way. The liturgy of the future (and the present) needs to be adapted in a creative way, and those concerned about adapting liturgy can participate by expanding the world of those with whom we worship. This is a task of suffering and humility since it means not only an intellectual understanding of the other, but the feeling of another's feelings. It implies mutual correcting and criticizing, as well as cooperation, all of which are directed to preserving the good that has already been achieved.

How can we be creative in liturgy today? Through a balancing of symbols. This is what is meant by a new liturgical dynamic. We are creative when we allow the symbols to be more closely tied to our religious experience, when there is a gathering together of the spiritual and psychological energies of the congregation around a centralizing image, when the worshipers have a focus for prayer that lives in the imagination rather than in the intellect or will. In the early church the assembly as a worshiping phenomenon provided such a dynamic. In the beginning it was the original experience of resurrection, then the possible immediacy of the eschaton or second coming, then Christian worship as a sacrifice of praise and thanksgiving in which the good Christian life defined the meaning of such sacrifice. But for a variety of historical, theological, as well as cultural and sociological reasons, the dynamic of the assembly of praise and sharing was replaced by the moment of consecration in the Mass of the medieval church. This concentration on the consecrated elements functioned like a black hole, swallowing everything into its great nothingness. Everything else in the liturgy was sucked into its visual magnetism. Divine presence was limited to the confines of the consecrated bread and wine. The liturgical assembly and the word of God were insignificant in comparison. It certainly caught people's attention and gave them a sense of awe. But it neglected other important aspects of Christianity. People expended so much energy on consecration that they had little left for Christian community formation, biblical spirituality, conversion as a process, and the evangelical value of social justice.

The Protestant reformers of the sixteenth century, and at other times before our own, made attempts to recover the liturgical dynamic of the early church. Often the musical aspect of the liturgy and the preaching served as a focus of the assembly's energies, and one or other or both magnetized the worshipers aurally as the medieval consecration had done visually. But the Reformation's emphasis on intelligibility and accessibility to the word of God caused a change in the liturgical dynamic, one which Roman Catholicism has now assumed with a vengeance. In most of our contemporary liturgical reforms we have moved to the classroom model. Liturgy is called celebration, but more often it is better described as "ongoing religious instruction." We see this in contemporary Roman Catholic liturgies with the proliferation of theme Masses. A theme is drawn from the scriptural readings, and this is then used to plan the liturgy in terms of preaching, music, actions, and environment. It is the imperialism of the instructional model.

This new dynamic has not received universal acclaim from the people in the pews. The common complaints are well-known: "Too wordy, too instructional, too boring, we are suffocating in verbiage." This is why there are complaints that there is a lack of reverence, mystery, and beauty in our worship. And so liturgists have been studying the ways humans ritualize, the nature of symbolism, the place of the affective human response, and the meaning of the sacred today in order to counteract this trend toward classroom worship. Imaginative dealing with symbols has been seen as a way of providing material for a new dynamic. It is not clear how this will go, but there are some hints. In any event, it will be the creativity of the adaptor that will bring about a balancing of symbols directed toward an encounter with mystery.

Practically, what this means for the planners is that they must weave together two symbol sets: those of the Christian tradition as bread, wine, water, oil, gestures, and the like with the symbols of daily life. Good worship here means a blending of the mundane and the sacred ritual actions of the Christian tradition. Sacramental bread and wine must show how the material of life as work, our families, our relationships, our play, our education, our problems are a true meeting with God. By balancing in worship these two sets of symbols, life symbols and Christian symbols, the imagination of the worshipers will be moved to a sense of mystery and this balancing will interpret their daily lives.

One of the reasons this balancing can work is the intimacy that is brought about. Physical symbols and images referring to such actions as eating, sexual union, bathing, and anointing strengthen the closeness between ourselves and God. In eucharist, baptism, and marriage we have actual bodily contact between the worshipers themselves and between the worshipers and physical objects. Christianity is fundamentally incarnational, and so the use of physical symbols and gestures is demanded by the nature of our faith. These stimulate people's imaginations and send reverberations to the level of the unconscious from which symbols derive their power. So financial needs and neighborhood conditions must be linked with blessings, altars, crosses, and ashes. In the juxtaposition comes an intimacy and a feel for God, that God is in our daily life as well as in the church's liturgy. Ritual repetition over a period of time should intensify this intimate assurance.

There are several areas that need attention in the balancing of symbols to bring about a liturgical dynamic that goes beyond the pedagogical model. 1) *Word and action*. Gestures, movements, and action can prevent an excessively verbal service. 2) *Activity and stillness*. Periods of silence blended with song, prayer, and action are necessary so that the word may sink in and the liturgy not give the impression of busyness. 3) *Ancient texts and present life*. Biblical texts and traditional prayers must be rephrased in terms of contemporary concerns, current language, and life experiences. 4) *Official prayers and spontaneous expression*. Ritual forms need balancing with improvisation. It is a question of where and how. 5) *Appointed minister and congregation*. The liturgy does not belong to the presider. Yet it is not purely democratic. Good ritual needs leadership. But the leader must pray in the midst of the people, not in front of them, or in place of them. 6) *Festive and prophetic elements*. Seriousness and joy should intermix. People need not come to church for bad news. Points can be made with humor.

By concentrating on this mix, a feeling can gradually build up of how God is coursing through people's lives. This means that worship does more than rehearse what we already know about life. It draws us into our imaginations where we find a sense of balance and an enhancement of our self-dignity. This provides the basis for spiritual transformation and the deepening of the presence of God. Through the liturgy we enter the mysterious aspect of our lives because through the interiorization process of the liturgy we become at home with ourselves, we become close to ourselves. We can possess that sense of intimacy which we must have before we can be intimate with others. Creativity in adapting the liturgy, then, is directed toward mobilization of the human imagination.

The third and final task of this fourth phase of liturgical renewal requires creativity of the highest kind. It is the task of inculturating our worship. This is a relatively new term as applied to worship. Inculturation refers to the way that the Christian faith relates to any culture and finds a home in that culture. How is the faith to be incarnated in any culture? Sometimes we refer to liturgical localization which stresses the idea of something that must come about on the spot where the Gospel is actively received, and in that being done in the living context of the liturgy. Today I believe that liturgical inculturation means the same thing as liturgical experimentation.

There is very little, if any, real experimentation going on in the churches today. This is clear from the fact that experimentation is not the same as adaptation. Changing the place of the kiss of peace, moving the confession rite, or singing the eucharistic prayer are not examples of experimentation. To experiment is to engage in a scientific process of discovering what you do not yet know. It means locating certain faith communities, whether they be parishes, campuses, retirement homes, hospitals, and the like in any culture and officially encouraging the worshipers there to find rites that best express their religious experience. They may start with any ritual, old or new. But their explorations must be done in conjunction with the consultation of liturgists, theologians, the professionals of the human sciences, as well as experts in other disciplines. The data must be analyzed and fed back into the larger denominational or universal church. Reflection will then call for further revisions and the process will need to continue in that way for some time. When one adapts a liturgy of the church, one ends up with that same liturgy, although in a changed form. This is not so with liturgical experimentation. This results in a liturgy of a particular culture, the shape of which cannot be easily predicted in advance.

As already noted, the relationship of liturgy and culture is a complicated one and, therefore, there is a need for careful experimentation. Liturgy, when it becomes Australian, Indonesian, American (if such large categories are even possible), cannot simply be the convenient support of one of these cultures, baptizing all its values and institutions. In the United States we need to distinguish between American liturgies and those which would celebrate our civil forms of religion. Liturgy is also judgment. It reflects a culture, but it cannot stop being a transforming, saving encounter with Christ who is operative in that culture. Liturgy must retain its essentially prophetic and redemptive character in society, but this is hardly possible if it is so absorbed by the culture as to lose its identity. Yet if liturgy is to pass judgment on any culture, it must do so in forms that are part of that culture. This is necessary if it is to communicate the judgmental thrust of the word of God. In this sense liturgy will move against the world. It will be reserved about what is immediately graspable in the culture. But this also demands that liturgical experimentation extend to the very core of the liturgical celebration for only then can liturgy be transformative. Inculturation cannot be limited to touching only the peripheral elements of the liturgy. Otherwise liturgy will not be able to confront a culture with any depth and honesty. Liturgy and culture should exist in a state of symbiosis, which means that although separate, they are in fact inseparable. This means that for the liturgy to be the expression of any group of Christians intent on proclaiming the kingdom of God, all historical forms that no longer communicate must be changed.

We come, then, to inculturation's most difficult question: What can be changed in the liturgy and what remains unchangeable? I think that the unchanging elements would include these three. 1) Christian liturgy is tied in its roots to the person of Jesus Christ and we cannot give that up. 2) Christian worship is communal in character. It is the worship of a visible community. God did not choose to save Christians individually but chose them as a people who would acknowledge God in truth. 3) The liturgy must be carried out in visible signs. It must be part of our world in such a way that its actions and words can be experienced as a fully human activity by the participants. One might also want to add that the church needs to live out its life of worship in terms of the basic functions of proclamation and response. Everything else could change.

Inculturation may be described as re-symbolization, and liturgical inculturation is then the searching for the signs of the sacred in any culture. These may be traditional signals of transcendence or they may be new expressions of the holy that are only now becoming prominent. But an inculturated liturgy is one whereby contact with the sacred is established through these symbols. So the question of inculturation is first the identification of the sacred in any culture, the symbols communicating that sacrality, and then the integration of that symbol system into the liturgy. Or better, whatever liturgy will be in any culture will be the way in which the celebration of Gospel values is done in terms of these native symbols of the holy. We are not only talking about far off exotic cultures. The liturgy in the Western cultures also needs to be inculturated. But the question facing us and those interested in restoring the proper relationship to liturgy and culture is: What are the signs of the sacred in any particular culture? Obviously, they will differ in the concrete. The search for the symbols of sacrality is where this book began in the first essay, "Symbols of the Sacred Today."

As the churches move on toward the twenty-first century they will be continually challenged by the demands of liturgical implementation, adaptation, and inculturation. But perhaps the greatest challenge is only now confronting us, especially those of us who worship as Americans, for a problem has arisen in the last twenty years which may be particularly American. It is certainly having repercussions on the way Americans worship.

There is a form of narcissism in American culture. This excessive individuality, this cultural egoism, this vain self-regard, this communal overpreoccupation with self, this societal self-conceit has made a difference for liturgy. Liturgy now has trouble with its public character. A narcissistic society which no longer has a balancing form of ideals such as the New Frontier or the Great Society will lead to fragmentation and dehumanization. In these terms the liturgy becomes something performed for the purposes of self-gratification. In the desire to make the liturgy safe and manageable, uniformity is imposed on the liturgy. Liturgy becomes not the place to experience creative ritual, a more powerful community bonding, but rather a place to lick one's wounds after the daily struggles with affectivity. The recovery of the imagination which enables us to befriend our symbols can be a helpful antidote to the kind of poisoning that takes place through this narcissistic approach.

We are now dealing not only with the cult of the liturgy but the cult of the individual. Between 1800 and 1960 we witnessed in the United States the age of the self-made person. There were some balancing beliefs such as the political system, national civil religion, capitalism, free enterprise, the nation, democracy. But many of these beliefs have now been weakened, we live with diminished expectations, and the present Reagan administration is not able to counteract this. In answering the question of newspaper interviewers of why they voted for Reagan, many people responded in terms of a hopefully more positive economic development. But these same people exhibited diminished expectations of what they want in life, namely, to feel good and that everything is OK. Behind this feeling good is actually a lack of hope and a sense of self-isolation. We find this same kind of narcissism among many of the ordinary worshipers. Often these people have a fear of the future and really do not expect a great deal. They seek gratification in the present and they look to the past to learn lessons of how to move forward. It is the immediate and the short term which is significant in their lives. There is an unsureness about individual worth and identity. These vague anxieties about personal significance make relations with others difficult. There is a desire for the good opinion of others and yet a distrusting and disdaining of those who offer it. People identify with the heros and the stars and yet reject them for reminding them of their own insignificance. This makes a great deal of difference regarding the public character of worship. There is a shallowness in emotional relations, an avoidance of personal commitment, impulsive behavior, and much unarticulated anger and depression. But most significantly, what it means is that the place of the sacred has been changed from something like public ritual to the area of human affectivity. What people expect from liturgy is not public witness and community building, but personal satisfaction and more personal encounter. At a time when politicians are assuring us that all is well, there will be little interest in receiving the challenge of word and sacrament which must necessarily sit in judgment on the present situation.

These are the challenges before us. We need to do more than put flesh on the structures of the revised rites and texts given to us by the churches. We are asked to make them available for this time and place through our creativity. And most challenging of all, we are called to permit and encourage every people and nation, including our own, to subject their symbols to reinvestigation. For if these symbols are to continue to give integrating power, their context must be reinterpreted as the culture grows. In this sense, even our most cherished symbols of God, Christ, and the liturgy have but a transitory significance.

13

The Liturgical Year: Questions for the Future

ON 14 FEBRUARY 1969 POPE PAUL VI IN HIS APOSTOLIC LETTER, *Mysterii paschalis*, promulgated the changes in the Roman Calendar. In a later consistory he described the purpose of these changes as follows:

> You will notice that the liturgical year has not been altered radically. Rather the criterion for its revision was that the elements making up the individual parts of each liturgical season would give clearer expression to the truth that Christ's paschal mystery is the center of all liturgical worship. Further, to the extent possible, the General Roman Calendar has retained the celebration of the saints' "birthdays," but in such a way that for the whole Church those saints have been chosen who seemed to be the most important both historically and as examples. Other saints of less general significance were left to be honored by the local Churches. There has also been care to ensure the historical truth of the elements pertaining to the saint's lives and feasts. The purpose of all these measures has been to bring out clearly that holiness in the Church belongs to all parts of the world and to all periods of history and that all peoples and all the faithful of every social rank are called to attain holiness, as the Dogmatic Constitution *Lumen gentium* has solemnly taught.[1]

The new calendar went into effect on 1 January 1970.

1. *Documents on the Liturgy, 1963–1979: Conciliar, Papal, and Curial Texts* (Collegeville: The Liturgical Press, 1982) 238.

The liturgical calendar changes were long in coming. Back in 1911 Pius X gave Sundays precedence over minor feasts. In the following fifty years there was continual pressure to ensure a more appropriate observance of Lent. Pius XII made it possible to choose the Lenten daily Mass over the feast of a saint. The Constitution on the Sacred Liturgy stated that "the minds of the faithful must be directed primarily toward the feasts of the Lord by which the mysteries of salvation are celebrated in the course of the year. Therefore, the Proper of the Time must be given the preference which is its due over the feasts of the saints, so that the entire cycle of the mysteries of salvation may be suitably recalled" (art. 108).

All this has happened. Sundays have a special position in the calendar. Only major feasts of the Lord such as Baptism of the Lord, Holy Trinity, and Christ the King take precedence. Only the feasts of John the Baptist, Peter and Paul, the Assumption, All Saints, and patronal feasts can be celebrated on Sunday and, during Advent, Lent and Easter, Sundays reign supreme. Sundays are more clearly tied to the celebration of Easter. The new calendar does not really solve the question of whether the liturgical year begins with the first Sunday of Advent or on the former Septuagesima Sunday. This debate still goes on. The introduction to the calendar simply states that the paschal celebration of the Lord's death and resurrection is the culmination of the liturgical year. And then next in the order of importance is the Sunday. In fact Sunday is older than Easter. It was the original feast of the church celebrated by the apostles, and from it the celebration of Easter as an annual event is derived. Next in importance, is the Easter season itself. Including the Easter triduum, the Great Fifty Days is the most important season of the church year, although one would never know it even if one went to church every Sunday of the year. This season which concludes with Pentecost is the continuation of the paschal mystery. It is clear that the focus of the calendar, even with its inconsistencies, is on the paschal event.

The season of Lent has been restored to its more pristine meaning as a time of preparation for Easter. It is to be characterized by flourishing of the catechumenate as well as prayer and penance. It extends from Ash Wednesday to the evening liturgy of Holy Thursday. Palm Sunday has become Passion Sunday and the last liturgical event of the Lenten period would often be the chrism Mass. In any event, the main lines of the Lenten season are clear: they refer to the saving work of Christ.

Throughout the rest of the year, various of these saving works are highlighted for special consideration. Of special importance is Christmas which extends from the eve of December 24 to the Sunday after Epiphany. This season comes to an end with the baptism of Jesus. Advent which has been an ambiguous season has been more clearly identified as the preparing for the first coming of Christ and of the second coming. It is a season of joyful expectancy and so the penitential aspect is suppressed. The season consists of two parts: the first extends to 17 December and the second part extends from that date to 24 December. These latter days are concerned with the coming of Christ in his human birth, and so there is a stress on the roles of Mary, Joseph, and John the Baptist. The seasons of the Sundays of the year, called Ordinary Time, are celebrations of the mystery of Christ in its fullness.

The new calendar of saints has proved to be more controversial than that of the temporal cycle. Pius V in 1568 reduced the number of saints' days to about 150. But since that time, the number had doubled. The revisers of the calendar attempted to make it more universal in character, both from a geographical and chronological point of view. All five continents are represented, Eastern Europe being poorly represented. As one might suspect, Italian and French saints still abound. As far as time goes, the early martyrs have the favor here. Most of the dubious saints have been removed.

There has been some shifting of dates of saints and that has been an improvement. But here the attempts should have taken more care to consult local churches. The concern for universality does not require that the saint be celebrated on the same day in every part of the world. But the basic thrust of the reform of the sanctoral cycle has been sound. Saints tend to take over the temporal cycle. With the calendar reform a healthy balance was achieved between the two cycles of the church year.

The question of a fixed date for Easter still remains open. This is a question of considerable ecumenical concern. Also, common calendars with the other Christian churches need attention in the future. The matter of holy days of obligation is upon us at the present time because of the publication of the new code of canon law. At the very least we should reconsider the 1980 proposal, which was withdrawn, of the Bishops' Committee on the Liturgy that 1) Christmas, Immaculate Conception, and All Saints remain as holy days of obligation in all dioceses of the U.S., 2) that the observance of the Ascension be moved to the seventh Sunday of Easter, 3) that the canonical obligation be removed from the Solemnities of Mary, Mother of God (1 January) and the Assumption (15 August), and 4) no changes be effected without prior catechesis. I, for one, could never understand why the only days of obligation apart from Sunday, were not the days of the Easter triduum. The recommended universal minimum for holidays, namely, one Marian feast and Christmas, makes a lot of sense. It is the present Canadian practice.

Here are some recommendations for clearing away some of the inconsistencies in the calendar as well as restoring a more scripturally oriented emphasis to the church year. These suggestions are not my own but are a summary of points being made by a number of liturgical scholars today.

(1) The feast of the Immaculate Conception continues to remain ambiguous, coming in the early part of Advent. The fact that it is the patronal feast of the U.S. will prevent it being downgraded liturgically. The original choice of 8 December apparently had something to do with the date of Mary's nativity, but the lectionary now places this feast into a larger perspective of salvation history, that is, God's plan for humankind through God's beloved Son. This biblical emphasis is also that of the fourth Sunday of Advent. So why be repetitious and not place the Immaculate Conception on the fourth Sunday of Advent, making some modifications so that the character of the Sunday remains? Then, the feast's true link to the incarnation would be even more safeguarded. The Immaculate Conception is not an isolated event, but the inauguration of the incarnational reality.

(2) January first in the last twenty years has had an identity crisis. What is it? Circumcision, octave day of Christmas, or Mary, Mother of God? True, all these mysteries have some connection, but liturgy is concrete and when something means everything, it means nothing. There is no particular reason for placing an incarnationally focused feast on this day. One might attempt to baptize the secular new year's day, but that in no

way ensures the biblical basis for the feast. The feast would best be abolished, in light of the fact that this season is too over-crowded with our attempting to go through Advent, Christmas, Holy Family, Mother of God, to say nothing of Epiphany and Baptism. And who knows what the Sunday after Christmas is to be about? Perhaps it would be better if it were given back its original meaning of the presentation in the temple rather than this mystery of Christ being cycled with the finding in the temple and the flight into Egypt. This might enhance the intimacy of the relationships of the feasts that all act as satellites around Christmas itself. One writer has suggested the following order: fourth Sunday of Advent-Immaculate Conception; 25 December-Christmas; first Sunday after-Presentation; second Sunday after-Epiphany; third Sunday after-Baptism.

(3) The problems of the Easter Cycle refer more to the end of the Easter season. Ascension need not be celebrated on the numerical fortieth day. In fact, historically this feast was linked with that of the Spirit's descent on the last of the fifty days of Easter. We could easily transfer Ascension to the seventh Sunday of Easter. Also, the feast of the Trinity needs to be challenged. Ordinary Time should begin after Pentecost. But the metaphysically strange feast of Trinity seems to disturb or artificially prolong the Easter Cycle which should end with Pentecost. On the second Sunday after Pentecost, the cycle is again interrupted by the transferred feast of Corpus Christi. The isolated feast of the body of Christ tends to stress the externalized and objective presence, a presence which is divorced from the living reality of the body, the church. It has been suggested that a way to alleviate that problem would be to transfer Corpus Christi to the third Sunday of Easter. This is the time of the living awareness of the early church and the feast could take on the meaning of those early Christians who met their crucified Lord in glory in the eucharist. This would also bring the feast closer to the Easter Vigil where the eucharist is clearly seen as the climax of the initiation event. Even at the present time, there are eucharistic references in the scriptural passages for this Sunday.

(4) We need to do something about All Saints and All Souls. Originally All Saints was kept in the month of May, but was transferred to the autumn for reasons having to do with food supply and the harvest. But it is really a paschal feast wherein

Christ is celebrated in the diverse members of the church. The Byzantine Church celebrates it on the first Sunday after Pentecost. A couple of options are possible: keep it in the Fall but integrate it into the eschatological series of readings characteristic of the last Sundays of Ordinary Time, or place it between Easter and Pentecost, perhaps being related to Memorial Day. Memorial Day has lost its connection with the Civil War and is now a memorial of all the dead. As for All Souls, the feast is redundant. Because of the revised texts in the sacramentary and the lectionary, it celebrates the same thing as All Saints. It should be dropped from the calendar.

(5) Also some change is required for the feast of the Assumption. It needs to be integrated into the temporal cycle. Mary, precisely because she is the greatest of the saints, requires a similar treatment as that given to all the saints. Thus, this feast could be moved to the Easter Cycle so that it is more intimately related to the paschal mystery. However, its special tie to the book of Revelation may make the more suitble time the eschatological Sundays of the year. Psychologically, the feast might work best in September or October.

What lies behind these suggestions is the need to make the liturgical year more than a series of unrelated festivals. These key celebrations must be more fully integrated into the paschal character of the liturgical year. There is no question of simply trying to sacralize everything. While Thanksgiving Day in the U.S. might achieve greater liturgical visibility, there can be no question of splashing holy water on Mother's Day or the Fourth of July.

Problem: The Historicization of the Liturgical Year

The whole mystery of salvation is celebrated every time the church brings itself to expression through the liturgy. But because this mystery is so rich, it is extended over the whole year so that this complexity can be expressed in different moods. Since the cycle of one year is our cultural heritage, this mystery of salvation is gradually unfolded over twelve months.

Since the Middle Ages with the historicization of the liturgy, the church year has been understood as beginning with Advent. To historicize the church year means to treat it as a kind of year long biography of the life of Christ. For instance, in such an understanding, Holy Week becomes a kind of historical walk-through of the last week in Christ's life. A more theological approach, one which respects the symbolic character of the liturgical year, would envision Holy Week quite differently. Palm Sunday would be the feast of Easter in anticipation, with the triumph of the entrance into Jerusalem placed next to the passion of Christ in the gospel. Thursday, Friday, and Saturday would all be celebrations of the paschal mystery as a unit. Each day would be Easter under a different formality and image. There would be no question of pretending that on Thursday Christ instituted the eucharist and suffered in the garden, that on Friday he died, and that on Saturday evening he arose. Such would be to treat the church year as an historical run-through of the Jesus of the gospels.

A more theologically oriented year would begin with the period of promise. Then it would move to the time of this promise fulfilled. Next would come the period of the promise lived out, and finally the last stage of this year would be that of the future promise. These four stages are the theological divisions of the history of salvation. To move from one to the next in the liturgy is to treat the liturgical year as a symbol which contains the reality that it expresses. The liturgical year need not point back to events that happened two thousand years ago, but should celebrate the Christ now present in the liturgy and the Christ who is always before us.

We need to recover the theological dimension of the liturgical year. That is, we must once again experience the church year on the level of symbolic reality rather than on the level of historical imitation. We have reduced the liturgical year to the level of sign, to a one to one relationship. What greater denigration of the symbolic content of the church year can be found than in the situation of the feast of the Annunciation nine months before Christmas? Is Annunciation really about the beginning of Jesus's earthly life, presuming, of course, that life begins with conception? Is Christmas concerned with the date of Christ's birth? Christmas began because of a theological emphasis on incarnation that was not adequately handled by the Easter experience as well as by a desire to counteract certain pagan festivities. We do not know when Christ was born. Whatever Christmas is, it is not a birthday celebration as we understand them to be.

There is an ancient way of mapping out the church year which has more theological cogency and has a greater sensitivity to the theological meaning of the texts. In what ways can we once again recover some of that meaning? In this older structure of the liturgical year there are four moments to which I have already referred.[2]

(1) *The Period of Promise:* This time which begins close to the beginning of the secular calendar is concerned with the promise to the Hebrews and is a time when the church recalls that it has been chosen to be the heir of the great promises that God has made. This period begins on the Sunday after the Baptism of Christ. It concludes with the Holy Thursday liturgy which is also the end of the time of Lent. The church year in this perspective begins theologically, that is, with the promises of redemption. The year does not begin with the looking forward to the coming of the historical Jesus at Christmas time. The trouble with starting the year with Advent is that the Advent images become too easily historicized. They are twisted to refer to the predictions of the coming of the Messiah. Advent, Christmas, and Epiphany become the first part of Jesus' autobiography spread over the several months at the beginning of the church year. The incorrect theological presupposition is instilled in the worshiper's mind that we begin the liturgical year at this time, because we are celebrating the beginning of Jesus' life. In other words, the liturgical year is the church's biography of the historical Jesus, beginning at the physical beginning of his birth.

(2) *The Period of Fulfillment:* This is the time of the paschal mystery par excellence. It begins with the sacred triduum of Holy Thursday, Good Friday, and Easter and includes the Great Fifty Days, the time between Easter and Pentecost. During this time Jesus Christ is recognized as the final and full promise. He is the one who gives significance to our lives as Christians. Promise and fulfillment are theological categories, not chronological stages in time. What is climactic in the church year is the meaning of the historical Jesus and not his advent or coming to us. Even the fact that God comes to us in Jesus Christ must be subordinated to the fact that God redeems us in Christ. That is what

2. See Peter Fink, "Preface," in *Eucharistic Liturgies,* ed., John Gallen (New York: Newman Press, 1969) 3–5.

Easter is all about. Of all four periods, this is the most important one theologically and should be the dominating and determining period as far as the rest of the liturgical year is concerned. Theologically, it is important to see Easter, Ascension, and Pentecost as basically the same feast. Although in the development of the liturgical year the feasts were separately enhanced with their own ceremonies, still a symbolic understanding of liturgical time does not allow us to conclude that something historical is being affirmed. That is, the Easter event is so rich in meaning that one feast is insufficient for adequate celebration. Thus, the same mystery is spread throughout the Easter season. Pentecost and Ascension are also Easter. What the liturgical year, even in its division of the feasts, is affirming is that Easter, Ascension, and Pentecost are all one. Christ rose, ascended, and sent the Spirit as one action. In other words, no claims should be made for an historical division of this Christ event based on the divisions in the Easter season. Christ did not rise on Easter, walk around as a ghost for forty days, go up to heaven, and send a Holy Spirit ten days later. The major question that confronts us here is how to restore the symbolic and theological character to this season and avoid the implicit play acting which is still going on.

(3) *The Period of the Promise Lived Out:* This is the time of the church. This is the former Time after Pentecost, what is now called Ordinary Time. The fullness of Christ must be realized continually in time and so this is the period of struggles and failures, of hopes and glories. The church is fulfilling its mission of making Christ accessible to the world. The church under the guidance of the Holy Spirit is preparing the world for the final coming of the Lord. The major questions here are two. First, how is this time to be more adequately tied to the secular calendar since this is the period of the church in the world? Is it possible to incorporate more secular feasts such as the Fourth of July? This is also summer time for many of us and so is dead time, at least, psychologically speaking. This is time of relaxation to a certain extent. It is vacation time for many. But secondly, we must ask the question here about the mixed results of the stripping of the liturgical calendar which has taken place over the last decade or so. The intention has been the good one of restoring Christ and his mysteries to the center of the liturgical year and so liturgical worship, but in fact have we not made him

more remote? Is the Christ of the revised calendar more unattainable than ever because he is all too clean, too clinical, not sufficiently human?

Having restored the centrality of the paschal event to the time of Easter, can we be content with only one paradigmatic event in our church year? How is this one event to be opened up through other events? For instance, the Jews while focusing on the Exodus event, also found other occasions for celebration in their history. Where in the past the excessive number of saints' days in the calendar may have been detrimental to the centrality of Christ, do we not have the possibility that day after day of continuous readings of seasonal days, or even Sundays which are all very ordinary have in fact placed Christ in the realm of abstraction and therefore no more available to the worshiping community than the Christ of former times hidden behind an overblown sanctoral cycle?

(4) *The Period of Future Promise:* This is the final stage of the church year which takes in Advent, Christmas, and Epiphany. This is the eschatologically oriented conclusion of the liturgical year. The Christ of the end-time dominates this stage in the year as the church prepares to experience once again, but in a new way, the promise that has been given to it. The liturgical year ends where it began in the time before Ash Wednesday. The Baptism of Christ becomes a pivotal time between future-promise and promise. The major question here is how to restore a sense of the future coming of Christ, who has come, but must always come again and again in this time. The first Sunday of Advent is not the time to wish the congregation a Happy New Year. Advent is not the time of the Israelite community, Christmas and Epiphany the time of the gospels, and the whole thing a kind of birthday celebration of the historical Jesus.

What to Do about the Christian Passover

Triduum planning must focus on Easter as three days. The revision of the triduum is a major consideration here. The vigil was ordinarily a night watch charged with salvation themes. It was a watch of praise because of the death/resurrection event. Only later was it seen primarily in terms of Christian initiation, the time when the church renews itself by bringing in new members. Both of these aspects should be clearly articulated in the vigil service. The triduum itself needs to be experienced as the second stage of the church's retreat. Maundy Thursday, Good Friday, and the Vigil are not three separate feasts but constitute the unitary feast of Easter. It is one liturgy both theologically and ritually speaking. Although there are special services attached to each of these days, there is only one liturgical experience as there was only one liturgical celebration in second century Christianity. The elaboration of the liturgies of the so-called Holy Week throughout the ages has obscured this original unity of the paschal feast. Holy Week became an historical revisiting of the last week in Christ's life on earth. Can we promote the demise of the title "Holy Week"?

The paschal event is indivisible just as the Passover of the Jews includes all of their events of passing over to freedom from slavery in Egypt to the contemporary experience of the holocaust. Jesus does not die on Good Friday and rise on Easter. Easter is three days. What kinds of reforms are needed so that the liturgy of the sacred triduum can affirm that it is impossible to separate death and resurrection in Christ and that in his glorification are still found the signs of his suffering and death?

This tendency to historicize the liturgy has also been true of the third stage of the time of the church on retreat. Here the one Easter-event is ritually spread over the fifty days of Easter time through the separate celebrations of the feasts of Ascension and Pentecost. But this breaking up of the Easter feast is not an historical description of what actually happened chronologically in the post-resurrectional life of Jesus. All are a unified event in Christ. But the richness of the paschal mystery demands ritual time during which the various facets of this mystery can be incorporated into Christian living.

Questions that need to be raised are: How can we celebrate Holy Thursday so that it is not seen as some kind of enactment of the last supper? How is it possible to make the washing of the feet gospel narrative become more concretely the theme of the eucharistic event? Maundy Thursday is not about the institution of a sacrament, nor a time which is primarily concerned with the adoration of that sacrament. Rather it proclaims that our eucharist is verified in our acts of loving service. Thursday's liturgy says that now that we have completed our Lenten reconciliation process, we are prepared to confront the glorified

Christ at the personal cost of stripping ourselves and washing the feet of marginal people. Not only is this not the feast of the institution of the eucharist, it is not the time to commemorate the origin of the ordained priesthood. It does not seem to be the time to stress the unity of the ordained by means of concelebration. The chrism Mass might be more appropriate for that.

How are we to pray on Good Friday. Not with funereal sadness but with the exhilaration of the suffering servant who sees the light of the fullness of days, of a people who have a high priest who has opened the way for us, and of a chosen race whose king reigns from a tree. The more ancient tradition of Good Friday is the adoration of the cross, not the crucifix. It is the cross of victory that we proclaim. "We should glory in the cross of our Lord Jesus Christ" is in fact the theme song for the whole triduum, and so is sung at the beginning of Maundy Thursday.

The Easter Vigil may need revision to bring it back into focus. It is liturgical story telling time done by means of flashbacks. The new fire is hardly cogent these days when lights can easily be turned on and off. But the Easter proclamation needs to be made early in the service so that the stories of the liturgy of the word can be properly contextualized. These stories elaborate the major themes of passover: liberation and freedom and new life. They are not about crucifixion as such. But the stories are about the goodness of God and the ways that we are called to suffering so that resurrection is possible. These stories climax in the new life of the church as experienced in its new members. But Christian initiation is about both resurrection and death, and so the Easter Vigil is not simply unrestrained jubilation. Death and life are irreversibly wedded together and this ambiguity must pervade the vigil service as it moves to its high point in the ritual of baptism. Water is both life and death. Christ has come through death to victory but still bears the scars of his trials. Often because we are uncomfortable with such ambiguity, we tend to historicize these chief mysteries of Christ. We feel we only have the strength to take on one such reality at a time. And so we separate Friday from Sunday. But while Friday is serious, it is not funereal and while Sunday is joyous, it is realistic in its expression of such joy. The question is how can we experience once again the Passover of Christ as one symbol which incorporates the creative tension of both life and death?

What to Do about Lent

Often the period of Lent is described as the time of the church "on retreat." In fact, it is only the first step of such a retreat, the other two being the triduum and the Great Fifty Days. But the idea of retreat may be the most helpful way of looking at this somewhat faded and dysfunctional time of the liturgical year. At one time, Lent took its whole meaning from the preparation of the community before receiving its new members at Easter-time. Thus, the baptized prepared through different renewal projects to celebrate public reconciliation before Holy Thursday. The catechumens underwent the final stage of their process, the immediate preparation for the initiatory mysteries. And all fasted, an extension of the early but briefer fast which was connected with the Vigil. But in a world where there are still too few cat-echumens, and where the fast has been mitigated to the point where it is imperceptible, it is difficult to find a meaning for Lent. To see it as the time when the church takes the first step in a program of renewal may be the way to restore the signifi-cance to this time of the liturgical year.

What does it mean for the church to be on its annual retreat? It is not a private journey of spiritual growth. It is not necessarily a time of individually structured acts of sacrifice, service or prayer. The church's retreat is a communal one. It is the opportune time for the local community of Christians to advance together in the process of becoming the sacrament of the church. The conversion experience of this retreat is not equated with turning away from sin or turning to some virtue. It is a reshaping of consciousness of what it means to be a Christian. The conversion is not one that we decide to do, but one that God does to us. Peter Fink has pointed out that this conversion can take place on four levels as they are spread over the Lenten and Easter seasons and the rites of the church point to these levels: 1) *Personal conversion to Christ:* the first three weeks of Lent are concerned with this level and the liturgy of the word for these Sundays calls the com-munity to such conversion; 2) *Conversion as a Community:* this relational dimension of conversion is the preoccupation of the second half of Lent which culminates in the death and resur-rection of Jesus, an event which establishes the church; 3) *Con-version as Sacramental:* our communal conversion as visible is the focus of the liturgical celebrations of the post-Easter Sunday period; the resurrection of Christ does not negate his incarnation since he is still embodied in us; 4) *Conversion as Missionary:* the conversion referred to in this period from Ascension to Pentecost leads to an awareness that the church lives in its proclamation, announcing the kingdom of God to the world.[3]

But Lent is also a time of the church on retreat on its own. Originally, this meant that the Christians of the local community served as a support system for the catechumens to be initiated at the end of Lent. They did this by engaging in the process of reconciliation. Lent is penitential to the extent that penance is a renewal of baptism. At the end of Lent before the catechumens underwent the initiation ceremonies, the baptized members of the community were absolved in the liturgical rite of Holy Thursday. Were adult initiation truly normative today, it might be possible to recover the meaning of Lent along these lines. But it seems that we need to make some adjustments in our attempts to make this period significant once again.

It is important to stress the meaning of Lent in our Sunday liturgies. I believe that at the present time, with the exception of a growing number of parishes, doing it in terms of the catechumenate is unrealistic. And so it seems that highlighting the reconciliation aspect is both feasible and desirable. To do this we can bracket the season of Lent from Ash Wednesday to Holy Thursday by keeping the community aware that it is both a reconciling and reconciled community. Practically, this would mean that Ash Wednesday must become the kind of liturgy which would lead to Holy Thursday. This could mean that Ash Wednesday would be best non-eucharistic since it should culminate in the eucharist of Maundy Thursday. During the Sundays of Lent there would be brief ceremonial reminders of what began on Ash Wednesday. There perhaps would be adaptations of the present scrutinies, although they would be more directed to the baptized on retreat and would emphasize reconciliation rather than initiation. Perhaps we should not try to save Ash Wednesday at all since it developed out of a literal sense of the forty days of Lent, but that is another matter.

Whatever is done to make Lent live again in Christian living, I believe that it must be done in terms of the renewal of the

3. Peter Fink, "Is Lent a Retreat?" *Hosanna* 6:1, 6.

sacrament of penance, reconciliation. Is Lent the time for pastoral counseling with confession with general absolution on Holy Thursday? Are the Sundays of Lent to stress the reconciliation aspect of the eucharist, thus taking on the character of communal reconciliation with public pronouncement of absolution or forgiveness on Holy Thursday? How can what goes on in the reconciliation room be related to Lent and the Easter triduum? However, most liturgists see Lent's meaning as coming from initiation and the catechumenate. Should the Christian initiation of adults become significant in the life of the church, then it will give that meaning to Lent.

Can we get rid of the idea of Holy Week? It is a misnomer. There is no such thing as Holy Week. Nothing starts on Palm Sunday. The Triduum starts Thursday night. Rather, Passion/ Palm Sunday stands in the liturgical year as a final encouraging moment in the Lenten journey. This Sunday is an abbreviated Easter event. It is the entire paschal triduum in miniature with the glory and triumph of the palms and the degradation of the passion. It is Easter in anticipation. It is the final hint of what is to come. It is the penultimate moment in Lent. There is no need to start again on Holy Thursday because we have pretended that Christ has undergone his passion on Palm/Passion Sunday.

Ordinary Time

What can we do about Ordinary Time? This is not an infrequent question on the lips of liturgical planners, having exhausted their creativity in the preceding weeks of the Easter triduum and the pre-Pentecost period. The answer is to be found not so much in what can we do with Ordinary Time, as in what does the liturgy do with it. Does the liturgy only give us a taste of time in its climactic celebrations of Christmas, Epiphany, Palm Sunday, the Easter triduum, and the other key feasts? Is Ordinary Time little more than a celebration (?) of duration? What happens when Ordinary Time is ritualized? Is time endured? Tolerated? Wasted? Is liturgical time different in Ordinary Time? Or does Ordinary Time have any theological meaning whatsoever? Common sense indicates that for many worshipers what goes on in church at this time is little more than a series of random liturgical acts which, however energetically performed, represent but a succession of inconsequential moments in the liturgical cycle.

Few people are actually satisfied with the ordinary in life. They hunger for the surprise in a fresh awareness of the familiar aspects of the human condition. Were this not the case art and music would never break out of a narcissistic enclave to become public. Behind the variety of ways in which people deal with time, whether tasted or wasted, is the urge to find out the meaning of mortal time. Few are content to experience time as a one-way and irreversible process. Most of us would like to find ways to celebrate our duration. Is that not the same as the desire to find meaning in life, to enjoy oneself, to be comfortable with growth, and seek after intimacy? What art can do for us is to arrest time, to capture that evanescent moment, and to place it in the theatre of our personal stories. Can we allow the liturgy to do less?

Time is too short for us humans. Thus there is a need to celebrate our ordinary time. That we are not comfortable with the brevity of life is the reason that often we quickly go from highs to lows, passing each other as in a perpetual carnival. For many of us living is a constant costume changing, going from one mask to another amidst a medley of hails and farewells, or worse, sneers and retorts. How little time we have to accomplish what we want in this world! Do not many of us regret the lack of time left for personal growth because it has taken us so long to come to the necessary insight?

The liturgy, sensitive to human limitations, in Ordinary Time assists the worshipers in dealing with their own impatient and ever changing selves and thus with the inevitability of death. How does worship take on such a seemingly impossible task? By providing the possibility of experiencing what we might do with the shortness of our lease on earth. It is more than a matter of calling us to come to terms with the limitations of time and death. Most liturgies already try to do that. Rather, the special challenge of Ordinary Time is to be creative with those limits.

What should be brought to liturgical expression in Ordinary Time is the transmutation of time itself, that whatever is of value in life is determined by the quality of our lives. While the great festival times in the church year speak eloquently about patient waiting in our humanity (Advent/Christmas) or about new life from death (Lent/Easter), it is ordinary time which images for us how our individual lives can be durable symbols. It is as if we were a work of art such as a great novel which survives the current fashions and the moments of great enlightenment and entertainment. We too must survive beyond the dramatic moments of our personal histories. We too must exist in between the Easters and Christmases of our lives, times usually spoken of as dull, as lacking in color passion, and as our desert experiences. In these very prosaic periods, the liturgical celebration of Ordinary Time lifts up our lives as a parable, where there is embodied in human flesh an original and penetrating view of human life and events from our individual perspectives.

Liturgical Ordinary Time is that portion of the year when we hope to make our particular Christian vision durable, one which can withstand unpopularity in a secularized society or one that need not seek easy applause by demonstrating its contemporary relevance. Ordinary Time brings to ritual visibility our faith conviction that all of our life has a future and will outlast our present way of being in the world. But Ordinary Time says more. It says that those times of our lives between festivals are like a book waiting to be read. We are affirmed in being readable books, ones which entertain and enlighten the best and the worst, the most simple and the most complicated of the people who live with us.

In the end, paradoxically, Ordinary Time must remain ordinary. The special Christian celebrations do not necessarily determine the mark of a Christian. It is not the drama and intensity of Christian worship which adequately defines the follower of Christ. There is also a need for the depth of vision, the breadth of understanding, and the universal appeal of life with are found in the ordinary. It is the power of the quiet, seemingly pedestrian, ordinary existence which makes it possible for us to become parables which sustain others when they are lost in darkness. This is not to say that beautiful and solemn liturgical celebrations of the great Christian feasts do not also have this quality of parable. Surely they do as much to promote human living as the music of Mozart and the painting of Cezanne. But in the long run, a work, whether a painting, music, the Christian life, or liturgy, must endure. It must have quality. Ordinary Time is about quality.

Ordinary Time must be part of any liturgical cycle, lest the great festivals conceal our inner poverty. Much of the limitation and negativity of our lives will be forgotten or hopefully perish along the way of our spiritual journeys. But the best of us will be saved. Just as posterity preserved the plays of Sophocles and Shakespeare, the portraits of Rembrandt, and the quartets of Beethoven, so do our high liturgical festivals present God with the best of our lives. But why did history make its particular selectivity? Because the great artists of the past had the continuing power to illuminate and elevate human thoughts and emotions. They had quality and durability. Celebrating these characteristics of the Christian vocation is what the liturgy does in Ordinary Time.

The Rediscovery of Advent

The secret for understanding Advent is found in the images that fill the liturgies of this season. Some of these images are: watch, calf and lion cub feed togther, speak to the heart of Jerusalem, the hills flow with milk and honey, spring on you suddenly like a trap, the bow of the mighty is broken, no need to worry, all the trees of the forest will clap their hands, the child leaping in her womb, the night of the waiting world, there will be no end of peace, the rising sun will visit us. There is a lot more here waiting and welcoming a babe in swaddling clothes with angels and shepherds crowding around. Rather, this season speaks of Christ coming in our own time. One of the three major figures which dominate this period is Isaiah. He provides the rich messianic texts which speak of Israel's belief that God would send the anointed one. But this notion speaks especially to today's world which is longing for adequate human leadership. The second Advent figure is the evangelical John the Baptist who announces the present time of salvation where what has been prefigured has been realized. And in the faith and the *Magnificat* of Mary, the third dominating figure, we have an anticipation not only of the birth of Christ but also of his resurrection.

These images and figures reveal Advent to be a progressive entering into Christmas. But the meaning of these images and figures is governed by the meaning of Christmas itself. If we move beyond the historicization of Christmas, the meaning of Advent will surely have to change. The images of Christmas control the images of Advent. The stars, the angels, the shepherds, the magi, Mary and Joseph: all reverence the Christ. But the focus is not on the Jesus of Bethelehem who has already been announced, born, and manifested. He has already had his first epiphany. The Christ who is expected at Christmas is the only Christ that Christianity has: the risen Christ of glory. Advent, then, becomes the gradual expectation that the Christ of glory will come to save us. While Advent attends to the nativity of Christ, it takes its meaning primarily from his final coming. For this reason it is more helpful to view Advent as the end of the Church year. When it is clustered with Christmas and Epiphany it becomes part of the primary eschatological period in the church's annual experience of the Christ-event rather than being an historicized way of preparing for the birthday celebration of the Infant Jesus. The seasonal theme, then, is one of emerging eschatology, namely, that in Christ all things are fulfilled. And as Christ's living body in the world, the church continues to witness to this fulfillment and anticipates in its liturgy the end of all things.

Advent, Christmas, and Epiphany are not to be treated as three distinct and isolated feasts with their own easily distinguishable meanings. In the same way that Easter is three days, so these three festivals form a single liturgical unit. What meaning Advent, Christmas and Epiphany have is derived from the significance of this period in the church year, namely, the celebration of the coming of Christ, especially Christ in his glory. This change of emphasis is not an attempt to play down the incarnational presence of Christ in all of creation. The point is that this incarnational emphasis becomes the basis of our hope that Christ will come at the end of time. The Advent/Christmas/Epiphany season directs the church to look to and anticipate the future coming of Christ. When our liturgical celebrations clearly indicate that historical factuality does not exhaust the meaning of this time of the liturgical year, when the truth of the Christian Gospel proclaimed during this season is the fact of Christ, not his originating setting, when in our spirituality the event of the birth of Christ is more important than the circumstances, when the meaning that is being ritualized at this time of the yearly cycle is in the fact of Christ, not the cards and carols with their vivid descriptions of the Christ-happening, when we rejoice that we hear the meaning of our lives not from angels in the sky but from our fellow human beings, then we will know that we are on the way to experiencing once again, the year, precisely as liturgical.

THE CHURCH YEAR AS SYMBOL

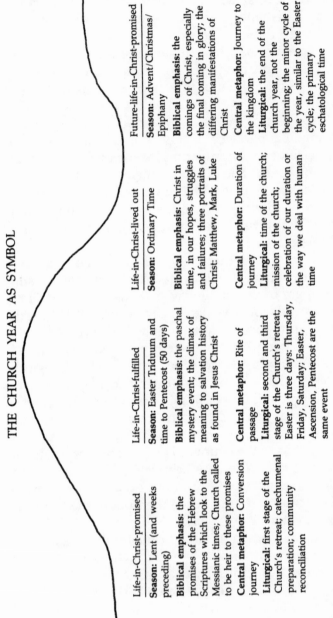

Life-in-Christ-promised	Life-in-Christ-fulfilled	Life-in-Christ-lived out	Future-life-in-Christ-promised
Season: Lent (and weeks preceding)	**Season:** Easter Triduum and time to Pentecost (50 days)	**Season:** Ordinary Time	**Season:** Advent/Christmas/Epiphany
Biblical emphasis: the promises of the Hebrew Scriptures which look to the Messianic times; Church called to be heir to these promises	**Biblical emphasis:** the paschal mystery event; the climax of meaning to salvation history as found in Jesus Christ	**Biblical emphasis:** Christ in time, in our hopes, struggles and failures; three portraits of Christ: Matthew, Mark, Luke	**Biblical emphasis:** the comings of Christ, especially the final coming in glory; the differing manifestations of Christ
Central metaphor: Conversion journey	**Central metaphor:** Rite of passage	**Central metaphor:** Duration of journey	**Central metaphor:** Journey to the kingdom
Liturgical: first stage of the Church's retreat; catechumenal preparation; community reconciliation	**Liturgical:** second and third stage of the Church's retreat; Easter is three days: Thursday, Friday, Saturday; Easter, Ascension, Pentecost are the same event	**Liturgical:** time of the church; mission of the church; celebration of our duration or the way we deal with human time	**Liturgical:** the end of the church year, not the beginning; the minor cycle of the year, similar to the Easter cycle; the primary eschatological time

The Three Portraits of Ordinary Time

Mark: mystery of the Messiah; emphasis on miracles; true discipleship. Son of Man: gradual recognition of Messiah as suffering; ministry of Jesus is the revelation of his function in the kingdom; candid.

Matthew: Jesus as rabbi; Jesus as new Moses, New Israel; fulfillment of the law and the prophets; Son of God and Son of David; Jesus as Lord of law; commandment of love; serious, majestic setting.

Luke: Jesus as prophet; kingdom = universal salvation, Gentiles must be included; gospel of mercy for those lost, of the poor, for the insignificant; detachment and renunciation; joy, wonder, admiration.

14

The Church Year and the American Experience

THE RESHAPING OF THE LITURGICAL YEAR WHICH WAS MOBILIZED BY the Constitution on the Sacred Liturgy may well be the most successful of the reforms which emerged from the Second Vatican Council. Yet the question keeps arising about the viability of this "new" calendar for the American Church. Is this restructuring still too unspecified to thematize the American religious experience? Is the present liturgical year still a grid which is imposed on a national ethos which differs from cultures in which the Roman Rite still rings a resonant note? In other words, the question of the inculturation of the church year is still with us. Not only are we searching for cultural equivalents to the Latin liturgy, but we need to examine the naturally recurring patterns in a culture which are not that of the Roman Rite.

To raise this issue is not to denigrate the positive gains of the calendar. One need but recall the more significant changes such as the restoration of the primacy of the Sunday, the recovery of the unity of the Easter triduum, the recognition of the eschatological character of the Advent/Christmas/Epiphany Cycle, and of course, the enlivening of the Lenten season through its close connection with the catechumenal process.

What is at issue here is the matter of the inculturation of the liturgy, a task which in principle was embraced by the Second Vatican Council. The indigenization of worship is the proclamation of the Good News in relation to the experience of the churches and their cultural settings. It is not a matter of merely transposing worship forms from one culture to the other. Rather the biblically based worship of God must become more meaningful to local Christians. They must be able to feel at home with their normative rites. They need to be able to receive the Gospel actively in their own language and cultural patterns.

What this means specifically is that in the case of the liturgical year for the U.S., the organization of the church's time must be founded on certain principles. These principles are: 1) that while religion and American culture are distinct, they are not independent or opposed; 2) that while America has become a secularized society, there are still religious elements influencing the culture; and 3) that the split between Gospel and culture that has occurred means that the culture needs to be evangelized and the Gospel needs to be inculturated. This inculturation takes place through the identification and acceptance of an American vision as located in common goals, sets of values, environments, and patterns of behaviour. This vision is transmitted through symbols and embodied in artifacts and so becomes incarnated in the American tradition which can be identified as the American experience. Following are some of the characteristics of the American experience which must be considered in structuring an American Church calendar.

(1) Most cultures are traditional and rooted in the past. They are concerned with preserving and conserving. American culture represents more a break with the past. This is not a complete rupture, but it does mean a preoccupation with the concreteness of the present. For this reason an American theology is not abstract. It will be pragmatic. The self-understanding of the church places priority on human conscience rather than abstract principles of authority, on diversity and marginal existence rather than global identity, and experimental life-styles rather than a universal notion of community.

(2) Americans, with some quite noticeable exceptions, will have trouble with the doctrine of original sin. America as nature's nation or as the country of the new Adamic innocence is still with us. The character of our society is still nourished by the possibility of a radical innocence. This is one of the reasons that Americans cannot deal well with sin, evil, or death. Innocence seems to be a more natural category. This is reflected in the passion with which Americans insist that their governmental

officials be publicly honest, despite other deficiencies they might have. They must participate in this communal innocence.

(3) The key to American spirituality is transformation. Americans do not want to be immobile. They desire to be new people. This flows from their drive to return to an original innocence. This is one reason why revivalism and fundamentalism have been powerful forces and are still present today. In fact the more sophisticated the technology and the more pervasive the aesthetic dimension in American living, the more influential is the tradition of Billy Graham, the liturgy of the Crystal Cathedral, and the judgment of the moral majority. Even the intellectuals are attracted to a charismatic spirituality.

(4) The American experience is dominated by the eschatological. Historically, this has been seen in the American consciousness of the frontier as illimitable. The East looked upon the West as a place without beginning or end. The promise and hope of a young nation was articulated in the language of the open frontier not only with its broad humor but especially with the feeling that democracy was the solution to endless problems. And once the physical frontier vanished, the conquering spirit moved to technology as a new wilderness to conquer. The American spirit is reluctant to come to terms with boundaries, limits, or ends. Although more sober than in recent past, Americans still hope that technology will correct environmental disorders.

Our European predecessors were time oriented, especially in terms of tradition and culture. For the American, space has been the field of pragmatic operations. We have been short on time but long on space. Space has overshadowed time so that even the concept of freedom has been spatialized. But now the movement is to restore the balance between space and time. Life in historical time cannot now be confronted and promises fulfilled by sheer movement in space. What one does in space, one does by moving. In time what is accomplished is achieved through decisions. And the person of space and time looks inward upon the issues of human life. So for example, the problems of the American cities cannot be resolved by flight. Americans are now asked to confront the realities of limit and boundaries by coming to terms with life where one is and must remain.

This brief overview of some characteristics of the American world view highlights certain preferences. In general what is preferred are: experience rather than reason, the present rather than the past, innocence rather than sin, revolution rather than the status quo, concrete alternatives rather than synthetic solutions. The preferences are pragmatic with a thrust to explore and probe for change, create choices, and engage in further experiences. These are the cultural values which need to be incarnated in the symbol system of the church year so that these values become part of the religious tradition of American Catholics. What follows are some selected examples of ways in which our recently revised liturgical calendar can reflect these American characteristics.

(1) The priority of the theological over the historical in the structure of the church year. As is evident in so much writing about the church year, there is a move away from the historicization of the church's time to an understanding of the church year as a symbol. Since the Middle Ages the celebrations of the liturgical year have been confined by an historicizing mentality which treats the church year as a twelve month long biography of the life of Christ. Advent is the time of the Old Testament and looks to the coming of the infant Jesus in Bethlehem. Holy Week is a kind of historical walk-through of the last week in Christ's life. To historicize the year is to use the time machine approach where one can leave the present moment and go into the past for a brief, artificially constructed period of time.

A more theologically oriented perspective to the church year treats it as a symbol. The emphasis is not placed on chronological time but the truths and experience of the major Christ events. Liturgical time spread over the secular twelve months is a rhythm of Life-in-Christ. Structured symbolically, the church year begins with Life-in-Christ-Promised, then successively proceeds through the stages of Life-in-Christ-Fulfilled, Life-in-Christ-Lived-Out, and Future Life-in-Christ-Promised. This symbolic approach to the liturgical year was developed in the previous chapter.

The church year as a series of events corresponds to the American search for innocence, for something new under the sun. Each yearly celebration is a shedding of a sinful past. The American spirit is to move on. To stay with one's sin, especially the sin of the past, is not appealing. Americans would prefer a church year which is also on the move. As in the case of other symbolic events, there is the possibility of transformation through the church year, whereas a looking toward the past does not allow for personal and communal change. The newness of the transformed person must come from the intersection of the present and the future. One may be forgiven of the past, but this is a negative experience. When one moves from major event to event, the experience is more that of the transforming journey. It is no surprise that the eschatological image of the church year will respond more to the American experience. Life does not end and begin again. The liturgical year is on an ever ascending spiral. It does not conclude and then start up again. That would be too space oriented. Life in historical time has changed for Americans. It must also change in the liturgical year.

(2) When should the church year begin? This question is closely related to the first point, the symbolic character of the year. The historicized and traditional approach began the year with the first Sunday of Advent for obvious reasons. The stress was on chronological time. Christmas moved in the direction of the physical birth of Christ. Advent represented the period of Israelite longing and waiting for the Savior. The symbolic approach to the church year places the beginning around the time of the commencement of Lent. This is logical since the first theological event, the time of the Promise, coincides with the Lenten season. Which of these two approaches is more appropriate for the American Church? The first is not since it requires a sense of pretense so opposed to the American pragmatic mentality. It would seem that the second choice, beginning with the Lenten period, would be more appropriate. But is it? What immediately comes to mind is that the church year's opening should correspond to the secular calendar's opening. But experientially when does that take place in the United States? New Year's Day is now more characterized by broken resolutions, rowdy behavior, an orgy of football games, and the calming of the effects of the previous night. It celebrates the beginning of very little. It ends a festive mood or serves as a pause from work or the hangovers.

Perhaps, Americans begin the year with the deadline for income taxes. And some do turn this event into a ritual. But this time is also quite insignificant for many, even those who are required to pay taxes. Some say that the opening of school which signals the end of summer and provides merciful relief for parents is the beginning of the year. Again this is not universally shared. Beginning school is usually an ambiguous experience for Americans. Usually, it is more ending than beginning. I suggest that we have no clear and definitive beginning of the secular year. We begin at different times depending on our circumstances and the beginnings themselves. And the beginnings have more a literal and pragmatic meaning than a symbolic one.

Thus, I believe it unrealistic to emphasize the beginning and ending of the liturgical year in terms of a twelve month period. There might be a utilitarian beginning and ending for the purpose of organizing the lectionary readings, but in fact such boundaries are artificial and do not respond well to the eschatological dimension. Such a view is too rational, too tied to the past to be effective. Americans will need, on the one hand, to experience the year as a whole and, on the other hand, to live in the major festivals as the breaking through of their limits. The image of the liturgical year is not linear chronological time or even an ever recurring circle, but a helix, an ever ascending spiral, impelled by major thrusts of energy, in this case, the chief seasonal celebrations.

(3) Sunday for Americans. Sundays have a special position in the new calendar. Sunday is more clearly tied to the celebration of Easter. It is the day to remember the resurrection of Jesus. It has an eschatological emphasis, looking to the time of future fulfillment in the coming of Christ. Sunday is the day of the Christian assembly. On this day Christians do their "special thing" in terms of their major symbols and rituals. It is the Christian day of praise.

Theologically, this view of the Sunday is unchallengeable. It is also abstract and general. Church on Sunday is in competition with the national experience. For Americans the weekends belong to themselves. The office, professions, factories, farms, and schools demand their time and attention during the rest of the week. Often this is true of Saturdays so that the weekend is reduced to Sunday. The weekend, or minimally Sunday, is the time of leisure where large institutions such as the church should not be making demands. Who wants to spend one's free time in church?

The general characteristics of the American experience may provide some insight in handling this conflict. American culture's distantiation from its past does not allow one to encourage

Sunday worship in terms of what has been the tradition. Abstract theologizing here will do little. Only a pragmatic, or better, experiential, solution will work. Any promotion of Sunday, if that is desirable, must be based on practical experience. The legal approach of insisting on Sunday Mass attendance has been losing its force for years. With the American propensity for an original innocence, it becomes increasingly difficult to use the "guilt trip" method for getting people into the church building on Sundays. Too many simply do not feel guilty if they do not participate in Sunday worship. Thus, we need to provide a context for a weekly liturgy which is useful and is freed from legal demands from the institutional church. The recent reinstatement of the holy days of obligation (Notice the language!) has only shown how authority lacks credibility in this area.

In searching for ways to make the liturgical experience feasible it is important to accept in a realistic fashion that most parishes are not communities. They are not a theological phenomenon. They are sociological in character. They are an administrative umbrella under which are situated many communities which are diverse in character as well as many individuals who belong to no community. As a facilitating unit the parish will offer liturgical services on Sunday for those who want them. The Saturday evening Mass should not be seen as a regrettable second choice. Whatever happened to the understanding that the liturgical day begins the evening before? With the sleeping habits of many Americans as well as the mobility of the population, Saturday evening worship may be a more realistic approach. The Easter triduum begins Thursday evening. Why is the "First Vespers" experience appropriate for a feast but not the weekly eucharist? Should we not admit that Sunday obligation needs can be "fulfilled" through weekday eucharists for the smaller faith communities in the parishes? Hopefully, these same people would also participate in the Sunday assembly several times a year. At the present the liturgy does not correspond sufficiently to the American experience of pluralism, the pragmatics of people's life-styles and the realism that church going cannot compete with leisure time. It may be that the Sunday will remain the day of *actual* worship for most Christians. But greater emphasis on hospitality will be needed to make it the kind of time which can be incorporated into leisure.

(4) Americans celebrating seasons and festivals. It has been observed by liturgist, Michael Joncas, that the Roman approach to a liturgical season can be visualized by an upward curve which reaches a climax and then slowly descends to a lower level. On the other hand, Americans build up to a climax and then immediately descend from that peak. The most obvious example of this is the practice of singing Christmas carols several weeks before 25 December and their disappearance on 26 December. I do not believe that the solution is to become countercultural, trying to resist the commercialism of Christmas by refusing to sing Christmas carols until the midnight Mass. The problem is not simply American commercialism. It is also due to the fact that the church treats Christmas as too oriented to the past and the physical birth of Christ. Most traditional Christmas carols are blatant examples of religious historicization.

Singing Christmas carols during Advent might contextualize them as more eschatological in character. Since the Advent/Christmas/Epiphany Cycle is concerned with the manifestations of Christ and especially the final one, the songs need not be tied to a certain date. Nothing new begins on Christmas Eve or, better, Christmas Day. It has already begun. Thus, I advocate joining secular society in the use of carols before 25 December, but extending the Christmas experiences through Epiphany through their use. In general Christianity needs to provide an alternative to the shortcomings in the culture, while at the same time it is engaging in the process of indigenization. In the use of carols after Christmas the church does not follow the consumeristic society. The main reason that radios stop playing carols on the 26th is that they are preparing for the next advertizing campaign.

Some liturgists view the early celebration of the "midnight Mass" with apprehension. Midnight Mass should be at midnight. But is that not too literal in application? The first Mass of Christmas should function more as does the Easter Vigil. A celebration of the evening before makes sense theologically from an American point of view. The evening before can be very important for Americans. It is often the evening before an event which is more highly intense emotionally and more energy filled by the heightened experience of preparation. Although liturgy is primarily praise, it is also hard work. Our mistake is to see worship as the ritualization of leisure time. It sounds good theoretically. But it does not appear very workable practically. This does not mean that there would be no liturgies on Christmas Day or Easter Day. I suspect that pluralism will always be an overriding consideration in the United States.

It is fruitless to insist on the separate celebration of days which have no secular analogate. Christmas and Easter are always national holidays. But Ascension, Immaculate Conception, All Saints, and the Assumption will continue in a marginated and dysfunctional state unless thay are moved to Sundays. In the previous chapter I summarized the many suggestions made by liturgical experts to alleviate the problem of such a great dissonance between the church year and the secular year.

Additional feasts could emerge from the secular culture. Perhaps, Martin Luther King's birthday could be incorporated into the church calendar. If we need a holiday of obligation, try Thanksgiving, or, better, the eve of Thanksgiving. The Fourth of July may not require religious ritualization, but we need to be open to that in the future. It may well be *the* special celebration of the Christian family since this summer holiday often brings families together in a way that has little direct connection with our country's independence.

What lies behind so many of these suggestions, which may be but a prelude to deeper inculturation efforts, is the need to make the liturgical year more than a series of unrelated festivals. It must be experienced as a whole, as a symbol. There is no question of simply trying to sacralize everything such as splashing holy water on Mother's Day. But the indigenization of any ritual or ritual time presupposes that the rites of the liturgical year are like a musical composition. They have their own integrity and internal dynamism. There are rests in music. But one cannot keep stopping and starting. The liturgical year, once in motion, must continue on with its own flow and rhythm. Like music it comes alive in the living. When the church year becomes the musical piece of the worshipers in the United States, it will be American.

15

Liberation and the Imagination in the Liturgy

OPPRESSION HAS MANY MEANINGS. HERE I DEFINE IT AS BURDENING with cruel and unjust impositions and restraints. It means to subject someone to a burdensome or harsh exercise of authority or power. In analyzing how the imaginative process in liturgy can alleviate human oppression, other meanings are relevant. For instance, one can be oppressed by the psychological factors within oneself. But the interest here is that oppression which is caused by an unjust imbalance of power in human social interactions. The most obvious example of this is the system of rule of an oppressive government. It is a situation of one party or group overpowering or pressing down another.

To be oppressed, then, means to be the subject of unjust or excessive exercise of authority or control. In itself authority is not oppressive, but it is the manner of operation which causes an imbalance of power between groups or people. Members of one group experience themselves powerless to change a situation. Such oppression becomes so much the fabric of life that not to cooperate with it requires a special effort, a courageous action with possible negative consequences for oneself. Oppression may be so institutionalized that it becomes a cultural way of thinking. It is interpreted as the normal course of events. This is true not only of oppressive physical constraints, but also of a person's consciousness in which the world is perceived as essentially oppressive. And so, oppression exists in the realm of attitude as well as behavior. Patterns and ways of thinking contribute to the oppressiveness of certain situations. Behind oppression there is some kind of force. It need not be physical force. It can be economic, military or legal. Whatever form it takes, it is threatening.

There are clear negative effects that oppression has on the individual or the society to which the individual belongs. *Self and group deprecation* is perhaps the most obvious. It comes from a negative self-definition which is based on internalization of the opinion that the oppressors hold of the oppressed. In turn, the oppressed adopt their oppressors' guidelines for their behavior. Thus, some groups accept the opinion that they are good for nothing, know nothing, are incapable of learning anything. Some studies of anti-Semitism have identified a tendency toward self-hatred, which minimizes the achievements of Jewish people. This self-hatred is often unconscious and so can be accompanied by feelings of superiority and chauvinism. If members of a group experience discrimination because of group membership, they may react by overemphasizing their group identity or by trying to hide it. In any event there will be feelings of anxiety and unworthiness.

Personality development which takes place in the context of this experience of oppression will be distorted. One finds this in women who equate self-development with self-sacrifice or in black children for whom skin color is symbolic of low self-esteem. Some tests with black children have indicated that in their color drawings, black and brown refer to the soil or ground, while their drawings of white children are larger and more lifelike than those of black children. It would be easy to quote from the literature today to illustrate how the oppressed come to internalize the belief systems that define them negatively. It is the very beginning of their experiencing themselves to the contrary that breaks this oppressive cycle. It is here that the imagination comes to the rescue. It is here that oppression and liturgy must meet and confront. The oppressed must believe in themselves, but it is precisely their self-understanding which is converted into a negative self-image through the experience of oppression. Liturgies which are enriched by the human imagination can provide the proper antidote to a poisonous and unjust social atmosphere. For instance, liturgies celebrated by gays/lesbians can counteract their low self-estimation as well as their anger and hurt which stem from their being treated as marginal people by the larger society.

Another negative effect of oppression is *emotional dependence*. Often there is a hidden desire on the part of black children to be white. Peasants, while fearing their oppressors, have an almost magical belief in their power. Rather than letting off steam at the employer, a worker will do it at home. In their alienation the oppressed want to resemble and imitate their oppressors. This desire to follow the oppressors is especially true of the middle class. They dream of being in the place of those who "lord it over them."

It is no surprise that such experiences of oppression lead to *grief and depression*. There is the loss of human dignity; there is the conscious repression that takes place when one is the underdog; there is the regret over what one's life might have been but is not. There is the manifold suffering of those of one's group who have gone before and will come after, as well as one's contemporaries. Often there is violence involved, such as killings, beatings, and rape. But most of all there is the experience of hopelessness to stop the tyranny. It is a kind of death-experience. Imagine the depressed state of Mario who can never be Mario the human being, but must always be Mario the Hispanic. Because he belongs to a certain class of people, others have permission to act toward him in a certain way such as with harassment or violence. This appears to be an inevitable part of his life.

We also need to take into account that *rage and anger* are part of being oppressed. This reaction is not the same as depression because it is usually more pronounced, probably because depression takes place when the anger is turned in on oneself. But again, this anger is manifested against one's peers rather than those who are in a privileged position. Studies show that there is considerable hostility toward those who prosper on the part of those who are fatalistic about their situation. This anger stems from envy, lack of trust of the outside world, feelings of individual aggressiveness, and fear and doubt because of discrimination. Often the oppressed become more open and free as they redirect their hatred toward their tormentors. Through the imagination such redirection of energy can become productive and liberating within a Christian context.

Finally, there is a particular kind of *fear* found in the oppressed. It is the fear of freedom. If free, the person must reject a negative self-image and move toward autonomy and responsibility. But this involves risks more than many are willing to accept. Thus the paradox that people experience a fear of thinking and acting in ways other than those prescribed by the oppressive consciousness. For example, this is often the case with gays/lesbians. It is saddening to see some of this world's most creative people confine themselves to certain unimaginative and imprisoning aspects of their life-style.

The way in which the oppressed have been able to survive these negative experiences through the centuries is largely through their capacity for celebrativeness and humor. This resilience amidst rejection and powerlessness often takes the form of fun, good times, and frolic. Again, some research has shown that Blacks' downcast and sour moments were often in the presence of white people and when the latter were not around, they were forgotten. Often this liberating humor is expressed in the music of the oppressed people. It is this notion of liberation through celebration which points to the power of the imagination to be a force confronting and transcending oppression. For celebration presupposes imagination. It is in the human imaginative process that we must look for the resources for the victims of history to change the drama of power games and self-depreciation. The nuclear arms race is the ultimate exaggeration of the kind of injustice which pervades society. It is too late for either simple exhortations or complicated recipes to overturn the oppression which afflicts so many of us caught in the midst of the nuclear conflict. Now we must move toward a transformation of our whole Christian spirituality. This is a task which will demand all the creativity of our imaginations that we can generate.

The most effective way in which we can reconceptualize and re-experience our spirituality is in overcoming the dichotomy between the vocations of spiritual union with God and the pursuit of social justice ministries. Such separation left the holy to the individual interior life while the poor and oppressed were left to public charity. Capitalist as well as socialist societies are equally at fault here. The church which at times reduced itself to its sacramental professionals merely aped either the hierarchy of one or the bureaucracy of the other. In order to overcome this misconception which isolates Christian spirituality from the ministry of social justice, we will need to recover our consciousness of God in our daily living. It is through the imagination that such a task can be accomplished.

Basically, this means a shift from understanding God as a form of dominating power, a divine potentate who manipulates the world and is in control of the human race, to one who is deeply involved in our making of ourselves. God invites, but does not force us to respond to one another. Christian spirituality which is based on this experience of God takes us just as we are and calls us to attend responsibly to who we are so that we can gradually discover our humanity. And if we do this, we shall find that we are intrinsically related to all other human beings. We are a mystery to ourselves and we can understand ourselves only when we are united to other people. This format for Christian living offers another scenario than that of a final nuclear holocaust. As we live in this world racked by the worst kind of injustices, we must pay attention to what we are as human beings. It is through images, symbols, and myths, workings of the imagination, that we can be converted from racism, sexism, economic exploitation, environmental pollution, and persecution to responsible hope and love, seeking to redeem the human situation.

This need for the imagination flows from our disillusionment that empirical science and industrial technology can be the means of saving humanity from the deep fears and aggressions that hound us with the horrors of massive destruction and untold oppression. In one sense the answer lies in the very old and traditional call for religious conversion, a leap leading to a radical change. But the difference now is that it is not an intellectual conversion with resultant changes in ethical behavior. It is a wholistic conversion in which the imagination is both the catalyst for transformation and the field where this conversion takes place. As our God-consciousness gradually personalizes all reality, this God revealed in symbols, narratives, and sacraments in Christian Scriptures and liturgy, will move us into the struggles for freedom and liberation. The reign of God will not come about like some act of a divine bureaucrat or transcendent businessperson who manipulates history to bring about a better world.

Rather, our God chooses to struggle with us and with special victims of history. The kingdom takes place when we respond to this struggling God through personal and social conversion.

The kind of God-consciousness which grows in the religious imagination is one which always leads those who are informed by it to seek out the victims of oppression, to strive for solidarity with the poor, to engage in the struggles for justice. It is this kind of God-consciousness which must be ritualized in Christian liturgy, which must be the ground on which our liturgical experiences are based. Worship is an organized pattern of religious symbols. Because these symbols are born in and fed by the human imagination, they make the liturgy an experience where oppression can be transcended. There are several characteristics of symbols which make them enablers of this individual and communal freedom: 1) their ability to point to several different meanings at the same time; 2) their attractiveness, their call for response. It is impossible to remain indifferent to them; 3) their capacity to stir up the emotions and desires even in the seeming absence of a rational cause; 4) their triggering effect, that is, every symbol tends to make one think of another symbol; 5) their directional character, that is, they point the perceiver in a particular way. Symbols produce presence by means of concentration of awareness. All of these qualities of symbols make it possible for us to live in another way. We can inhabit another world by means of symbols when these symbols are nourished by the imagination. Thus symbols can do many things. They can point to a person's need to do something. They can be the avenue whereby persons get in touch with their inner lives. They can focus the common objectives of a group. Because symbols have an ambiguous quality they can articulate a variety of relationships, while bringing these relationships together through a central focus. Symbols bring together the energies of a society.

When there is a convergence of the socially functioning symbols with the symbols responding to individual psychological needs, two things happen to the perceiver, and in liturgy, to the worshiper: 1) a deepening of the interior life by bringing the social and individual dimensions of life together and 2) an intimacy in which the worshipers feel a nearness to themselves. Together these qualities of the symbolic experience bring about unity in the person of the worshiper. This is another way of speaking about the imaginative life of the person. In liturgy as well as the aesthetic experience, the imagination works within a structured symbolic framework. The result of this process is the attainment of equilibrium or balance. The imagination equalizes the various polarities we experience, the subjective and the objective parts of our lives, new and old information, the conscious and unconscious motives to which we are subject. It is this balancing power of the imagination which makes it possible for liturgy to confront oppression.

This imaginative activity when channeled through liturgical ritual can be the source of creativity. It can be the stimulant for further human growth. The equilibrium referred to here is more than mere intellectual or emotional adjustment. It is total integration. It is through the symbolic imagination that one's past, present, and future can be brought together. The imagination transcends time and superimposes the images of our total life one on the other. The balance needed to overcome oppression is above all the experience of stepping out of one kind of time, breaking away from a fixation on the past, a stagnation in the present and a preoccupation with the future.

As already noted, this integrality is possible because of the way the imagination brings about interiorization. To put it simply, this means the ability to respond to reality around us. By means of our imaginations we so modify our world that we can responsibly engage it. Nothing from the outside so dominates us that we are forced to a standstill. The other way the imagination facilitates integration is through the feeling of intimacy that we have within ourselves. It is how we feel about our inner lives. It is a sense of being at home with ourselves, being familiar with ourselves. It allows us to move out of ourselves because we feel our goodness in an inner way.

When this kind of integration takes place, there is the restoration of balance in one's life. Both interior and exterior threats are relativized. Dangers are reduced so that they can be handled. In all of this the dignity of the individual is asserted in the face of denigrating opposition. When we are beginning to fall apart in our inner selves, the imagination comes to the rescue providing images of our goodness, our personal uniqueness, and our relationship with our world. Out of this enhancement of personhood, we can overcome the oppression that surrounds us.

The imagination has ways, then, of helping a person deal with oppression. If the oppressive situation or images become too threatening, our symbolic life counters by bringing other images into consciousness. These counter images reduce the power of the oppressive ones and relieve excessive anxiety. Or the imagination will transform a threatening image by having part of it transferred to other images, thus weakening the original image. What is threatening can be displaced to another area of consciousness. When the imagination operates in this fashion, it is following the principle: divide and conquer.

Another approach of the human imagination in dealing with oppression is more indirect. It is to undercut the oppressive influence by building up inner security. For instance, repetition can take the wind out of a threatening situation. The sense of familiarity mollifies the images and dissipates some of the fears. In fact, intimacy may actually result. Or the imagination may simply pile one image upon another. This conglomeration of images triggers a whole network of meaning and this in turn makes us more comfortable with our existence. Finally, the imagination has the ability to fuse many images into one. Each of these images may be the cause of fear on their own. But several images keep each other in control and within bounds. This assists the person to move away from the influence of oppression in any given situation.

Perhaps, in no place does the imagination's confrontation with oppression show up so clearly as in the liturgy. The extensive symbolic character of the liturgy allows the imagination full play. The sacramental actions of liturgical worship are especially adapted to bring about human integration which is characterized by the balanced personality, the overcoming of anxiety, and the inner feelings of personal dignity and intimacy. All this is possible because the connection between the symbols of the liturgy are not only logical, but also imaginational. Through the dynamics of the imagination the waters of baptism speak of an inner transformation which is not readily made by reason alone.

The way in which the imagination works in liturgy is especially clear in the matter of intimacy. The sacraments can foster a closeness with God through ritual repetition. Through continual contact with the liturgical experience, worshipers can enhance the quality of their own lives. Again, intimacy is possible because the liturgy employs concrete physical symbols. So many of the images in worship are those of the body: eating, drinking, touching, kissing, sexual union. As these images and liturgical actions become a ritualized way of meeting God, they enable the worshipers to become more immediate to themselves and more assured of their individuality. Images of sex, food, and life when brought into a sacramental context can bring the believer close to God and dispel some of the sense of hopelessness occasioned by an oppressive culture.

The main purpose of recovering the imagination in the liturgy is the same as that which frees the worshiper from oppression: to restore balance to people and to enhance their self-dignity. This, then, provides the basis for spiritual transformation and deepening of the presence of God. The power of the oppressors often comes from the way in which they can make contact with our hidden fears and anxieties. Through the liturgy we can enter the mysterious aspect of our lives and counteract these oppressive influences. The interiorization that takes place through the imagination enables us not only to respond to the faith-content of the liturgy but also to create the kind of sense of closeness and reassurance which is our protection from oppression. It is a paradox of grace that in the liturgy the oppressed, far from succumbing to self-deprecation, emotional dependence, grief, depression, anger, rage, and fear may be more open and more capable of celebration than most other worshipers.

16

Creativity: Variations on a Sacred Theme

An hour's snow:
Heaven and earth settle briefly
All their old differences.

THIS LOVELY HAIKU POEM WAS ON A CHRISTMAS CARD I HAD RE-
ceived from my late friend and colleague, the poet James Luguri.
It spoke of the meaning of Christmas in a far more imaginative
way than the hundreds of cards I have received with their expected message of "Peace on Earth, Good Will to Men" or their
nondescript holiday tidings. Two more haiku Christmas cards
from Jim graced my life.

Winter branches:
In an abandoned nest
A new egg of snow

Christmas eve walk:
First quince in blossom
Before the year ends.

How the human imagination soars when confronted with these
parable-like poems: parable-like because they have no endings
but invite us to further exploration. Whatever else it is, creativity
moves us to further pursuit. It does not conclude. It offers no
definite answers.

The creative imagination is the source of those qualities that make us most human. To take one example, it assists us in dealing with loss, the frustration of our desires. Many of you remember the poem by Blake, which is good advice for all of us lovers.

> He who binds to himself a joy
> Does the winged life destroy.
> But he who kisses the joy as it flies
> Lives in eternity's sunrise.[1]

If we take the pronouncements of our society seriously, imagination and fantasy are for kids. Mature people don't daydream. They work. They do something. They don't just stand there. A fantasy life is a nuisance. It is O.K. for children at their particular stage of growth. But no self-respecting adult would be caught dead with it. Our language gives us away. We say we *indulge* in fantasy. This is presumably like having a triple ice cream cone or a second piece of chocolate decadence.

And it is true that many of us adults are uncomfortable with many, if not all, forms of fantasy. We feel guilty that we are wasting our time, time that could be spent (notice the verbs) on keeping our noses to the grind (note the image). What would happen to our world if *everyone* wanted to fantasize!

And yet the ability to fantasize is a primary quality of the creative person. Through this imaginative process we can blend the rational and non-rational components of our experience into something entirely new. Fantasy is not the kid's stuff we grow out of as we pass into adulthood.

But are not liturgy and fantasy seen as antithetical? Fantasy belongs to that which is unreal, nonexistent, unattainable. But can liturgy be unreal and beyond grasp? And if fantasy is made equivalent with being out of control and if liturgy becomes the paradigm of a controlled situation (many examples here), then the two can never meet. Many of us are threatened by that which seems beyond our control. About such important things as life and death, my personal meaning, and the existence of God, we want to be sure. We don't want vagueness or ambiguity about

---

1. William Blake, *The Complete Poetry and Selected Prose of John Donne and the Complete Poetry of William Blake* (New York: Random House, 1941) 579.

that kingdom of God on which we use up so much of our energies (note the image).

But consult Jesus about the kingdom and what do we get? Stories, metaphors, and parables. In his book, *The Third Peacock,* Robert Farrar Capon calls Christianity the ultimate fantasy, *the* fairy tale. What this means for those who care for the worship of the church is that we do not have to reinvent the wheel. The story is already there. We need but apply our imaginations and retell it.

To claim that creativity is a must for liturgy and its artists is but to say that we will not get much further in our liturgical renewal if we do not engage the human imagination, whether that of our selves or of our congregations. After all, how much more historical work, revisions of liturgical texts (yes, I said texts, not gestures and symbols), or catechesis do we need? You don't change people's minds, you change their experience. We need a new liturgical magnetism, one that had all the attraction of the moment of consecration of the former, well-orchestrated Solemn High Mass. That moment of consecration was the liturgical black hole that sucked up all the spiritual and psychological energies of worshipers. What we have now resembles too often the classroom.

As liturgical artists we must present the world of the liturgy, the world of the liturgical texts in sonic, plastic, and visual dimensions. In our liturgy, we must make present the world that is there in front of the liturgical texts, a world often hidden, unnoticed, and unattended. We cannot ignore the obvious: that our psychic lives are both conscious and unconscious, hidden and revealed. And so we must take our cues from the world of the arts, a world that binds together the conscious and the unconscious so that the world of the liturgical text can be presented by means of a more imaginative world. If we want to know what creativity in liturgy means, we can be helped by our experiences of creativity in the arts. A few examples will suffice to make my point.

Like the film, our liturgy is a combination of fiction, drama, poetry, dance, music, painting, sculpture, religion, and philosophy. But does the liturgy, like the film, heal the separation between the real and the unreal world? Actors in the film often come off better than most of the real live people we live with.

We do not have enough beauty in our lives and it is one of the things we need most. That is why we continue to make and look at movies, hoping for the best.

A painting is a reality of its own. Few would consider it an ordinary reproduction like some photographs. The painting represents its own world. Painting makes worlds for us to see; sometimes these worlds remind us of worlds we know, and sometimes painting leads us into worlds unknown. How can the liturgy do the same? In the same way we do not think of a play as like real life. It is really an exaggeration of real life in its manners and characters. But good drama has a world of meaning and sensibility that it makes available to those who wish to enter it. The liturgy can and must do the same.

Poetry is always a distillation. Even long epic poems like the *Iliad* or *Beowulf* could hardly be more compact. In poetry the song (the heart) and the insight (the mind) are combined as nowhere else. Auden said that "a sentence uttered makes a world appear." Poetry gives us a world that is already familiar but that we did not know very well before we read the poem. We did not know that such a world mattered so much. Poetry gives us the world in which we can come to live.

"Music sounds the way emotions feel," according to Aaron Copland. What does music mean? is a nonsensical question. Although we may analyze it into tones, melody, and rhythm, what music is dealing with is our response to time. However inharmonious may seem the sequence of sounds, music is an order expressed within the flow of time. We have many rhythms in our lives and music can express them all, sometimes in obvious, sometimes in subtle ways. The whole range of our emotional life can be heard through the musical imagination. A performer can say: "I play what I live" and a listener can say "I will live what I hear." Such should be the case in our Christian worship. Our liturgical music should help us make sense of our time.

What is creativity? Let us look at two definitions. One comes from an important American philosopher and theologian and the other comes from a storyteller. Let us begin with the more theoretical one. Our theologian, Henry Nelson Wieman, has written this paragraph of description of human creativity:

Human creativity consists of bringing together these two sides of discovery, open *awareness* on the one hand and *theorizing* on the other—with its analysis, discrimination, definition and experimentation. When these two are united and rightly balanced human life leaps forward like an open spillway or a hound unleashed. Life becomes suddenly and marvelously abundant. When these two are brought into fruitful interaction, the richness of the world and the fertility of life is shown to be amazing. The artist, the prophet, the moral and social reformer, the scientific genius, the religious seer, all rise up in numbers and power when awareness of the wide, rich, novel fulness of concrete experience can be combined with the scientific method. But wide open mystic awareness flounders helplessly and blindly when unassisted by scientific method. And scientific method becomes a barren definition of concepts without yielding when not supported by open awareness.[2]

What is important in this description of creativity is what Wieman calls *creative interchange.* Creativity is not just intuition and not just intellectual understanding. It is this process of interchange that helps us to discover what it means to be creative in the liturgy. I will sketch four characteristics of this creative interchange: 1) a new perspective, 2) a progressive integration, 3) an expanding appreciation, and 4) a setting in community.

(1) In this interchange a *new perspective* emerges. We become aware of our experience and that of others through communication. This is the reason that artists live in colonies and that we need a mobilizing image in liturgy around which our meanings can be gathered. Images unite; ideas divide. I share something of importance to me and you do the same in this kind of human interchange. Creativity will remain imprisoned unless there is that kind of sharing where new perspectives can arise. One of the paradoxes of creativity is that in order to think originally, we must familiarize ourselves with the ideas of others.

This is more than a sharing of ideas. It is a sharing of values. How often have I heard liturgical planners exclaim: "I have this

2. Henry Nelson Wieman, *Religious Experience and Scientific Method* (New York: Macmillan, 1926) 197. (Republished: Carbondale: Southern Illinois University Press, 1971)

great idea." Notice how often they use the word, idea. Frequently this is little more than a sharing of recipes. Many times people have creative ideas but they exist in isolation because they have not identified their new perspective in which to ground the ideas. What is the point of being creative in offertory processions if one comes from an old perspective that sees this part of the liturgy as an offering of bread and wine rather than the new perspective of setting the table? Take next Sunday's readings and locate an image around which to pray rather than identifying a theme. You will experience what I mean by a new perspective.

(2) *Progressive integration.* We integrate the meanings we have received from others and integrate them into those we already have. Our thoughts and feelings are enriched by being exposed to others' values in life. The integration is largely subconscious, unplanned, and uncontrolled. But it does mean that one must draw apart and cease from a great deal of activity or input; otherwise the constant stream of new meanings will prevent deeper integration. A period of loneliness and quiet provides for incubation and creative transformation. In the words of the poet, Porchia, "To be someone is to be someone alone." That is why I begin planning liturgies early, take a fair number of ideas and images and then let the relevant ones emerge (usually while I am jogging). One who is continuously in association with others is not likely to be the medium through whom a great deal of creativity will occur. Creativity is not the same as frenetic activity. That is the problem with the planning session with its exclamation: "I have this great idea." It becomes the tail wagging the dog.

(3) *Expanding appreciation.* Once we have shared our values and have had a chance to integrate them, our appreciable worlds will expand. The range of our experience will increase. After all, reality is what we pay attention to. A richness of quality is lacking for people whose consciousness remains untransformed; there is a narrow range of possibilities. For those whose imaginative life is wider, possibilities occur that previously did not exist. I have found that working with professional artists as I do, and especially with dancers, I can make a number of choreographic suggestions, although I am not a choreographer. The point is that my own world has widened and I can see possibilities where even the expert dancer might not, at least in a liturgical situation.

This new appreciable world in which we live is not one that is constant. It expands and contracts with great variation from day to day. But once acquired, it is not lost. It is at least a memory and a conceivable hope. This larger appreciable world does not mean more pleasure, enjoyment, and happiness. But it does mean that the experiences will be deeper and higher and that our longings and fulfillments will be more profound, but that does not mean that they will be less painful.

(4) If you and I have expanded our worlds as individuals, then our relations *with our communities* will grow in ways that will be transformative and healthy. This is a task of humility and suffering since it means intellectual understanding of the other, the feeling of the other's feelings, mutual correcting and criticizing, cooperation directed to preserving the good that has already been achieved. Community here is more than backslapping geniality but includes the discernment of illness and evil in one another. Community means both suffering and freedom. Refusal to take suffering is perhaps the chief obstacle to the increase of creativity in one's life. One of the most helpful and effective bits of advice to give people when they feel depressed and are questioning the meaning of life, is to encourage them to do something creative, although it may require effort and pain. Creativity rather than logical reasoning is called for in such a situation.

Creativity for Wieman, then, is the way any person combines theory (the intellectual) with openness (the intuitive). This combination is found equally in the writer who transforms his or her experiences of the human scene into a novel or play and in the scientist who tests and probes the collected data in order to come up with a new theory. Both work through intuition as well as intellect. Both work with ideas that are as much feelings as they are thoughts. Both writer and scientist depend on inspiration and the workings of the subconscious mind. Creativity is that unique combination of abstract theory and expanding experience.

But let us listen to a quite different description of creativity. J. Ruth Gendler in her collection of short stories entitled, *The Book of Qualities*, speaks of creativity this way.

Creativity is not efficient. She has a different relationship to time than most of us. A minute can last a day and a day can last an hour. She loves all the seasons. She is on intimate terms with the sun and the moon. It is New Year's all year long at her house, what with celebrations for the Celtic, Hebrew, Tibetan, Chinese, Japanese, and other New Years too numerous to mention. Creativity loves to gossip with the birds and put on her masks and beads and dance with the animals. Although bright colors amuse her, she most often wears neutral tones. She is especially partial to off-white.

Some people consider Creativity selfish because she does what she wants. I have always found her to be gracious and most generous. She is certainly complex. If you have only met her in a serene mood, her flair for drama may offend you. She is not your aunt with the porcelain teapot who plays chamber music. If you are one of those people who only go to see her when she is starring in a major melodrama, you will not hear her rain songs. If you insist she is mad, you will never see how still her face is when she returns from a dream.

Sometimes Creativity disappears completely or wanders around the back alleys for weeks at a time. She has a strong need to be occasionally anonymous. If you run into her at the post office line during one of these periods, you will probably not recognize her. She is in a different place. It is almost as if her blood has slowed down. When the blank period is over, Creativity brings her free self home with her. Her skin is new. She is ready to work. More than anyone else, Creativity understands the secret meanings of the months when nothing seems to get done.[3]

What can we learn about Ms. Creativity who has this somewhat unreliable relationship with time? She refuses to be categorized by bright colors. She has not one, two or three, but multiple New Years. It means that creativity is not a kind of problem solving. For those who believe that the creative process is to terminate in answers to questions, the resolution of complex situations, planning a music liturgy would not differ fundamentally from an electrician deciding how best to wire a redecorated room. But creativity lives her own life and she has her own rhythm and time.

Creativity cannot be forced. But like love, it will come if we

3. J. Ruth Gendler, *The Book of Qualities* (Berkeley: Turquoise Publications, 1984) 64.

are open to it. We let a lot of creativity pass by because we are too busy to note it. The imagination is not bound by schedules but tosses its ideas into consciousness at any time of day or night. Perhaps, if we miss the creative moment, it will return in different guise. But we cannot always recapture the insight in its original form. We must attend to our thoughts and feelings during the time of incubation. Creativity is not bound by our appointment books. We may have to wait while she gossips with the birds or we may join her as she dances with the animals.

Creativity consists largely in rearranging what we already know in order to find out what we do not know. We need to look afresh at what we normally take for granted. Unfortunately, we tend not to ask questions about that with which we are acquainted. We ask questions about unusual events. But creativity often wears neutral tones, especially off-white. If you wish creativity to join you in your quest, look where you are not looking. After all, reality is what you pay attention to.

Creativity goes her own way and she is a complex person. She is a classic nonconformist. She spends little time with the emotionally repressed, with the intellectually inflexible. She avoids those dependent on others and lacking in self-confidence. She passes over those weak in faith, the authoritarian personalities, and those who close themselves to experience. She also does not wish to be identified with counter-conformists who flout convention because they feel a need to be different. Creativity is not into the task of being alienating. Creativity has a balanced attitude. She is original in ideas and open to new experiences, but she is not unconventional for its own sake. She remains attuned to the thinking of others.

But she is complex because originality is her broadest trait. Being more flexible than most people she tries a variety of approaches. Give her a brick and it becomes a paperweight, or a part of a walkway, or something to grind into red powder, or something to throw at someone. But creativity consists not in novel responses alone. The creative person not only has new ideas, but also follows them up. And this is where the trouble begins. Copernicus and Galileo were denounced as blasphemers. Darwin's theory of evolution brought down the wrath of the clergy. And Stravinsky's *Le Sacre du Printemps* provoked a riot.

Creativity may adopt highly bizarre devices to make for more favorable conditions for inspiration. Some of our most creative people have been most idiosyncratic. Schiller, for instance, filled his desk with rotten apples. Proust worked in a cork-lined room. Mozart took exercise. Dr. Johnson surrounded himself with a purring cat, orange peel, and tea. Hart Crane played jazz loud on a victrola.[4]

Creativity can help us reeducate ourselves to remain open to new experiences. Perhaps in our younger years at school we learned what our teachers said we should know. If our teachers always knew the answers to our questions, it was because we were trained to ask the kind of questions they would be able to answer. Our creativity will be found in the way we keep asking the question.

Finally, creativity takes time. There may be a long period of time when our ideas go underground. As far as we can tell, creativity actually moves in recognizable phases. Not all agree that this is the way to slice the pie, but I believe that the creative process does go somewhat like this.

There is the *first insight* when the germ of creation is born. This may be a poet's response to the death of a friend or a painter's sight of sun on the lake in late afternoon. The second phase is that of *preparation* when the creator reads, discusses, questions, and explores. For instance, the painter may sit day after day on the hillside, observing colors, figures, and changes in light. Immersion into the subject matter is a condition of creative thinking because it gives the materials with which to work as well as acquaints one with the difficulties of producing something.

After the conscious mind has done its work, the unconscious takes over. This is the period of *incubation*. This time may be long or short. This may be a time of discouragement. Hart Crane would work on a poem for months, even years, jotting down lines on scraps of paper as they came. *Illumination* brings the creative process to a climax. It may be sudden as when whole stanzas of a poem will come. It is at this time that integration occurs and the imagination takes command. The final stage of *verification* is the time when intellect and judgment complete the work of imagination. Creativity is not a single flash of intuition.

4. Many of the examples in these paragraphs are from George F. Kneller, *The Art and Science of Creativity* (New York: Holt, Rinehart, and Winston, Inc., 1965) passim.

It requires analysis to separate significant factors from less important ones. This is the time when the composer plays her piece for a friend in the hope of an objective assessment.

There seems to be, then, a creative cycle of five identifiable phases: 1) the impulse to create, 2) the gathering of materials and investigation of methods, 3) time of incubation when the work proceeds unconsciously, 4) the moment of illumination when the unconscious mind suddenly announces the results of its labors, and 5) a process of revision and verification.[5]

Because the liturgy is the place where the story of Jesus Christ, the story of the paschal mystery, takes place, pastoral musicians like other liturgical ministers are to be storytellers. The liturgy provides the opportunity for all of us with our small and limited stories to get caught up into the larger incorporating story of Jesus Christ. The liturgy is storytelling time because like good stories it can pull us out of ourselves, can transport us to the world of the story where we undergo its trials and thrills and return to our own reality with renewed appreciation. Storytelling is not the kind of experience we should leave behind because we grow up. Stories are for adults too. All people want to move out of their skins and return from a journey slightly different.

Liturgy is storytelling time because it is narrative in structure. Stories have a beginning, middle, and end and so capture the temporal dimension of human existence. They deal with people in their moments of decision while they are carving out a future by understanding and reappropriating the past. Human stories speak of freedom and making choices. Storytelling is part of the human process because time and freedom are. The liturgy is a kind of story. In worship we tell and retell stories that have more than ordinary impact: the stories of salvation, life in Christ, and the journey in the Christian community. When we retell these stories Sunday after Sunday, they become part of our self-identity as Christians and they shape our permanent attitudes towards life. These attitudes bring about a greater sensitivity in our lives and so we become "holy" in so far as we go out to others from a more integrated position.

In the liturgy we tell our stories again and again. We do not usually get it right the first time. We need to retell it repeatedly in hope that we will come up with a satisfactory story. In this

5. Ibid. See chapter three, "The Act," 47ff.

way the story of the liturgy is allowed to have an inner impact. And the whole liturgy is storytelling, not just the liturgy of the word or the homily. Liturgical musicians help tell this story in sonic form by creating a coherent unity in the liturgical experience. The musical quality of liturgy is one of the most important ways to get at the stories that lie too deep in the consciousness of people to be told directly. The liturgy presupposes the story that cannot be told. But the story that is told is a true one. To say that story, song, or musical work is true is to say that it reveals, suggests or reflects deeper meanings. Thus, how the story comes to light in the liturgy itself raises certain questions peculiar to the musician.

How does the musical dimension of the liturgy require that the assembly has a familiarity with the Christian story, not simply as historical past, but as a present event that achieves its meaning from the future? The obvious examples here are: does music reinforce the idea of Christmas as a past event, Advent as a time of Old Testament longing, Holy Thursday as the celebration of the institution of the sacrament of the eucharist, the Ascension and Pentecost as feasts separate from Easter? If so, the music is hindering the story of the liturgical year, which is not concerned about historicization or creating a biography of Jesus Christ.

Second, is music an integral part of the story? You have all been at musicals where this was not the case, where the songs were interspersed as to be only loosely connected with the story or where the story was but an excuse to sing some fetching tunes. Does the story narrative stop while we take out time to sing à la Donizetti or Bellini bel canto opera? Is the sung liturgy like a dramatization that is deficient when there is no advancement of character by means of song? One thing is certain. The four-hymn Mass is not the way to tell the story liturgically. The four hymns actually set up a pattern counter to that of the eucharist, disguising its basic shape. The four hymn mentality (which can be present even if there is singing at the other parts of the liturgy) tends to stress secondary elements of the rite and so changes the liturgy's transforming thrust.

Third, if the liturgy as storytelling is to be musical, how can the texts of the story be sound? Usually, the texts that advance the narrative—prayers, readings, the eucharistic prayer—are not sung. Creativity is called for here in a special way. For recitation of these parts can prove to be dissipating in energy, with boredom as the result. In what way is the Christian story carried in hymns and chants? If Pentecost falls on the first Sunday of May, marian hymns may not advance the story but rather create a distracting subplot.

Fourth, how can we help tell the resurrection story? Stories have power when we can identify with them and feel that they are true for us. Christianity grew because of the engaging power of its story. It is a truly human story. That is the reason for the appeal of the Christmas story. But we find it difficult to place ourselves in the story of the resurrection, and only at certain times in our history has it been palatable to see ourselves on the cross. But everyone can welcome the birth of a child. For a mobilizing story, how can you beat the stable of Bethlehem with its chorus of angels?

But the central New Testament story is the death and resurrection of Jesus Christ. "If Christ has not been raised, your faith is futile" (1 Cor 15:17).

Paul tied this story to human experience by putting it into the context of conversion. Death is death to sin. Resurrection is new life. The resurrection story works if it fits our experience. Does it tell the story of our experience? Paul's theology of resurrection is abstract for us today. More people are engaged by the empty tomb. The four gospels give different stories of the resurrection, which are filled with minor contradictions. But as stories, rather than history, they are powerful in asserting that death is not the end of Jesus of Nazareth. Death is not the end of life. These are mysterious things that can only be grasped in story forms that provide possible ways of imagining them. We should take our cues from such creative people as Emily Dickinson, who becomes theologian in her poetry when she speaks of the resurrection experience.

Who has not found the Heaven—below—
Will fail of it above—
For Angels rent the House next ours,
Wherever we remove—[6]

6. *The Complete Poems of Emily Dickinson*, ed., Thomas J. Johnson (Boston: Little, Brown and Company, 1960) 644.

The liturgical musician can help us develop the kind of imagination that can converse with angels at an empty tomb and envisage a world beyond this one, a world in front of this one. Music is one of the ways that the story can make sense of our experiences. We feel foolish reciting *alleluia*. But to sing it can be the height of human religious expression. The liturgy needs creative pastoral musicians and pastoral musicians need to be creative. The reason is wonderfully stated by theologian/poet, Emily Dickinson:

> Through the great Waters sleep,
> That they are still the Deep,
> We cannot doubt—
> No vacillating God
> Ignited this Abode
> To put it out—[7]

---

7. Ibid. 661.